THE THIRD REICH, 1933–1945

CANADIAN REVIEW OF STUDIES
IN NATIONALISM
(Vol. 7)

GARLAND REFERENCE LIBRARY
OF SOCIAL SCIENCE
(Vol. 384)

CANADIAN REVIEW OF STUDIES IN NATIONALISM

Series Editor: Thomas Spira

THE THIRD REICH, 1933–1945
A Bibliographical Guide to German National Socialism

Selected, Annotated and Edited by
LOUIS L. SNYDER
Professor Emeritus
Ph.D. Program in History
The City University of New York

GARLAND PUBLISHING, INC.·NEW YORK & LONDON
1987

Library of Congress Cataloging-in-Publication Data

Snyder, Louis Leo, 1907–
The Third Reich, 1933–1945.

(Canadian Review of Studies in Nationalism; vol. 7)
(Garland Reference Library of Social Science; vol. 384)
Includes index.
1. National socialism—Bibliography.   2. Germany—
Politics and government—1933–1945—Bibliography.
I. Title.   II. Title: 3rd Reich, 1933–1945.   III. Series:
Canadian Review of Studies in Nationalism; v. 7.
IV. Series: Garland Reference Library of Social
Science; v. 384.

Z2241.N27S65   1987   [DD256.5]   016.943085   87-7608
ISBN 0-8240-8463-2

Printed on acid-free, 250-year-life paper
Manufactured in the United States of America

121356

For
Ida Mae Brown Snyder
"In every gesture dignity and love."
Without whom . . . .

CONTENTS

INTRODUCTION

Any historical phenomenon merits attention by scholars seeking to clarify what happened as well as by those readers who prefer non-fiction to fiction. But the historiography of German National Socialism, concerning the personality and character of Adolf Hitler, the rise and development of the Third Reich and the role of Nazi Germany in World War II, all of these have proved to be of special importance. Hitler boasted of his Thousand-Year Reich, which fortunately for civilization lasted just twelve years, but this was an era in which every German, every European, eventually almost every person in the world, all were influenced in one way or another by the ideology of National Socialism and its effects.

National Socialism has become a subject of enormous interest. To meet an insatiable demand there has been a huge supply of published materials about it — documents, biographies, autobiographies, essays, articles, encyclopedias and reminiscences. Not only the scholarly journals but also newspapers and magazines devote space to every conceivable aspect of the Nazi regime. Recently, for weeks the newspapers of the world were filled with front-page stories about the reported death of Dr. Josef Mengele, the notorious Angel of Death at the extermination camp Auschwitz, who for four decades had escaped the wrath of an outraged society.

The task here is to comb the enormous and cascading literature on National Socialism and provide a guide to the material that has been published about it. An attempt is made to give as wide a range as possible without including too many of the publications of lesser value. The size of the entries is kept to a minimum — just enough coverage to describe the author, the publication title, the city of publication and date, with a highly condensed summary of the contents. Because generally there are highly contradictory estimates by reviewers of almost all books published, no attempt is made here in the body of the entries either to praise or criticize the contents. The reader attracted by a given subject on National Socialism is urged to consult the book and make his own judgment as to its value.

Documentary Materials

For the scholar seeking to throw light on any special phase of National Socialism, the existence of documents is of prime importance. For example, any study of Hitler's foreign policy is dependent upon documents of the German Foreign Office during the Nazi regime. In this respect, historians have been fortunate. In the confusing later days of the Third Reich, when Germany was being bombed pitilessly into submission, many important documents could well have been lost. Instead, the triumphant Allies, especially the Americans, were able to rescue them from destruction.

This happy circumstance was described by Shepard Stone, one-time foreign correspondent for *The New York Times*, who returned to Germany after the war as a staff member of United States High Commissioner John McCloy. In an interview with *Die Zeit*, held on 1 April 1983, Stone told of his experiences as an officer with the United States Army in the final days of the war:

> We were passing through some villages in the Harz region. One day, we came upon a castle deep in a forest. As it turned out, the place housed the entire Foreign Office archives from 1870 to 1944.
>
> A man came out of the house – I think his name was Baron von Griesheim – and since I was in charge of the unit, the building was turned over to me. Then he showed me a telegram he had received from von Ribbentrop: "Destroy the entire Foreign Office archives."
>
> I instantly asked him whether he had done so. He escorted me to the basement and pointed to a pile of ashes in a corner. I asked him what that was, and he answered: "a month's worth of *Völkischer Beobachters!*"
>
> In another place, there were all the documents. He had them beautifully wrapped in yellow wrapping paper.
>
> Later, my men arrived. They asked me: "Why must we guard these packages? There's some fabulous wine here."
>
> But we were able to prove how civilized Americans are. Our colonel instantly ordered all the documents loaded on trucks and taken to Marburg, where they were photographed.
>
> I'm glad they're back in German hands again at the Foreign Office and that nothing was stolen.

These documents were published both in the United States and later in Germany. They were by no means the only papers captured by American troops in the final days of the war. Others were confiscated, brought to Washington, DC, photostated, and the originals returned to Germany as the property of the Bonn Federal Republic of West Germany.

Such archival material will be worked on by scholars for years to come. At the same time, the broad category of documentary material presented here includes much of interest to the amateur armchair historian who is fascinated by a regime that was clearly one of the major aberrations in the history of civilization.

Historiographical Controversies

Experienced historians realize that members of their craft can take the same set of facts and come to exactly opposite conclusions in interpreting them. This happens so often in historiography that it is no longer an unexpected *modus operandi*.

Behind these confrontations is a curious development in the writing of history. Leopold von Ranke, leading German historian of the nineteenth century and called the father of modern historiography, was noted for his insistence on careful and methodical research. He set a standard operational procedure for his fellow scholars by insisting that the historian's task is to be completely objective and to relate *was ist geschehen*, exactly what happened.

Ranke's advice was important and to the point. At the same time, it raised a number of perplexing questions. Does it not tend toward a calendar-like narration of events? What is the purpose of writing history without adequate interpretation? Is it not necessary for the historian to give his own judgment on the documentary material he has unearthed in his research? These questions serve to reinforce the conclusion that von Ranke was not an analyst but a "visual" historiographer – and analysis has become the heart of the historian's credo.

Since the era of von Ranke, historians, while praising his sense of objectivity, have concerned themselves more and more with the analysis of a given set of facts. The current fashion is to lean in the direction of interpretation. The result has been a proliferation of debates among scholars on the meaning of what happened. In the process the background, personality and milieu of the individual historian has become of major importance. Consciously or unconsciously, his writing is influenced by personal motivations and beliefs. The result has been a plethora of differing interpretations of the same set of facts. Unfortunately, there is no academic Supreme Court to decide which historian has presented the plain and simple truth.

These confrontations are often fascinating. Some historians, aware of the difficulties involved in their work, adopt a courteous and conciliatory tone and present their findings cautiously. Others, especially in England, where eccentricity is prized, come at each other like battling gladiators, hurling barbs of irony and acid wit, and then retire together graciously for the traditional and valued tea — as if nothing unusual had happened. Witness the case of Oxford historians A. J. P. Taylor and Hugh R. Trevor-Roper in their scathing difference of opinion on the origins of World War II, a curious debate which will be described later in this introduction.

The historiography of National Socialism is filled with such scholarly antagonisms. One of the reasons for this is the extraordinary complexity of the Nazi regime. The maxim that there is nothing new in history has its limitations. There have been many examples of mass murder in the past, but nothing to compare with the genocide of the Holocaust. There have been many dictatorships, but few can match the barbarism and vulgarity of Hitler's Third Reich. Nothing like the Nuremberg Trial has ever taken place on this planet. Only a few of these historiographical debates will be mentioned here.

Functionalists versus Intentionalists. A recent controversy among historians concerns the nature of the National Socialist regime and Hitler's role as its leader. On the one side are the functionalists, who call the Third Reich a polycracy, in which an anarchic state of administration reigned. The functionalists, led by historians Hans Mommsen and Martin Broszat, hold that decisions in Nazi Germany were made by conflicting authorities and that Hitler did not and could not determine the course of policy. They insist that he did not make decisions himself and, instead, was driven into them. In the long run, say the functionalists, Hitler was really a weak dictator.

The opposing school of historians, the intentionalists, presents a fundamentally different interpretation of Hitler's role in the Third Reich. Among them are such authorities as Gerald Reitlinger, Raul Hilberg and the majority of scholars specializing in National Socialism. These observers maintain that Hitler had a definite program, described in his blueprint *Mein Kampf*, and that he sought to implement it by making the appropriate decisions. In short, he was a harsh dictator who knew his goals and pursued them relentlessly. The argument continues in full force. The functionalists insist that the Nazi regime was subjected to all kinds of conflicts on the domestic scene. In this polycracy Hitler was forced to maintain his control by playing one group against the other and seeing to it that no one collection of his minions assumed too much power. Always, say the functionalists, inconsistency and confusion were rampant in the Third Reich.

The intentionalists claim that, despite the views of the functionalists, Hitler remained the guiding spirit of the monocracy, *his* dictatorship and *his* totalitarian state. They contend that he had his own list of objectives, priorities and conditions. He was the ultimate power in the Third Reich, despite all claims to the contrary. No matter what is said, the intentionalists cling to their belief that the *Führer* remained the supreme decision-maker in the state and the ultimate repository of National Socialist ideology.

The antagonistic schools clash especially on the nature of Nazi genocide. The functionalists deny that Hitler ordered the atrocities, and claim that the program evolved from a series of slaughter operations in 1941 and 1942 and from the fact that further evacuation of Jews from Europe had become impossible. The intentionalists hold that, while Hitler was careful to avoid any specific written orders, as head of state he had all along advocated systematic killing in his books, speeches and conversation. To him, "elimination" meant slaughter.

A German *Sonderweg*? There is an ongoing debate among historians about the meaning of the Nazi phenomenon. Was it evidence of the *continuity* factor in German history, a development with roots running deeply into the past and a program identified with traditional tendencies and ambitions (Hans Kohn, George L. Mosse, Peter Viereck, Eberhard Jäckel)? Or was it the result of the *catastrophe* theory, which considers Nazism a catastrophe that hit the German people like a bolt of lightning (Friedrich Meinecke, *et al.*)?

Added to this is the scholarly clash on the existence of a *Sonderweg* — the peculiarity of German history. Here again, the Kohn school, as *Sonderweg* advocates, holds that, indeed, basic differences exist in the development of German and other European nationalisms. They point out that neither Italian nor Spanish Fascisms, despite their dictatorial aspects, accepted the kind of racial ideology which led to the Nazi system of genocide. They reject the idea of a "problematic nature" of the *Sonderweg* and maintain that Hitler monopolized the traditional nationalism of apolitical Germans and turned it into a berserk nationalism altogether different from other European nationalisms.

Opposed to this point of view are the historians, many of them Germans, who deny that there is anything "peculiar" about German historical development leading to Hitler. They insist that what happened in Germany was merely a part of the general European-wide phenomenon of Fascism. German National Socialism, they claim, was merely a part of similar developments elsewhere in Europe. They see several types of German nationalism which are not different from those in other countries. They criticize advocates of the *Sonderweg* as favoring an "older notion" of a monolithic, uniquely evil and special German nationalism severed from the more benign and rational Western tradition. They accuse the Kohn school of being composed of "moralistic authors" (the Kohn school replies that its critics are confusing morals with Rankean objectivity). Among opponents of the *Sonderweg* thesis are such historians as Karl Dietrich Bracher and bibliographers Dieter Buse and Juergen Doerr.

Reichstag Fire. On the evening of 27 February 1933, shortly after Hitler came to political power, the imposing *Reichstag* edifice in Berlin, housing the German Parliament, was burned in a sensational fire. A controversy soon arose among historians and has persisted to the present day on the origins of the conflagration. In 1960 German investigator Dr. Fritz Tobias published in *Der Spiegel*, a popular magazine, an article which claimed that Marinus van der Lubbe, a young mentally retarded Dutchman, had acted alone in setting the fire. Tobias wrote that van der Lubbe had himself started the arson. He also charged that the Dutchman, in the days before the burning, had tried without success to use a torch on other public buildings. He concluded that there was no Nazi participation whatever, as was widely believed. Professor Hans Mommsen, historian at the Ruhr University in Bochum, supported Tobias's thesis in several scholarly articles.

In March 1973 Swiss historian Professor Walter Hofer, of Bern University, accused Tobias and Mommsen of resorting to non-scientific methods in presenting the lone-arsonist theory. Hofer, together with his international team of experts, held that there was documentary proof that the detectives in charge of the Tobias inquiry had worked for the Third Reich and that some of them had been Nazi-minded even before the fire. Mommsen refused to retreat: "Professor Hofer's rather helpless statement that the accomplices of van der Lubbe 'could only have been Nazis' is tacit admission that the

[Hofer] committee did not actually obtain any positive evidence in regard to the alleged accomplices' identity." The debate continues unresolved.

Roles of Psychohistory and Psychobiography. So unexpected was the advent of National Socialist Germany and so bizarre were the personalities of its leadership that the historiography of the era saw the application of new interdisciplinary techniques to help explain what had happened. The result was that much more attention to the nature of the Third Reich was given by behavioral scientists, including social psychologists, psychiatrists and psychoanalysts. Added to these scholars were such social scientists as historians, political scientists and biographers who sought to combine historical interpretation with psychological analysis. They utilized the new disciplines of psychohistory and psychobiography, which combined historical and biographical research with psychological insight.

The new approach attempted to analyze motivations of Nazi leaders, especially Hitler, by attention to their early formative years, relations with their fathers and mothers and sexual drives. As was to be expected, differences of opinion arose among historians about the value of the new technique. Those defending psychohistory see it as a most important way to explain Hitler's almost hysterical hatred of Jews that led to the terrors of genocide and the Holocaust. They describe the new approach as of great value in understanding what happened in the Third Reich. On the other side are the skeptics who condemn the behavioral sciences as in their infancy and deprecate the value of psychiatry and psychoanalysis (from the theories of Freud to those of Adler and Sullivan) as much too controversial to be of any value. After all, they say, no one was able to get Hitler on a psychoanalyst's couch in order to study his mind. Then why indulge in guesswork? And what about the psychiatrists who testify for the prosecution and defense in a murder trial and give exactly opposite conclusions on the same set of facts? Like other intellectual controversies, the debate on the value of psychohistory goes on.

Social Milieu. Still another controversy has arisen among historians and sociologists about the part played by social classes in the successful drive of National Socialism to political power. Scholars of both disciplines agree that Hitler exploited all social classes in his campaign for the chancellorship — the rightist and élitist upper class, which feared communism; the embattled middle class, burdened by inflation; and the masses, which were entranced by the Nazi bread-and-circuses, the glamor of the Nuremberg rallies and the oratory of Hitler. But historians and sociologists differ on the matter of which class played the most important role in the doom of the Weimar Republic and the rise of Hitler to power. Some insist that it was the bourgeoisie, disgruntled by its loss of status, which played the dominant role. Others reject this point of view and claim that a movement of this kind could only have been successful if it attracted the mass support of the proletariat. Driven to distraction by unemployment and poverty and impressed by the hugely successful propaganda campaign of Dr. Goebbels, the workers, say these analysts, gave Hitler the overwhelming support he needed to promote his revolution. Here again the scholarly disputes continue, with books appearing regularly to support one view or another.

Industrialists and Bankers. Another debate arose among specialists on the role of industrialists in easing Hitler's drive to political power. In the early days of the Nazi party (the National Socialist German Workers' Party), Hitler was hard-pressed for funds to enable the expansion of his little-known followers. He managed to acquire the *Völkischer Beobachter*, an anti-Semitic sheet in which he could trumpet his ideology. Then he began to turn in several directions seeking money to expand the work of his growing party. Some scholars insist that such industrial magnates as Hugo Stinnes gave Hitler his main support during the early days and were really responsible for the rapid development of National Socialism. They say that funds began to flow into the coffers of the Party from wealthy Rhineland industrialists who saw in Hitler their best safeguard against annoying unions and the inroads of communism. They point out that wealthy banker Kurt Freiherr von Schroeder contributed vast sums to Hitler and became the midwife of Nazism by bringing Hitler and Franz von Papen together on 4 January 1933, in a historic interview at Cologne which led to the National Socialist government.

Yale historian Henry Ashby Turner, Jr., in his *German Big Business and the Rise of Hitler* (1985), attacked this thesis and insisted that, on the basis of his research in German archives, the financial contributions of big business were negligible, outside of some support by Thyssen, Kirdorf and Schacht. He concluded that the truth is that Nazism was self-supporting because of the dedication of its members and a variety of supporting funding devices. Again, the same set of facts led to an unresolved historiographical controversy.

Holocaust. There are varying estimates of the tragic Holocaust, the horrible genocide in which millions of Jews fell victim to Hitler's monomania and were incinerated in the ovens of extermination camps. A bitter historical controversy has arisen on the role of the Catholic Church and especially Pope Pius XII, in the Holocaust. Several stud-

ies, especially Guenter Lewy's *The Catholic Church and Nazi Germany*
(1964) and Saul Friedländer's *Pius XII and the Third Reich: A
Documentation* (1966) criticized Pius XII because of what they say was
his silence in the face of Nazi mass murder. On the same theme, Rolf
Hochhuth's drama, *Der Stellvertreter* (The Deputy), aroused international attention. Those who held this view published documents from
various sources indicating that the Pope had repeatedly received accurate reports through diplomatic and other channels about the mass
slaughter of Jews in occupied Poland, as well as facts about the
deportation of Jews from Germany, France, the Netherlands and other
countries to the death camps. Allegedly, the papacy did not view the
plight of Jews with expected moral courage or real urgency. Further-
more, these critics claimed that the Vatican ignored many calls for the
excommunication of Hitler.

Catholic writers heatedly defended the papacy. They published
portions of the Vatican archives covering World War II to defend the
Pope against the charges leveled against him, and asserted that public
protests would have been unsuccessful in helping Jews and might well
have caused additional danger for Catholics in Nazi-occupied Europe.
The Vatican had to protect its good name with the Germans and could
not risk its status of neutrality. The Vatican also did not propose to
undermine the German struggle against Soviet Russia.

Added to the controversy were studies accusing American President Franklin D. Roosevelt of doing far less that he could have done
to rescue Jews from their plight in Nazi Germany. The debate on Pius
XII and President Roosevelt was notable for its emotional tone of re-
crimination.

Nuremberg Trial. There was also a confrontation, especially
among legal scholars, about the legality of the Nuremberg Trial.
Twenty-two German principals of the Nazi regime were tried before an
International Military Tribunal from November 1945 to October 1946.
The triumphant Allies, flushed with victory, were divided upon most
policies except one – the German war criminals were to be punished.
They were charged with crimes against peace, against humanity, and
against defenseless minorities.

The defendants complained angrily that this was victors' justice,
with an unfair, illegal trial against responsible leaders, who were only
working in defense of their country. This viewpoint was echoed in an
ongoing debate among historians, political scientists and legalists. One
side contends that these were *ex post facto* proceedings with no justification in international law and that the judges could not possibly have

been objective under the circumstances. The authors of these books were troubled by the questionable legality of the trial and tended to agree with the accused that this was plainly victors' justice.

Other scholars rejected these views and claimed that evidence presented at the trial indicated clearly that monstrous crimes were committed, that precedents must be established for future conduct, and that perpetrators of crimes were to be held accountable for their actions.

Revisionist Historiography. After World War I several revisionist historians, led by American historian-journalist Harry Elmer Barnes, presented a point of view absolving Germany of guilt for the outbreak of war and set the order of guilt for direct and immediate responsibilty upon Serbia, France and Russia, with further culpability equally divided among Austria, Great Britain and Germany. This conclusion was rejected by most historians, but it was greeted inside Germany with gratitute by German scholars then in the midst of a campaign to combat what they called the *"Kriegsschuldlüge"* ("war-guilt lie").

A similar debate erupted among scholars after World War II. Most historians, although admitting that the general economic, political and psychological climate in the late 1930s was such that war could be expected, agree that Hitler's plan of aggression provided the spark that ignited the conflagration and that the German dictator was primarily responsible for the immediate origins of the war. This view was taken by British scholars such as John H. Wheeler-Bennett and Lewis Namier, and American historians William L. Langer, Norman Rich and Gerhard Weinberg, all of whom saw continuity in Hitler's thinking and his policy of aggression to achieve what he called *Lebensraum,* or living space.

The new revisionist historiography began in 1961 when A. J. P. Taylor, a Fellow at Oxford University, published *The Origins of the Second World War.* Like Harry Elmer Barnes a historian-journalist fortified with a brilliant writing style, Taylor enjoyed irritating his scholarly colleagues with far-out and unexpected judgments. The British public received Taylor's revisionism with delight, but serious scholars rejected the Pecksniffian opinions of their colleague as altogether false and misleading.

Briefly, Taylor argued that Hitler was not bent upon conquest, but that he was a traditional German statesman in the category of Frederick the Great, Bismarck and Stresemann. What Hitler wanted, in Taylor's view, was not war with Great Britain or France, but merely a revision of the Treaty of Versailles. The Hitler who turned on the Soviet Union in 1941 was no longer the Hitler of the prewar era. The only war, Taylor wrote, that Hitler desired in 1939 was a war of nerves, in which he excelled. He had no way of knowing that Great Britain and France would go to war over Danzig. Taylor held that *Mein Kampf* was a grandiose day dream and that Hitler's *Table Talk* was only fantasy. Documents presented at Nuremberg were only "lawyers' briefs." All other historians, Taylor challenged, were dead wrong on war responsibility.

Other historians denounced Taylor's revisionism as a naïve whitewashing of Hitler and an apology for appeasement. Hugh R. Trevor-Roper, Regius Professor of Modern History at Oxford (a post which Taylor publicly admitted he deserved more than Trevor-Roper), charged that Taylor had wilfully misused documents and in reality was acting as an apologist for the Nazis. This work by Taylor, said Trevor-Roper, was presented "with all his old resources of learning, paradox, and *gaminerie*" and was "demonstrably false" and "utterly erroneous." Where Taylor described Hitler's "patience," the critic saw indecision. Hitler's ultimate purpose, said Trevor-Roper, was emphatically not that of traditional German statesmen, but aimed at "the destruction of European civilization by a barbarous empire in Central Europe." Other historians were just as sarcastic in their condemnation of Taylor as the *enfant terrible* of British historiography.

Hossbach Memorandum. On the matter of Hitler's responsibility for aggression, another debate emerged on the meaning of a critical memorandum of a meeting called by Hitler and presided over by him. At a conference held on 5 November 1937 in the Reich Chancellery, Colonel Friedrich Hossbach, Hitler's *Wehrmacht* adjutant, wrote minutes of the meeting from his notes five days later. This memorandum was captured and presented as evidence at the Nuremberg Trial.

Most historians accept the Hossbach Memorandum as clear evidence of Hitler's program of conquest. At the meeting he asserted that "the solid racial core of the German nation gives it the right to greater *Lebensraum* (living space)." He stated that expansion could not take place without destroying resistance, and the problem was how to gain the most at the lowest cost. Once it was decided to use force, timing and execution were to be determined. The latest date would be between 1943 and 1945 — any subsequent date would be to Germany's disadvantage.

Revisionist British historian A. J. P. Taylor again was out of step with his colleagues. He deprecated the importance of the Hossbach

Memorandum and argued that it was simply an occasion on which Hitler dissimulated in order to confuse his opponents. Taylor held that Hitler merely wanted a free hand to correct intolerable conditions in the East and that he really had no ambitions directed against Great Britain or France. Other scholars again denounced Taylor's view as typically naïve. Trevor-Roper, Taylor's colleague at Oxford, decribed Taylor's analysis of the Hossbach Memorandum as too painful to be accepted by any scholar of academic standing.

Use as a Reference Tool

The discriminating reader will want to use these guidelines in finding exactly the right book.

Selection. These 850 titles have been selected to give a representative number of books and articles in the vast literature on National Socialism.

Content. The entries start with a note listing the author's or authors' name(s), title of book, city of publication, publisher and date of publication. Periodical articles give author's name, title of article, name of journal, volume number, date of publication and page numbers.

Annotation. The editor's annotation is limited strictly to a description of the contents of the book or article. What is the author's theme(s) or thesis(es)? What ground has been covered by the publication?

Editor's Choice. Virtually every book published has been either praised or criticized by reviewers. Very few receive either unanimous favorable attention or unfavorable reviews. For that reason the annotation has avoided critical comment one way or another. However, the editor has placed an asterisk before the author's or authors' names of those books and articles he regards as outstanding works on National Socialism. This procedure is purely subjective and need not be followed by the reader. At the same time it should be noted that inclusion of entries does not necessarily mean that all these books and articles are of superior merit.

Subtitles. For the reader's convenience, subtitles are given. Complementary topics are included at the head of each chapter.

Introductory Notes. An introduction for each chapter summarizes the contents and the ground covered.

Organization. There are so many categories in the treatment of National Socialism that this guide could be divided into an unwieldly number of chapters. To avoid the necessity of searching through too many divisions in the classification scheme, the categories have been limited basically to the traditional and time-honored divisions of political, economic, social, cultural, religious and psychological. For convenience, special subjects have been given chapters of their own. For example, while foreign policy might be included under political, it is set aside for a chapter because of its importance for the understanding of German National Socialism. Similarly, several other categories, such as biographies, resistance, and a few others, have been given special chapters.

Combinations. As a matter of convenience, several categories have been combined. Psychological developments include psychohistory, psychobiography and propaganda. Religious conflicts take into consideration Catholicism, Protestantism and "Positive Christianity." The material on Jews includes the general subject of the Holocaust. These are indicated in the Table of Contents and also in the chapter headings as subtitles and can be used for easy reference in finding the exact book desired.

Index. To find the book of a particular author, the reader is urged to consult the Index of Authors placed at the end of the guide. The numerals after the names in the index refer to the specific entries and not to pagination.

The reader, in common with the editor, will be fascinated by the extraordinary attention given by authors to every conceivable phase of the National Socialist regime in Germany. The impact of this failed government on the history of the twentieth century was so great that scholars in many disciplines have devoted their attention to many aspects of its origins, development and fall. There is also a vast popular literature devoted to the subject, especially to the life, personality and character of Hitler and the careers of the ambition-smothered rogues and ruffians who operated in his entourage.

It is a pleasure to add a note of warm thanks here to Eric Greenfeldt of the Princeton Public Library, and the staff of the Firestone Library of Princeton University, all of whom have rendered valuable assistance in the best spirit of the librarian's profession.

CHAPTER 1

DOCUMENTARY MATERIALS

Documents, Records, Reports, Speeches, Conversations, Readings

The term "documents" is used here in its broadest sense. It includes records and reports of all kinds as well as readings. The editors who present a collection of "documents" on Hitler and the Third Reich generally also include excerpts from secondary sources, newspaper stories, letters and the like.

After World War II, the victorious Allies captured official Nazi documents of all kinds, including records kept by the Foreign Office in Berlin, archives of the National Socialist Party, records of Nazi art plunder and various documentary materials. American troops who gathered this information sent it to Washington, DC, where it was photostated and the originals returned to the Federal Republic of West Germany. Thus, there is available at the National Archives in Washington a large volume of Nazi records.

There is always a problem in judging the value of official governmental documents, especially those on foreign policy. It is usually recognized that governmental administrators are most sensitive to what future historians will say about such major problems as war responsibility. After the outbreak of World War I, the belligerent governments issued Blue Books and White Books to justify their special courses of action and to place the burden of war responsibility on the enemy. Dangerous documents were eliminated or possibly rewritten. The process was repeated after World War II. For the historian it becomes a kind of higher intellectual game to find the truth in doctored documents.

The problem is especially acute when considering the unreliability of Nazi documents and documentation. It is no exaggeration to say that the Nazi regime was based on the efficacy of the lie. Hitler was said to have believed that the more times a lie was repeated the more it would be regarded as the truth. Nazi records are replete with falsifications, misstatements of fact, exaggerations and efforts to mislead. The historian judges Hitler and his work not by his speeches, contrived for effect, but by his actions.

BIBLIOGRAPHY

1. ACTES ET DOCUMENTS DU SAINT-SIÈGE RELATIFS À LA SECONDE GUERRE MONDIALE (Acts and Documents of the Holy See in Matters Concerning the Second World War). Rome: Libreria Editrice Vaticana, 1966 *ff.* Following the publication of a number of books on the silence of the Vatican during Hitler's "Final Solution" in World War II, notably Guenter Lewy's *The Catholic Church and Nazi Germany* (1964) and Saul Friedländer's *Pius XII and the Third Reich: A Documentation* (1966), the Vatican began the publication of a multivolumed series of acts and documents designed to defend the papacy and the Church from mounting criticism. Volume 1 (1966) concerns the Holy See and the war in Europe; volume 2 (1966) reprints the letters of Pope Pius XII to the German bishops; volumes 3 and 4 (1967) treat the Holy See and the religious situation in Poland and the Baltic countries. Volume 1, *The Holy See and the War in Europe*, appeared in English translation in London (1968). Volume 7, covering the years 1942-43, was published in 1973.

2. AKTEN DER HISTORISCHEN KOMMISSION DES REICHSFUEHRERS-SS. *Die Erhebung der österreichischen Nationalsozialisten im Juli 1934* (Documents of the Historical Commission of the *Reichsführer-SS*. The Rebellion of the Austrian National Socialists in July 1934). Vienna: Europa Verlag, 1966. Documents from Heinrich Himmler's files on the SS concerning the uprising of Austrian National Socialists in July 1934 reveal Hitler's intention to implement the Third Reich's union with Austria.

3. AKTEN DER PARTEI-KANZLEI DER NSDAP (Documents of the Party Chancellery of the German National Socialist German Workers' Party). New York: K. G. Saur, 1983, 1984 and 1985, 3 vols. in 491 microfiche.

    The files of the National Socialist Chancellery were supposed to be lost until they were published in this extensive microfiche edition — nearly 100,000 pages accompanied by index and six calendar volumes. The *Partei-Kanzlei* was not only Hitler's relay station for administration of the National Socialist German Workers' Party, it also enjoyed wider influence in the political events of the Third Reich. The files were "reconstructed" from copies of correspondence, minutes, memoranda and other documents scattered through German and other archives. List price of the microfiche edition — $4,000.

4. *AKTEN ZUR DEUTSCHEN AUSWÄRTIGEN POLITIK, 1918-1945, AUS DEM ARCHIV DES DEUTSCHEN AUSWÄRTIGEN AMTES (Documents on German Foreign Policy, 1918-1945, from the Archives of the German Foreign Office), SERIES C, 1933-1937. DAS DRITTE REICH: DIE ERSTEN JAHRE. Vol. 2, part 1, 14. OKTOBER 1933 BIS 31. JANUAR 1934; part 2, 1. FEBRUAR BIS 13. JUNI 1934; Vol. 3, part 1, 14. JUNI BIS 31. OKTOBER 1934; part 2, 1. NOVEMBER 1934 BIS 30. MÄRZ 1935. Göttingen: Vandenhoeck & Ruprecht, 1975.

    These documents on German foreign policy cover the period from Germany's withdrawal from the League of Nations and the World Disarmament Conference in October 1933 to the proclamation of military conscription in March 1935. The English edition appeared earlier in DOCUMENTS OF GERMAN FOREIGN POLICY, Series C and D (1949-1966). The entries reflect the efforts of the German Foreign Office professional diplomats to maintain a bit of autonomy and to neutralize the Ribbentrop policies. Yet, there is no doubt that the Foreign Office went along with Hitler in his policy of aggressive revisionism.

5. *AKTEN ZUR DEUTSCHEN AUSWÄRTIGEN POLITIK, 1918-1945, AUS DEM ARCHIV DES DEUTSCHEN AUSWÄRTIGEN AMTES (Documents on German Foreign Policy, 1918-1945, from the Archives of the German Foreign Office), SERIES D, 1937-1941. DIE KRIEGSJAHRE, Vol. 12, Part 1, 1. FEBRUAR BIS 5.

APRIL 1941; Part 2, 6. APRIL BIS 22. JUNI 1941. SE-
RIES E: 1941-1945. Vol. 1, 12. DEZEMBER 1941 BIS 28.
FEBRUAR 1942. Göttingen: Vandenhoeck & Ruprecht,
1969.
This is the parallel German edition to the next to last volume
of the completed Anglo-American series. The documents starting in December 1941, beginning after the United States entered
the war, reveal the German concern about difficult conditions
on the Eastern Front. Reports to the *Führer* told of the
dangerous situation in Russia, but the optimistic Hitler refused
to recognize the problem. Several of the documents concern the
Madagascar Plan as a place of exile for German Jews, but the
idea was soon abandoned in favor of the "Final Solution."

6. ARAD,   Yitzhak,   Yisrael   GUTMAN   and   Abraham
    MARGALIOT, eds. *Documents on the Holocaust.* New
    York: Ktav, 1982.
    A collection of 213 primary documents tracing the destruction
    of Jews in Germany, Austria, Poland and the Soviet Union.
    Drawing upon the Yad Vashem archives, the editors offer offi-
    cial documents from the highest Nazi levels as well as accounts
    of eyewitnesses caught in the Holocaust. The aim is to provide
    materials for an understanding of the nature and scope of Nazi
    genocide.

7. BAYNES, Norman H., ed.   *The Speeches of Adolf Hitler.*
    London: Oxford University Press, 1942, 2 vols.
    Offers representative passages from Hitler's public speeches be-
    tween 1922 and 1939. The editor cut the speeches drastically
    because of their overlong texts, and limits himself to what he
    sees as the core of Hitler's thinking. His aim is to present the
    personality and character of the *Führer* as revealed in his own
    words.

8. BOBERACH, Heinz, ed.   *Meldungen aus dem Reich* (Reports
    from the Reich). Neuwied and Berlin: n.p., 1965.
    A collection of reports on conditions in the Third Reich selected
    from the secret files of the *Sicherheitsdienst* (Security Service)
    of the SS from 1935 to 1944, including reports on morale, cul-
    ture, propaganda, press, radio, rumors and reaction to Hitler's
    speeches.

9. BOELCKE, Willi A., ed.   *The Secret Conferences of Dr.
    Goebbels.* New York: Dutton, 1970.

A record of the closed meetings held by Dr. Joseph Goebbels, Minister for Public Enlightenment and Propaganda, which details the programs inaugurated by Goebbels to maintain the German people's loyalty for the Nazi regime.

10. BROSZAT, Martin, *et al.*, eds. *Bayern in der NS Zeit* (Bavaria during the Era of National Socialism). Munich: Oldenbourg Verlag, 1977.
A volume of documents on resistance and persecution in Bavaria, illustrating the social situation and political relationships as seen in confidential reports. Seeks to show the grassroots actions of ordinary Germans in Bavaria during the Third Reich. The theme is "the interaction of social structures and political control." Included are police reports as well as comments by minor bureaucrats and party officials. The focus is the small town and the rural hinterland.

11. Bundesarchiv. Files in Bonn on the National Socialist Party, Reich Chancellery, Ministry of the Interior, Reich Ministry for Propaganda and Reich Ministry for Science and Education.

12. *DER HITLER PROZESS (The Hitler Trial). Munich: Deutscher Knorr & Wirth, 1924.
On 26 February 1924 Hitler was brought to trial on a charge of high treason because of his part in the Beer-Hall *Putsch* at Munich on 8-9 November 1923. This is the official record of the proceedings. The text reveals that Hitler took advantage of the court to attempt a propaganda triumph. Acting as his own lawyer, he gave a dazzling display of oratory. He took full blame on himself for the *Putsch*: "This is my attitude: I would rather be hanged in a Bolshevik Germany than perish under the rule of French swords." He predicted that the hour would come when the masses would unite with those who were ordered to fire on them. "Even if you judge us guilty a thousand times, the goddess of the eternal court of history will laugh and tear up the verdict of this court, but she pronounces us not guilty." Hitler was sentenced to five years' imprisonment at Landsberg-am-Lech, of which he served only nine months. His behavior before the Munich court made an enormous impression on the German public.

13. *DOCUMENTS ON GERMAN FOREIGN POLICY, 1918-1945, Volume 6, November 1, 1936-November 14,

1937 (The Third Reich, First Phase, series C, 1933-1937).
Washington, DC: U.S. Government Printing Office, 1983.
Continued project for publishing German diplomatic documents. The German Federal Republic joined the plan and issued its own version. This is the English-language edition of
series C. Major themes include German interests in East Asia;
attempts to draw Romania into the German orbit and to
neutralize Belgium; Hitler's troubles with the Vatican;
German-Polish relations; estrangement with the United States;
and efforts of the British and French to find a general settlement
with Berlin, efforts not reciprocated by Germany.

14. DOKUMENTE DER DEUTSCHEN POLITiK, 1935-1940
(Documents on German Foreign Policy, 1935-1940). Vols.
1-6, issued in Berlin: Deutsche Hochschule für Politik,
1935-39. Vols. 7-8. Berlin: Deutsches
Auslandswissenschaftliches Institut, 1940.
Official documents issued by the Hitler government from the
advent of the National Socialist regime to the outbreak of
World War II. The documents selected are chosen to inform the
world about the reasonableness of Hitler's foreign policy and
German efforts to circumvent the Treaty of Versailles while
pursuing a policy of peace.

15. DOMARUS, Max, ed. *Hitler: Reden und Proklamationen,
1932-1945* (Hitler: Speeches and Proclamations,
1932-1945). Neustadt a.d. Aisch: Schmidt, 1962, 1963, 2
vols.
A giant collection of Hitler's speeches and proclamations from
the year before the *Führer* assumed political power to the end
of World War II. These two volumes, along with Hitler's *Mein
Kampf*, give evidence of Hitler's ideology and plans. In 1965,
the Süddeutscher Verlag in Munich issued an extended version
in four volumes.

16. FOREIGN OFFICE, GERMANY. *Documents on the Events
Preceding the Outbreak of the War.* Berlin: German Foreign Office, 1939; New York: German Library of Information, 1940.
A German White Book, issued in reply to the British War Blue
Book on the origins of the war, offers 482 state papers and
documents. A prefatory note accuses the British War Blue
Book of being journalism, not history, and claims that its own
book is real history. "It is accurate, not superficial, genuine,

not juggled." Shows the trend of Great Britain's "bellicose policy" after the Munich agreement. Includes documents to reveal "Poland's systematic campaign of extermination against Germans in Poland and Danzig." Describes the *Führer* as statesmanlike in his efforts, "grand in outline and infinite in their patience," to find an "equitable solution." Emphasizes "Britain's will to war," as described by Foreign Minister Joachim von Ribbentrop.

17. FOREIGN RELATIONS OF THE UNITED STATES. *The Conference at Berlin* (The Potsdam Conference). Washington, DC: U.S. Government Printing Office, 1960, 2 vols.
Official documents on the Potsdam Conference. Under the cover name of Terminal, the meeting of the chiefs of state of the Big Three (Stalin, Attlee and Truman), their principal advisers and technical experts was held in Potsdam near Berlin in midsummer 1945 to clarify and implement earlier agreements reached for the future of defeated Germany. Political decisions were made on four occupation zones and Poland, attention was given to the effective deindustrialization of Germany and Germany was required to pay reparations.

18. *GILBERT, Felix, ed. and trans. *Hitler Directs His War: The Secret Records of His Daily Military Conferences.* New York: Oxford University Press, 1950.
Felix Gilbert of The Institute for Advanced Study, Princeton University, translates and edits the documents on Hitler's military conferences from North Africa and Stalingrad to the beginning of the end. First translated for the United States Army for official use, the record reveals in Hitler's own words the truth about the Nazis, the brutal political battles and the vicious infighting at the highest levels of the Third Reich. The top-secret transcripts disclose the *Führer's* daily meetings with leading military advisers — Goering, Goebbels, Himmler, Speer, Bormann, Jodl, Keitel and others. The documents reveal Hitler's refusal to face facts and his raging against the generals when they dared to tell him the truth about the military situation.

19. GÖRING, Hermann. *The Political Testament of Hermann Göring: A Selection of Important Speeches and Articles by Field-Marshal Hermann Göring.* Arranged and translated by H. W. Blood-Ryan. London: Long, 1939.

A selection of the important speeches and lectures, mostly extemporaneous, by Hermann Goering, No. 2 Nazi, from the birth of the Third Reich in 1933 to 1938. The editor shows how the German Air Minister always used public meetings to state a national grievance or argument, often quite foreign to the body he was addressing.

20. GREAT BRITAIN, MINISTRY OF INFORMATION. *How Hitler Made the War*. London: His Majesty's Stationery Office, 1939.
     This official publication offers the British version of the steps taken by the German *Führer* leading to war. Includes the report by British Ambassador Nevile Henderson in Berlin on the circumstances leading to the termination of his mission to the German capital. Attention is given to Hitler's methods and techniques during the final negotiations before Nazi armies invaded Poland.

21. *Guide to German Records*. Washington, DC: National Archives and Records Administration, 1985.
     Records microfilmed at Alexandria, VA. This Volume 84 offers Records of the German Armed Forces High Command (*Oberkommando der Wehrmacht, OKW*), part 7, *Wehrwirtschaft und Rüstungsamt* (War Economy and Armaments Office).

22. HERZSTEIN, Robert Edwin, ed. *Adolf Hitler and the Third Reich*. Boston: Houghton Mifflin, 1971.
     A volume in Houghton Mifflin's *New Perspectives in History*, this book is a collection of documents and readings on the Third Reich from 1933 to 1945. The author weaves his treatment alternately with documentations and comments by such experts as George F. Kennan, Gerald Reitlinger and others.

23. HITLER, Adolf. *Hitler's Secret Conversations, 1941-1944*. New York: Farrar, Strauss &Young, 1953.
     Hitler's minions recorded these conversations as if they were the wisdom of the ages. Samples: *Race*: "It's our duty continually to arouse the forces that slumber in our people's blood." *Self-estimate*: "There was a time when one could say there was *only* one Prussian in Europe and that he lived in Rome....There was a second Prussian. He lived in Munich and was myself." *Grandeur*: "When one enters the Reich Chancellery, one should have the feeling that he [*sic*] is visiting the master of the world." *Suspicions*: "I never met an Englishman who didn't say

Churchill was off his head....There's no doubt about it: Roosevelt is a sick brain." *Americans:* "There's nobody stupider than Americans. I'll never believe the American soldier can fight like a hero." Hitler dismissed as insane anyone who disagreed with his judgments.

24. HITLER, Adolf. *The Speeches of Adolf Hitler, 1922-1939.* London: Oxford University Press, 1942.
A collection of Hitler's speeches from the early days of political life to the outbreak of World War II.

25. HITLER, Adolf. *Tischgespräche im Führerhauptquartier, 1941-1942* (Table-talk at the *Führer's* Field Headquarters, 1941-1942). Stuttgart: Seewald Verlag, 1965.
A collection of Hitler's field headquarters table-talk from 1941 to 1942, recorded by assistants eager to preserve every utterance of the *Führer.* Hitler would talk far into the night about every conceivable subject and his words were taken down as the talk of a genius. This volume reveals much about the nature of Hitler's thinking as well as its uncommon shrewdness responsible for much of the early successes.

26. HITLER E MUSSOLINI. *Lettere e documenti* (Letters and Documents). Milan: Rizzoli, 1946.
Records of the exchange of letters between the German *Führer* and the Italian *Duce.* Documents are included.

27. HOFER, Walther, ed. *Der Nationalsozialismus: Dokumente, 1933-1945* (National Socialism: Documents, 1933-1945). Frankfurt am Main: Fischer Bücherei, 1957.
The Swiss historian of Bern University offers a selection of documents illustrating the history of National Socialism from Hitler's accession to power to the end of World War II.

28. INTERNATIONAL LABOR OFFICE, *Industrial and Labor Information.* Geneva: International Labor Office, 1934.
General information about labor and industrial affairs, including the texts of early laws in the Third Reich, such as the Law to Promote National Labor, 20 January 1934.

29. *INTERNATIONAL MILITARY TRIBUNAL. Trial of the Major War Criminals before the International Military Tribunal, 14 November 1945 to 1 October 1946.*

Washington, DC: U.S. Government Printing Office, 1949
ff.
Forty-two volumes of the proceedings at Nuremberg when 22
Nazi leaders went on trial for crimes against peace, war crimes
and crimes against humanity, cover the trial from beginning to
end, including the testimony of the accused, statements of
prosecution and defense counsel, cross-examinations and texts
of the verdicts. A typical entry provides extracts from the minutes of a secret conference Hitler held with his army chiefs on
23 May 1939. In shorthand notes, Oberstleutnant Rudolf
Schmundt reveals that Hitler, who always protested that he had
no intention of waging aggressive war, expressed his doubt of
the possibility of a peaceful settlement with England. "The
Dutch and Belgian air bases must be occupied by armed force.
Declarations of neutrality must be ignored....Albeit under protest, Belgium and Holland will yield to pressure." This kind of
testimony contradicted Hitler's oft-proclaimed protestations of
a peaceful policy.

30. IRVING, David, ed. *Breach of Security*. London: Kimber,
     1968.
   A collection of German secret intelligence files on events leading
   to World War II.

31. JACKSON, Robert H. *Report to the International Conference
     on Military Trials*. London, 1945. Washington, DC: U.S.
     Government Printing Office, 1949.
   A report by the American prosecutor at the International Military Tribunal on the subject of military trials.

32. JACOBSEN, Hans Adolf, ed. *Dokumente zum Westfeldzug,
     1940* (Documents on Campaigns in the West, 1940).
     Göttingen: Musterschmidt Wissenschaftlicher Verlag,
     1960.
   A collection of documents concerning Hitler's campaigns in the
   West in 1940 at the height of military success.

33. JACOBSEN, Hans Adolf, ed. *Kriegstagebuch des
     Oberkommandos der Wehrmacht* (War Diary of the
     Wehrmacht High Command). Frankfurt am Main:
     Bernard & Graefe Verlag für Wehrwesen, 1965.
   The German author of a history of World War II and an editor
   of five volumes of documents on National Socialism concen-

trates on Hitler's war strategy and presents the day-to-day war efforts of the *Wehrmacht*'s High Command.

34. *JACOBSEN, Hans Adolf and W. JOCHMANN, eds. *Ausgewählte Dokumente zur Geschichte des Nationalsozialismus* (Selected Documents on the History of National Socialism). Bielefeld: Verlag Neue Gesellschaft, 1961.
These five volumes of documents present the history of National Socialism from its beginnings to 1945, selected from the enormous number of documents on the Nazi era.

35. KEMPNER, Robert M. W. *Das Dritte Reich im Kreuzverhör* (The Third Reich in Cross-Examination). Munich: Bechtle Verlag, 1969.
The United States team of prosecutors at the International Military Tribunal at Nuremberg from November 1945 to October 1946 was led by Chief of Counsel Robert H. Jackson. Among his associates were sixteen American Assistant Trial Counsel, including the German-born Dr. Robert M. Kempner. Kempner provides the texts of his cross-examination of witnesses before the tribunal, including Hermann Goering and such minor figures as Hitler's interpreter Paul O. Schmidt, Crown Prince Friedrich Wilhelm of Prussia ("I knew that we would lose the war"), and Johanna Wolf, Hitler's secretary, who described the last days in the Berlin bunker.

36. *KENNAN, George F. *From Prague after Munich: Diplomatic Papers, 1938-1940*. Princeton: Princeton University Press, 1968.
Contains previously unpublished documents, letters and diary notes written by the diplomat-historian while serving as Secretary of Legation in the U.S. Embassy in Prague and Berlin. Includes material written by himself, although some of it was submitted to Washington as official reports under the signature of colleagues. Seeks a sense of perspective in chaotic and very dangerous times. The theme concerns "one of humanity's oldest and most recalcitrant dilemmas of a limited collaboration with Evil in the interests of its ultimate mitigation."

37. KIRCHE IM KAMPF, DOKUMENTE DES WIDERSTANDS UND DES AUFBAUS IN DER EVANGELISCHEN KIRCHE DEUTSCHLANDS VON 1933 BIS 1945 (Documents on the Resistance and the

Building of the Evangelical Church in Germany from 1933 to 1945). Tübingen: Wunderlich, 1950.
Documents on the militant Protestant Church concerning the resistance and renaissance of the Protestant Church in Germany from the beginning of the Third Reich to its fall in 1945. Pays special attention to the building of the Evangelical Church as a response to Hitler's new pro-Nazi "Positive Christianity." Pastors Dietrich Bonhoeffer and Martin Niemoeller emerge as ecclesiastical heroes.

38. KOHLERBERG, Friedrich P., ed. *Persönliche Adjutantur des Führers und Reichskanzlers* (Personal Adjutant to the *Führer* and Reich Chancellor). Koblenz: Bundesarchiv, 1970.
Records of the daily tasks and activities of Hitler's adjutants, including letters and official papers, as well as accounts of the personal attention of adjutants to Hitler's wants.

39. *MASER, Werner, ed. *Hitler's Letters and Notes.* Translated from the German by Arnold Pomerans. New York: Harper & Row, 1974.
A collection of Hitler's letters, notes and documents taken from archives and private sources, revealing insight into the *Führer's* thoughts, dreams, ideas, ambitions and philosophy. Seeks to prove that previous biographers incorrectly interpreted the *Führer's* mental development. Part 1 contains letters and postcards from 1906, when Hitler was seventeen, to 1945, with discussions on music, architecture, the weather, cockroaches in his Munich apartment, mutual acquaintances, and comments on history, democracy, economics, the military and anti-Semitism. Part 2 consists of notes for speeches, writings and plans for action. Several hundred letters and documents are rendered in facsimile, including several of Hitler's drawings.

40. MÜLLER, Hans. *Katholische Kirche und Nationalsozialismus* (The Catholic Church and National Socialism). Munich: Nymphenburger Verlagshandlung, 1963.
A collection of documents designed to clarify the relations between the Catholic Church and National Socialism from 1930 to 1935. Each of the four chapters has an introduction by the editor.

41. MURPHY, Raymond E., F. B. STEVENS, Howard TRIVERS and Joseph M. ROLAND. *National Socialism: Basic*

Principles. Washington, DC: U.S. Government Printing Office, 1943.

Prepared for the U.S. Department of State, this study was designed to show the characteristics of the enemy the United States was fighting. Included are the texts of documents Hitler used to solidify his position, such as the Enabling Act of 24 March 1933.

42. NAZI CONSPIRACY AND AGGRESSION. Washington, DC: Office of Prosecuting Counsel, 1946-48.

Multivolumed records presenting documents from the Office of the U.S. Chief of Counsel for the prosecution of Axis war crimes. Among the entries are the will and last testament and political testament of Hitler (both of 29 April 1945) before his suicide in his Berlin bunker.

43. NOAKES, Jeremy and Geoffrey PRIDHAM, eds. *Documents on Nazism, 1919-1945.* New York: Viking, 1974.

A collection of excerpts from official documents, memoirs, diaries, police reports, resistance memoranda and name index. The two English historians introduce the documents with their own special comments. They characterize the Nazi state and its impact on individuals and groups.

44. OBERKOMMANDO DER WEHRMACHT. *Fahrten und Flüge gegen England* (High Command of the *Wehrmacht.* Journeys and Flights against England). Berlin: Zeitgeschichtlicher Verlag, 1941.

Official reports of the German High Command Armed Forces on the air campaign against England. The documents include an account of the massive *Luftwaffe* attack on Coventry, the British Midlands manufacturing center, on 15 November 1940, in which the medieval cathedral was destroyed, a good part of the city wrecked, and its essential services paralyzed.

45. PRANGE, Gordon W., ed. *Hitler's Words, 1923-1943.* Washington, DC: American Council on Public Affairs, 1944.

A collection of Hitler's speeches during the twenty years from 1923, the early days of the Nazi movement, to 1943. The selections are shorter than in the two-volume collection edited by Norman H. Baynes (1942).

46. REMAK, Joachim, ed. *The Nazi Years: A Documentary History*. Englewood Cliffs, NJ: Prentice-Hall, 1969.
     A book of readings on the National Socialist movement, including its origins, eugenics, anti-Semitism, occupation policy and resistance to Hitler. Emphasizes the ideology of National Socialism and the operation of the totalitarian state. Special attention is given to German accounts of life under the Nazi dictatorship.

47. ROTH, Bert., ed. *Kampf: Lebensdokumente deutscher Jugend von 1914-1934* (Struggle: Documents on the Lives of German Youth from 1914 to 1934). Leipzig: Reklam jun. Verlag, 1934.
     A Nazi publication consisting of documents and readings about German youth during the two decades from the outbreak of World War I to 1934. Typical approach: "We National Socialist students did not go into working-class quarters to have our heads broken for nothing."

48. ROUSSY DE SALES, Raoul de. *My New Order*. New York: Reynal, 1941.
     A collection of Hitler's speeches designed to show the nature of the *Führer's* ideology.

49. SCHUMANN, Heinz and Heinz KÜNRICH, eds. *SS im Einsatz* (SS at Stake). Berlin: Deutscher Militärverlag, 1967.
     A documentation on the crimes committed by the SS, a collection sponsored by the Committee of the Anti-Fascist Resistance Fighters in the German Democratic Republic. Special attention is devoted to the protocols of the International Military Tribunal at Nuremberg (1945-46).

50. SNELL, John L., ed. *The Nazi Revolution: Hitler's Dictatorship and the German Nation*. Lexington, MA: Heath, 1973.
     A collection of readings in the Problems of European Civilization Series, edited originally by John L. Snell and revised in this edition by A. Mitchell. Features essays by such authorities on Hitler and Nazism as A. J. P. Taylor, Gerhard Ritter, Eugene Anderson, Karl Dietrich Bracher, Alan Bullock, Ernst Nolte and others. Attention is given to the Nazi movement and German history, Hitler's personality, politics, industry, the Army and the social impact of Nazism.

51. SNYDER, Louis L., ed. *Hitler's Third Reich: A Documentary History*. Chicago: Nelson-Hall, 1981.
    The author gives a running account of the history of the Third Reich through a variety of documentary materials, including official publications, reportage, speeches, excerpts from letters and diaries, radio talks and court records. The text is arranged chronologically with connecting notes to place the selections in historical context. The period covered includes the post-World-War-I years and the Weimar Republic, the rise of Nazism, World War II and Germany immediately after the fall of the Third Reich.

52. SONTAG, Raymond James and James Stewart BEDDIE, eds. *Germany: Auswärtiges Amt. Nazi-Soviet Relations, 1939-1941*. New York: Didier, 1948.
    Documents from the German Foreign Office as released by the Department of State. This compilation concerns captured German documents that trace the career of the German-Russian alliance during the early years of World War II. The documents are not easy to read and many can be suspected of being manufactured for the use of future historians. At the same time, they are of basic importance for any understanding of the diplomacy of Nazi and Soviet officials.

53. STROOP, Juergen. *The Stroop Report*. Translated from the German by Sybil Milton. New York: Pantheon, 1980.
    Starting in January 1943, guerrillas of the Jewish Combat Organization divided into some twenty-two groups, struck back at their Nazi tormentors in the Warsaw ghetto. In four days, twenty Germans were killed and fifty wounded. On the morning of 19 April 1943, German and Polish troops and police moved in on the ghetto in a "final action" to send all who were left to Treblinka concentration camp. The fighting went on for twenty-eight days as the guerrillas fought to the last. Many committed suicide at the moment before capture. This book is an illustrated report to Heinrich Himmler, head of the SS, by Major-General Juergen Stroop, who directed the destruction of the ghetto and who was executed in 1951. The essence of the report is given in the subtitle: "The Jewish Ghetto of Warsaw Is No More!" The text contains a facsimile of the record as well as the translation into English.

54. *TAYLOR, Telford. *Final Report*. Washington, DC: U.S. Government Printing Office, 1949.

The final report to the Secretary of the Army on the Nuremberg War Crimes Trials under Council Law No. 10. Taylor was the American Chief of Counsel for War Crimes. In this post he played a major role in unraveling the tangled details of the charges against the top hierarchy of Nazi leaders.

55.   TESTAMENT OF ADOLF HITLER. London: Cassell, 1961.
      After dictating his last will, Hitler issued a political testament in which he defended his work and career. He maintained that he did not want to go to war in 1939 and placed the blame for the conflict on "International Jewry." In Part II he expelled the "traitors" Hermann Goering and Heinrich Himmler, appointed his successors and outlined the form of government they should adopt. The text of the Hitler-Bormann documents is given in this book (Martin Bormann, Hitler's confidant and secretary, prepared the document, which he signed along with Dr. Joseph Goebbels; General Wilhelm Burgdorf, *Wehrmacht* Adjutant at the *Führer's* headquarters; and General Hans Krebs, Chief of Staff).

56.   *TREVOR-ROPER, H. R., ed. *Hitler's   War   Directives, 1939-1945* London: Sidgwick & Jackson, 1964.
      The text of Hitler's war directives was published originally in Germany as *Hitlers Weisungen für die Kriegsführung 1939-45, Dokumente des Oberkommandos der Wehrmacht*, edited by Walther Hubatsch and published by Bernard & Graefe Verlag in Frankfurt am Main (1962). These war directives, supplemented by later orders woven into the text, give an outline history of Hitler's war as conceived and controlled by the *Führer*. The documents show how Hitler envisaged the war, how he launched it, how he directed it and how he moved from intoxicating triumph to catastrophic defeat. In his notes, editor Trevor-Roper reveals the complications of the German command, and how military action and party politics were interrelated.

57.   *TRIALS OF WAR CRIMINALS.   Washington, DC: U.S. Government Printing Office, 1946-49, 15 vols.
      There were additional trials of accused war criminals after the major trial at Nuremberg in 1945-46. These documents give the record of proceedings before the Nuremberg Military Tribunals under Control Council No. 10, from October 1946 to April 1949.

58. U.S. DEPARTMENT OF STATE. *The Axis in Defeat.*
Washington, DC: U.S. Government Printing Office, 1945.
An official U.S. collection of documents on American policy
toward defeated Germany and Japan, including the important
JCS/1057, a U.S. Military Government directive for the
occupation of the American military zone in Occupied
Germany. "Germany will not be occupied for the purpose of
liberation but as a defeated enemy nation." The United States
Joint Chiefs of Staff sent the directive to General Dwight D.
Eisenhower to be used as a guide in occupation policies.

59. *U.S. EMBASSY. *Berlin Reports.* Washington, DC: National
Archives, n.d.
These reports from the U.S. Berlin Embassy to Washington
during the years 1930-39 emphasized the pace of Hitler's rearmament program, as well as the morale of the German people
under the Nazi regime. Most came from Ambassador William
E. Dodd, who served in the post from 1935 to 1937. Dodd's
extremely critical remarks on the Nazis provide a highly negative picture of what was happening in Nazi Germany.

60. *WIENER LIBRARY. *From Weimar to Hitler, Germany,
1918-1933* (Catalogue Series No. 2). London: Vallentine,
Mitchell, 1964.
The Wiener Library in London is a treasure trove for research
on any phase of National Socialism. Its catalogue series publications are indispensable for any understanding of the Nazi
phenomenon. The library is especially strong on documentary
materials. The records include indictments and judgments in
about 300 cases before the Nazi "People's Court" and "Special
Courts." Some 5,000 documents relate to the "Jewish
Question" from records of the German Foreign Office, the
Chancellery of the Nazi Party and local *Gestapo* offices. A
catalogue contains about 3,000 Nuremberg documents with
subject and name index, 1,500 reports from survivors of Nazi
persecution, as well as personal recollections. Available are records of 13 Nuremberg trials with transcripts of court sessions,
prosecution and defense documents, altogether some 40,000
documents on this subject. There are extensive records on the
Eichmann trial, transcripts of court sessions, about 1,600
prosecution documents and transcripts of the interrogation of
Eichmann.

CHAPTER 2

GENERAL

History, Historiography, Encyclopedias, Bibliographies

Historians of the Nazi era have busied themselves with the task of explaining the reasons for the decline of the Weimar Republic and the rise of National Socialism to power in the Third Reich. It is to be expected that there would be variations of concepts of causation, just as there are on such historical phenomena as the Renaissance, the Enlightenment, romanticism, nationalism and the two World Wars.

German historians have presented two diametrically opposed concepts of causation: *Kontinuitätslehre* (continuity concept) and *Katastrophentheorie* (catastrophe theory). The first holds that there is always continuity in historical causation, that roots always run deeply into the past. The catastrophe theory presents the view that on occasion something brand new can happen regardless of what has occurred in the past.

The confrontation of ideas may well be applied to the Nazi movement. The late American historian Koppel S. Pinson, in his *Modern Germany: Its History and Civilization* (1954), expressed a view held by most non-German historians: that the roots of Nazism can be found in the past from Luther to Frederick the Great to Bismarck to Hitler. In other words, the continuity theme is accepted by many historians as historically valid.

On the other hand, the distinguished German historian Friedrich Meinecke (1862-1954) leaned toward the opposite theory in his *The German Catastrophe* (1950). He reversed a lifetime of historical thinking and seemed to indicate that the rise of National Socialism was a kind of bolt of lightning which hit the unsuspecting German people.

Meinecke did criticize forces and entities such as the Prussian state for preparing the groundwork for Hitler, but he still maintained that Hitlerism was in reality an unpredictable phenomenon resulting in calamitous disaster. Other German historians insist that Nazism merely reflected European Fascism and was a part of it without special German features.

This chapter includes studies of general interest which do not fit comfortably into other categories presented in this bibliographic guide. Other books on the rise and fall of National Socialism will be found in Chapter 4.

BIBLIOGRAPHY

61. *ARENDT, Hannah. *The Origins of Totalitarianism*. Cleveland: World, 1958.
    Analyzes the more important characteristics of National Socialist and Soviet totalitarianism. Discusses all possible aspects of the movement in the Hitler and Stalin states. Devotes special attention to anti-Semitism in both dictatorships and describes the techniques used in concentration and extermination camps by totalitarian regimes. Notes that the first concern of Hitler was to purge the Jews from German life. He showed contempt for the narrowness of nationalism, the provincialism of the nation-state, while at the same time insisting on the "internationalism" of his own movement.

62. AYCOBERRY, Pierre. *The Nazi Question: An Essay on the Interpretations of National Socialism (1922-1975)*. Translated from the French by Robert Hurley. New York: Pantheon, 1981.
    Aims to explain National Socialism by examination of the works written about it. Discusses the books of one hundred authors, with special attention to Hannah Arendt, Hermann Rauschning, Carl J. Friedrich and Ernst Nolte. Criticizes the revisionist theories of A. J. P. Taylor on the origins of World War II, and points to the major dualisms of National Socialism: conservatism versus radicalism, élitism and populism, modernization and antimodernity, and fanaticism and opportunism. Uses statistical methodology in analyzing studies of Nazism, its sympathizers and adversaries.

63. *BAUMONT, Maurice, John H. E. FRIED and Edmund
    VERMEIL, eds. *The Third Reich*. New York: Praeger,
    1955.
    This study, published under the auspices of the International
    Council for Philosophy and Humanistic Studies and with the
    assistance of UNESCO, is edited by three historians, Baumont
    and Vermeil of the Sorbonne, and Fried of New York Univer-
    sity. Twenty-eight contributions cover many aspects of the
    Third Reich from its origins to the organization and efficiency
    of the German Fifth Column. The contributors include such
    specialists as Alan Bullock, A. J. P. Taylor, Otto Klineberg and
    Louis de Jong, in addition to essays by the editors.

64. *BLOND, Georges. *The Death of Hitler's Germany*. Translated
    from the French by Frances Frenaye. New York: Pyramid
    Books, 1958.
    An account of the last days of the Third Reich from the un-
    successful attempt on Hitler's life in July 1944 to "Apocalypse"
    in the *Führer's* Berlin bunker. Recounts the blunders and mon-
    strous tragedies attributable to the Nazi leader edging toward
    madness. Utilizes the archives of the German Supreme Military
    Command seized intact at Flensburg; orders, reports and per-
    sonal letters; documents of the Nuremberg Trial and many
    interviews. Explains how the German armies were smashed, the
    German nation pounded to rubble and wreckage and describes
    the ignominious end of the Third Reich.

65. BRACHER, Karl Dietrich. *The German Dictatorship: The
    Origin, Structure and Effects of National Socialism*.
    Translated from the German by Jean Steinberg. New
    York: Praeger, 1970.
    An almost encyclopedic account of the Third Reich by a
    German historian who wrote several works on the Nazi era.
    Analyzes the background of the Nazi movement and seeks "the
    multi-causal nature of German historico-political processes."
    Describes Hitler's system of totalitarian government and de-
    votes attention to the psychological and sociological causes of
    Nazi successes. Also discusses Hitler's foreign policy and role
    as a wartime leader. Bracher seeks to avoid dogma and myth.
    There is an extensive bibliography giving hundreds of entries on
    works by German scholars and journalists on the Nazi regime
    and its leaders.

66. BROSZAT, Martin. *The Hitler State: The Foundation and Development of the Internal Structure of the Third Reich.* Translated from the German by John W. Hiden. London and New York: Longman, 1981.
     Martin Broszat, of the Munich Institute of Contemporary History, presents a history of the Third Reich with special attention to its foundations and development of its internal structure. Describes Nazi Germany as a semi-fascist authoritarian state until 1936-37, when its drive for territorial expansion led to the outbreak of war in 1939. Perceives no systematic change of command. Hitler was substantially removed from both party and government, and governed from the periphery, not the center of the administration.

67. *BUSE, Dieter and Juergen DOERR. *German Nationalisms: A Bibliographical Approach.* New York and London: Garland, 1985.
     This is Volume 5 in a series of bibliographies on nationalism arranged by Professor Thomas Spira, editor of the *Canadian Review of Studies in Nationalism.* This is the first extensive bibliography of German nationalism. Provides nearly eight-hundred items covering some fifty years to 1981. The authors use the term *nationalisms* in the plural because of their belief that there were, and are, several different types of German nationalism beyond "the older notion" of a monolithic German nationalism severed from the more benign and rational Western tradition. There are entries on the origins of Hitler, National Socialism and World War II. Presents the opposing schools and their respective points of view.

68. CASINELLI, C. W. *Total Revolution.* Studies in Comparative Politics, No. 10. Santa Barbara, CA: Clio Books, 1976.
     A comparative study of Germany under Hitler, the Soviet Union under Stalin, and China under Mao. The ideologies of all three were based "on the belief in the possibility and inevitability of total change." Maintains that all three rejected the scientific and social principles of bourgeois civilization.

69. *CRAIG, Gordon A. *Germany, 1866-1945.* New York: Oxford University Press, 1978.
     This text by Gordon A. Craig, Professor of History at Stanford University, is included in the *Oxford History of Modern Europe.* Traces German development from the creation of Bismarck's Second Reich to the fall of Hitler's Third Reich. Is

concerned with the corruption of power at top levels and the failure of people at lower levels. Discusses the faults of the German Empire, particularly pointing to Bismarck's assault on the Roman Catholic Church as a dress rehearsal for Hitler's attack on Jews. The Army formed the strongest and most cohesive institution in Imperial Germany. A classical lack of proportion and absence of moderation led to the catastrophe of Hitlerism.

70. DILL, Marshall. *Germany: A Modern History.* Ann Arbor: University of Michigan Press, 1961.
A contribution to the 16-volume *Michigan History of the Modern World*, this book devotes special attention to the recent period. Emphasizes the development of modern German nationalism.

71. *EBENSTEIN, William. *The Nazi State.* New York: Farrar & Rinehart, 1943.
An early analysis of the structure and moving forces of National Socialism. The first five chapters concern the law and politics of the Third Reich, with attention to the fundamental politics of Nazism, the character of the national government, as well as state and local government, party organization, and law and justice. Five additional chapters discuss spiritual aspects of the regime, including control of art and literature, propaganda, training for leadership and religion. Also treats economic policies, labor and Hitler's foreign policy.

72. FRIEDRICH, Carl J., ed. *Totalitarianism.* New York: Grosset & Dunlap, 1954.
A collection of essays designed to explain the nature of totalitarianism. Presents the papers of a conference held by the American Academy of Arts and Science in Boston, 6-8 March 1953. Among the authors are Hannah Arendt, Karl W. Deutsch, Erik Erikson, George F. Kennan and Harold D. Lasswell. Altogether some forty leading scholars in related areas attempt to clarify this critical phenomenon. Although the accent is on totalitarianism in general, many of the essays direct their attention to National Socialism and the Third Reich.

73. FRIEDRICH, Carl J. and Zbigniew Kazimierz BRZEZINSKI. *Totalitarian Dictatorship and Autocracy.* Cambridge, MA: Harvard University Press, 1956.

This study of totalitarian dictatorship as a novel form of government devotes attention to the general model of dictatorship and the society in which it was created.

74. *GRUNBERGER, Richard. *The 12-Year Reich: A Social History of Nazi Germany, 1933-1945.* New York: Holt, Rinehart & Winston, 1971.

This history of Nazi Germany from its inception shows how Hitler, in order to enforce his grip on every German's allegiance, developed an unprecedented social system. It was rigidly hierarchical, with the ascetic figure of the *Führer* at the top as the focus for the aspirations of every German man, woman and child, injecting medieval rituals into every phase of German life. Examines in detail how the ordinary German citizen lived under such a system. Includes diverse subjects, such as education, sports, business, family life and the position of women. Gives attention to the Hitler Youth: "We are born to die for Germany."

75. HAFFNER, Sebastian. *The Meaning of Hitler.* Translated from the German by Ewald Osers. New York: Macmillan, 1979.

A German journalist examines the personality of Hitler and analyzes his fixation on race, contradictory policies and early achievements and successes. Believes that Hitler pursued two incompatible aims from the beginning: ultimate German domination of the world and extermination of the Jews. Defines Hitler as the greatest national traitor responsible for the death of seven million Germans, destruction of the state and national misery. Argues that Hitler was no Fascist, but was closer to Stalin than to Mussolini. Calls Hitler's declaration of war on the United States in December 1941 as simply stupid.

76. *HAMEROW, Theodore S. "Guilt, Redemption and Writing German History." *The American Historical Review,* LXXXVIII (1983), 53-72.

Historian Theodore Hamerow discusses the era between 1933 and 1945 as the watershed between an *ancien régime* and a new order, separating distinct political philosophies, civic ideals, social values and national loyalties. Writes about the work of historians as accusers and defenders, and treats the cycles of indictment and apologia, guilt and redemption.

77. HIDEN, John and John FARQUHARSON, eds. *Explaining Hitler's Germany: Historians and the Third Reich.* New York: Barnes & Noble, 1983.
A historiographical survey of seven topics, ranging from Hitler's personality to ideology and economic management. Attention is given to Hitler's social revolution, foreign policy and the general interpretation of National Socialism.

78. HILDEBRAND, Klaus. *The Third Reich* Translated from the German by P. S. Falla. London: Allen & Unwin, 1984.
Currently Professor of Medieval and Modern History at the University of Bonn, Klaus Hildebrand offers an account of Nazi Germany between 1933 and 1945, and analyzes the major problems of interpretation and the extent to which common ground has been reached by scholars in the field. Concerns himself with how far Nazism was a specifically German problem; Hitler as opportunist improviser or a follower of a predetermined program; the role of Big Business and Prussian militarism; and Hitler as old-style revisionist in foreign policy or an expansionist with broader aims. Emphasizes the evolution of the "Final Solution." The last chapter, "The Verdict of Historians on the Third Reich," presents the views of historians believed to be broadly in agreement with the "crude slogans" of Allied war propaganda, that Hitler's state was more or less a consistent result of the faulty development of the German nation. Challenges the continuity thesis that the roots of National Socialism can be found deeply buried in German history. Charges that this view is not even "worthy of discussion."

79. HILLGRUBER, Andreas. *Endlich Genug?* (Finally Enough?). Düsseldorf: Droste, 1982.
A distinguished German contemporary historian is irked by the cascading literature on National Socialism and calls for an end to the alleged overblown attention not only to the twelve years of the Nazi era but also to World War II.

80. *HOOVER, Calvin Bryce. *Germany Enters the Third Reich.* New York: Macmillan, 1933.
One of the earliest studies of the sequence of events leading to the Nazi revolution. Professor Hoover, who was in Germany for a year before Hitler's accession to political power, traces the development of National Socialism and analyzes its aims and influences. Seeks to understand the Nazi mentality. The opening chapters explain the alignment of economic interests for

which nineteenth-century terminology and eighteenth-century economic theory were no longer applicable. Describes the inflamed nationalism of the Nazi movement and the propaganda designed to hold the attention of the German people.

81. *JÄCKEL, Eberhard. *Hitler in History.* Waltham, MA: Brandeis University Press, 1984.
    Seeks to explain how Hitler came to power, his goals of living space and elimination of Jews, and the nature of his relationship with the German people. Maintains that all the major decisions in the regime were made by Hitler and that the *Führer* had already formulated his objectives before he came to power. Unlike Hitler's foreign policy and military decisions, the Holocaust was not the result of a single order, but the *Führer* was the prime instigator of the terrible event. Insists that, notwithstanding his own great responsibility, Hitler was no more than the executor of a longstanding tendency in German history.

82. JACKH, Ernest. *The War for Man's Soul.* Translated from the German by Andreas Dorpalen. New York: Farrar & Rinehart, 1943.
    Founder and head of the Hochschule für Politik in Berlin, the author left Germany in 1933 and settled in Great Britain. Analyzes the growth of National Socialism, presents Hitler as anti-God, and calls upon all free men to resist and defeat him.

83. KEHR, Helen. *The Nazi Era, 1919-1945.* London: Mansell, 1982.
    A British publication presents a select bibliography of published works from the early roots of National Socialism to 1980.

84. KOCH-WESER, Erich Friedrich Ludwig. *Hitler and Beyond: A German Testament.* Translated from the German by Olga Marx. New York: Knopf, 1945.
    Koch-Weser, leader of the German Democratic Party during the Weimar Republic, held many important posts, including that of Vice-Chancellor. He left Germany early and settled in Brazil. Examines Hitler's policies and methods at home and abroad, and reveals the shame many Germans felt about the Hitler era.

85. *LASKA, Vera. *Nazism. Resistance and Holocaust in World War II.* Metuchen, NJ: Scarecrow Press, 1985.

A bibliography limited to the role of Nazism in World War II, the nature of the Resistance movement, and the Holocaust. Lists 1,300 entries in twelve categories, including three on women. The book is intended for use by teachers, librarians and researchers who seek material on the Nazis limited to World War II.

86. LICHTENBERGER, Henri. *The Third Reich*. Translated from the French and edited by Koppel S. Pinson. New York: Greystone, 1937.
In one of the earliest books on the Third Reich, Henri Lichtenberger, professor at the Sorbonne and director of the Institute of Germanic Studies, presents an account of the rise of National Socialism, Hitler in power, his foreign policy, the racial myth, the religious problem and the Nazi economic system. Expresses his sympathy for the German desire for spiritual regeneration and for efforts to lift Germany out of postwar disillusionment, but deplores Hitler's deliberate intolerance and deep hatred for the Jews. Calls for German and French reconciliation. "We would like to hope that this is not too much for human powers."

87. LORD RUSSELL OF LIVERPOOL. *The Scourge of the Swastika: A Short History of Nazi War Crimes*. London: Cassell, 1954.
Of all the critics of National Socialism, none was more polemically-minded than Lord Russell of Liverpool. His short history of Nazi war crimes is a cold, factual indictment of Hitler and National Socialism. In brief chapters the author describes Hitler's instruments of tyranny, Nazi murders of prisoners of war, war crimes on the high seas, bestial treatment of civilians in the occupied countries, slave labor and concentration camps.

88. LUNAU, Heinz. *The Germans on Trial*. New York: Storm, 1948.
The author, who fled from Germany in 1936 because of his anti-Hitler stand and pacifism and became a naturalized American citizen, believes that the German people were not given a fair trial by world opinion. Insists that Fascism was not a peculiarly German disease, that even highly respected governments were fooled by Hitler and collaborated with him before the war, and that Germans have been no more aggressive, warlike, or greedy than other peoples. The *Gestapo* terror

allegedly was invented in order to make the German people obedient and acquiescent.

89. MEINECKE, Friedrich. *The German Catastrophe: Reflections and Recollections.* Translated by Sidney B. Fay. Cambridge, MA: Harvard University Press, 1950.
A distinguished German historian attempts to explain the reasons for the emergence of National Socialism. Rejects the concept of continuity in German history and favors the view that Nazism was a sudden "catastrophe" which struck the German people like a bolt of lightning. Hitler owed his success mostly to chance. Believes there was a long, perverted process leading to the Nazi regime. This explanation about the origins of National Socialism stirred much comment among fellow-historians in other countries. Some praised Meinecke for his liberal stance, but others criticized his analysis as historically unsound.

90. *NEUMANN, Franz. *Behemoth: The Structure and Practice of National Socialism, 1933-1934.* New York: Oxford University Press, 1942.
In one of the early studies of National Socialism, Franz Neumann discusses the close relationship in the Third Reich between politics and economics. Explains Hitler's vacillation and confused self-image. Describes the *Führer* as an inefficient administrator who lacked any coherent policies and often issued conflicting orders. Hitler was not at all sure of himself and often procrastinated because he was unwilling to make decisions. These views were substantiated by later scholars who came to the same conclusions on more evidence than that available to Neumann.

91. NOLTE, Ernst. *Three Faces of Fascism.* Translated from the German by Leila Vennewitz. New York: Holt, Rinehart & Winston, 1966.
A study of three Fascist movements – the French *Action Française*, Italian Fascism and German National Socialism, by Ernst Nolte, Professor of History at the University of Marburg. Treats Fascism as a metaphysical phenomenon and devotes approximately one-third of his space to National Socialism. Discusses the background – the race doctrine, history of the movement, its practice and fulfillment, and the ideology of Fascism. His aim is not merely description but understanding. Gives special attention to such details as young Mussolini's Marxist ideas as well as Dietrich Eckart's influence on Hitler.

92. NORDICUS, pseud. [Louis L. Snyder]. *Hitlerism: The Iron Fist in Germany*. New York: Mohawk Press, 1932.
This first book on National Socialism to be published in the United States was an attempt to alert the American public to the menace of the rising Nazi movement in Germany. From 1929 to 1931 the author, a German-American Exchange Fellow at the University of Frankfurt am Main, witnessed the activities of the Austrian demagogue and his fanatical followers in the chaotic battle of the streets against the Communists. He learned much from his fellow students about the nature of Nazism. Returning to the United States, he published this book on the Nazi movement. The author, Louis L. Snyder, used the pseudonym "Nordicus" as a satirical play on Hitler's concept of Nordic supremacy, the fulcrum of Hitlerite ideology. Emphasizes Hitler's aggressive drive toward war to reverse the verdict of the Treaty of Versailles. Devotes a chapter to a warning about the tragic status of Jews in Nazi Germany.

93. ORLOW, Dietrich. *The History of the Nazi Party, 1919-1933*. Pittsburgh, PA: University of Pittsburgh Press, 1969.
A formal history of the National Socialist German Workers' Party from the immediate post-World War I years to Hitler's assumption of power. Emphasizes the inside maneuverings during the critical year 1932.

94. PICARD, Max. *Hitler in Our Selves*. Translated from the German by Heinrich Hauser. Hinsdale, IL: Regnery, 1947.
A Swiss philosopher contends that Nazism was not merely a German phenomenon but a reflection of the general crisis of modern man. Sees Hitlerism as a terrible warning, and Germany, in a sense, as a sacrifice for the sins of humanity. Believes that Nazism emerged as a consequence of the spiritual chaos into which modern nations have fallen, a chaos in which continuity has been destroyed, values have become meaningless, and the individual has been reduced to a nullity.

95. *PINSON, Koppel S. *Modern Germany: Its History and Civilization*. New York: Macmillan, 1954. (Second edition with the collaboration of Klaus Epstein, 1966).
In this text on German history, the late Koppel S. Pinson emphasizes the recent era. Chapter 21 is devoted to "Germany Gone Berserk, 1933-1945," which includes sections on the rise of Hitler, ideology and power, historical roots of Nazism, the

totalitarian police state, German Resistance and road to world domination and ruin.

96. RHODES, James M. *The Hitler Movement: A Modern Millenarian Revolution.* Stanford, CA: Hoover Institution Press, 1980.
Sees National Socialism as a millenarian movement with Hitler as its prophet and a theology structurally similar to medieval Christian heresies and the Johannine tradition. Examines the ideology of heroic fanaticism and the *Volk*, and concludes that such a phenomenon as Nazism could recur in the future. Hitler's movement allegedly demonstrates a pattern of how human societies respond to the disaster syndrome if they are burdened by the sins of sloth and pride. Denies the concept of economic distress as a basic motivation for National Socialism.

97. *ROBERTS, Stephen Henry. *The House that Hitler Built.* New York: Harper, 1938.
The author, Professor of Modern History at Sydney University, Australia, spent sixteen months traveling in Germany during the height of the Hitler regime. Offers portraits of leading Nazis, including Hitler, Goering, Goebbels, Himmler, Hess and Schacht, and discusses various aspects of Nazi Germany's relations with the rest of the world. Believes the German nation has been duped because Hitler had led it down a road that could only lead to disaster. Exposes Nazi propaganda and ballyhoo from the viewpoint of a democratic individualist. Shows how little Germany could achieve self-sufficiency, and how far she had drawn on her financial and moral reserves.

98. RODES, John E. *Germany: A History.* New York: Holt, Rinehart & Winston, 1964.
This study of the entire course of German history devotes three chapters to the National Socialist era, with attention to the collapse of the Weimar Republic, the establishment of the Hitler dictatorship, characteristics of the Nazi state, and Hitler's success in foreign affairs. Covers the war years, and devotes special attention to the progress of German rearmament and Hitler's control over the military.

99. ROSENFELD, Alvin. *Imagining Hitler.* Bloomington, IN: Indiana University Press, 1985.
Expresses concern about the ghost of Hitler, and seeks to chart the course of an evolving myth. Believes that Nazism has been

lifted from its historical base and transmuted into forms of entertainment and political bad faith. What a generation ago was a historical or moral scandal is today a source of popular distraction, pornography and anti-Semitic slander. The movement seems intent on keeping Hitler alive and glorifying what he stood for, even in the process of attacking him. Attempts to account for the Nazi hold on our imaginations.

100. SCHÜDEKOPF, Ernst. *Fascism.* New York: Praeger, 1973.
The author, a German historian who served on the General Staff in 1942, seeks to clarify a subject filled with inconsistencies, contradictions and paradoxes. Describes the various Fascist movements that sprang up in Europe during the Long Armistice from 1919 to 1939, with special attention to the excesses of Hitler and Mussolini. Separates ideology from reality, the theoretical from the practical.

101. *SHIRER, WILLIAM L. *The Rise and Fall of the Third Reich: A History of Nazi Germany.* New York: Simon & Schuster, 1959, 1960.
A narrative text on the history of the National Socialist Third Reich. The journalist-historian author, an eyewitness observer of the Nazi regime, discusses the rise of Hitler, the triumph and consolidation of his movement, the road to war, the war with early Nazi victories and the turning point, the beginning of the end and the fall of the Third Reich. This book is widely regarded as a standard text on National Socialist Germany. Many later books on National Socialism based their accounts on Shirer's study.

102. SNYDER, Louis L. *Encyclopedia of the Third Reich.* New York: McGraw-Hill, 1976.
This attempt to present a compendium of every aspect of National Socialism, Hitler and the Third Reich gives attention to the men, the women, the events, the doctrines, movements, places and patterns, plots, words, acts and outcomes. Renders an alphabetized presentation of the facts and the images they provoke, the substance and the shadow, and information on the events, institutions and personalities of the Third Reich. Features more than 200 photographs and illustrations.

103. SNYDER, Louis L. *National Socialist Germany: Twelve Years That Shook the World.* Malabar, FL: Krieger, 1984.

This book, No. 125 in the Van Nostrand-Krieger Anvil series of original paperbacks in history, presents a concise history of the origins and development of National Socialism in Hitler's Third Reich. Strips the Nazi story to its essentials and presents sixty-seven of the more important documents to accompany the narrative text.

104.   STACHURA, Peter D., ed.   *The Shaping of the Nazi State.* New York: Barnes & Noble, 1978; London: Croom Helm, 1978. Nine avowedly revisionist essays on the National Socialist movement and the nature of Hitler's Third Reich.   Jeremy Noakes' chapter on the Catholic school struggle applies local history to the analysis of broader questions concerning the possibilities and limitations of resistance to the Nazis. Geoffrey Stoakes examines Hitler's ideas about foreign policy prior to the publication of the first volume of *Mein Kampf.*   Other essays concern Gregor Strasser, the background of SA membership, political indoctrination in the universities, the Nazi Women's Organization, the civil service bureaucracy and the German film industry.

105. *STERN, Fritz.   *The Failure of Illiberalism: Essays on the Political Culture of Modern Germany.* New York: Knopf, 1972. Presents a series of essays concerned with the culture of modern Germany.   Discusses the unifying theme of illiberalism in German history – not only the political structure, suffrage restrictions or class chicanery, but also a state of mind.   In this respect the book can be compared with Hans Kohn's *The Mind of Germany* (1960).   Emphasizes especially the collapse of the Weimar Republic.

106.   TAYLOR, Simon.   *The Rise of Hitler: Revolution and Counter-revolution in Germany, 1918-1933.* New York: Universe Books, 1983. Originally published in England as *Germany, 1918-1933*, this study presents the factors accounting for Hitler's rise to power. Attributes   Hitler's   political   triumph   to   three   major facts – disunity on the left, the fears of the middle class, and the ambition of German capitalists.   Attention is given to the political intrigues of 1932-33, which led to the chancellorship for Hitler.

107.   UNGER, Aryeh L. *The Totalitarian Party: Party and People in Nazi Germany and Soviet Russia.* London and New York: Cambridge University Press, 1974.
Published for the Centre for International Studies, London School of Economics, the book deals with the role of the totalitarian party in relation of the people to its rule. Traces the Nazi and Soviet approaches to organization and propaganda. Compares the impact of the two outstanding totalitarian parties in our era on their people. The author, attached to the Hebrew University in Jerusalem, shows the essential similarities of the two systems.

108.   WALSH, Edmund Aloysius. *Total Power: A Footnote to History.* New York: Doubleday, 1948.
Walsh, at that time Rector of Georgetown University, discusses the subject of geopolitics. Describes his interviews with Karl Haushofer (1869-1946), the German founder of geopolitics, who defended his theory, and analyzes the anatomy of power as represented by revolution, humanism and Hitlerism.

109.   *WEBER, Eugen. *Varieties of Fascism: Doctrines of Fascism in the Twentieth Century.* Princeton: Van Nostrand, 1964.
This volume in the Van Nostrand-Krieger Anvil series of original paperbacks in history analyzes the doctrine of revolution in the twentieth century with accent upon National Socialism and its development in Germany. Discusses the fundamental similarities and differences of the various forms of Fascism, their theories, doctrines, ideologies, goals, and the methods employed to carry them into practice. Readings consist of official documents, reports and speeches.

110.   WEINSTEIN, Fred. *The Dynamics of Nazism: Leadership, Ideology, and the Holocaust.* New York: Academic Press, 1980.
Discusses leadership, ideology, the early intellectual and conservative support for National Socialism, the wider social context in which the movement was allowed to develop, Hitler's leadership charisma and the phenomenon of the Holocaust. Sees his own approach as being within the range of the new psychohistorical methodology combining sociopsychological and psychoanalytical theory with history. Thrusts aside all traditional historical, economic and social techniques as insufficient in explaining the Nazi regime, and places his trust in

psychological and psychoanalytical techniques combined with history.

111.   WERTHEIMER, Mildred Salz. *Germany Under Hitler*. New York: World Peace Foundation, 1935.
A World Affairs pamphlet analyzing the causes of the Nazi revolution and some of its results. Gives attention to politics, government, the Nazi Party and economic conditions.

112.   *WHEELER-BENNETT, John W. *The Nemesis of Power: The German Army in Politics, 1918-1945*. London: Macmillan, 1953.
British historian John W. Wheeler-Bennett records that Prussia-Germany had been involved in no fewer than seven wars, of which four — those of 1813-15, 1864, 1866 and 1870-71 — were victories, while three ended in disasters even more resounding — Prussia at Jena and World Wars I and II. On each of these pronounced defeats the victors tried by every means to destroy German potential for war, but all such attempts were futile. Gives much attention to the army and Hitler from 1920 to 1933 and to Hitler and the army from 1933 to 1945. Shows the extent of the army's responsibility in bringing Hitler to political power and in tolerating the infamies of the Nazi regime.

113.   WINKLER, Paul. *The Thousand-Year Conspiracy: Secret Germany Behind the Mask*. New York: Scribner, 1943.
Attempts to identify the sources behind Nazism. Presents a special hypothesis: Nazism was not the product of spontaneous generation, crystallized by Hitler's evil genius; it was not a harsh reaction to the Treaty of Versailles; and it did not derive from basic traits in the German national character.

CHAPTER 3

BIOGRAPHY

Autobiography, Memoirs, Letters, Diaries

Scholars and journalists who have contributed to the literature on National Socialism have shown by far the greatest interest in biographies of the men behind the Nazi Revolution. Almost twenty percent of all books published on the Nazi era have been concerned with examination of the lives of the leaders and officials of the Nazi movement. Most attention is paid to the personality and character of Adolf Hitler as the driving force behind National Socialism, but many studies explore such Nazi leaders as Goering, Goebbels, Himmler and Hess. Not only the academician but also the general public seems to be fascinated by the lives of the cast of characters who brought such misery and degradation to the people of Germany and the world.

A striking characteristic in this realm of biography is the interest generated in the new psychobiography, an attempt to find psychological motivations in the lives of Hitler and his henchmen. Techniques have reflected the special interests of variant schools of psychoanalysis from Freud to Adler to Sullivan in the task of showing how the early years of Hitler contributed to the actions of his adult life. There is much difference of opinion among social psychologists, psychiatrists, and psychoanalysts in the matter of explaining behavioral characteristics, much of it coated with polemical barbs against those who hold an exactly opposing opinion.

Included in this chapter are such closely related subjects as autobiography, memoirs, letters and diaries. Attention is directed especially to diaries which are valuable for conveying a sense of how the situation appeared at the time to eyewitness observers.

BIBLIOGRAPHY

114. ABSHAGEN, Karl Heinz. *Canaris.* Translated from the
        German by Alan Houghton. London: Brodwick,
        Hutchinson, 1956.
      A biography of Wilhelm Canaris (1887-1945), director of the
      Abwehr, counterintelligence department of the High Command
      of the Armed Forces, and one of the leaders in the conspiracy
      against Hitler. Dismissed from his office in February 1944, he
      was arrested after the July 1944 Plot against Hitler and hanged
      at Flossenburg concentration camp on 9 April 1945. Canaris
      was one of the moving spirits of the German Resistance move-
      ment.

115. AINSZTEIN, Reuben. "How Hitler Died: The Soviet
        Version." *International Affairs*, XLIII (1967), 307-18.
      Reviews the Russian version of Hitler's death as described by
      journalist Yelena Rzhevskaya in *Berlinskie Stranitsy* (Moscow:
      Znamy, No. 5, 1965). "I am more inclined to accept the findings
      of the Red Army doctors regarding the cause of Hitler's death
      than Professor Trevor-Roper's version based on the hearsay
      accounts of Hitler's and Bormann's secretaries [and others]."
      Charges that Trevor-Roper's statement that Hitler had the
      courage to shoot himself was a myth. Accepts the Russian
      explanation that Hitler took poison and then ordered
      Sturmbannführer (SS Major) Heinz Linge, his personal attend-
      ant, to shoot him in the head.

116. ANDRUS, Burton. *I Was the Nuremberg Jailer.* New York:
        Coward, McCann & Geoghegan, 1969.
      Reminiscences of the American Army officer who was warden
      for the accused Nazi leaders tried and convicted by the Interna-
      tional Military Tribunal at Nuremberg after the war. Relates
      eyewitness reports about the personality and character of the
      Nazi leaders in confinement.

117. ANGRES, Werner T. and Bradley F. SMITH. "Diaries of
        Heinrich Himmler's Early Years." *Journal of Modern His-
        tory*, XXXI (1959), 206-24.
      Leading Nazi politician and ruthless practitioner of terrorism,
      Heinrich Himmler (1900-46), was born near Munich, the son of
      a secondary school teacher. Brought up in a devout Catholic
      home, he served in World War I and later obtained a diploma
      in agriculture. Member of a rightist paramilitary organization,

he came to the attention of Hitler and took part in the 1923 Munich Beer-Hall *Putsch.* In 1928 he became a poultry farmer, and the next year was appointed head of the SS, Hitler's personal bodyguard, the foundation of his later rise to great power in the Third Reich. The diaries do not reveal how or why this most ordinary man developed into a sadistic mass murderer.

118. ASTOR, Gerald. *The 'Last' Nazi: The Life and Times of Dr. Joseph Mengele.* New York: Donald I. Fine, 1985.
The first book on Dr. Joseph Mengele (1911-79), long missing World War II fugitive and notorious concentration camp director at Auschwitz in charge of selection to the gas chambers. Mengele conducted horrible, often fatal experiments on inmates at the Nazi death camp. Before the Russians liberated Auschwitz he escaped and made his way to Argentina, Paraguay and finally Brazil, where he lived unrecognized under a false name until he presumably drowned in the sea near São Paulo in 1979.

119. BALFOUR, Michael and Julian FRISBY. *Helmuth von Moltke: A Leader against Hitler.* New York: St. Martin's Press, 1973.
This biography of Helmuth James Graf von Moltke (1907-45), legal adviser of the German High Command and one of the leaders of the Resistance movement against Hitler and Nazism, traces the early life of this great-grandnephew of Field-Marshal Helmuth von Moltke, whose generalship had helped Bismarck in the foundation of the Second Reich. Moltke started on a brilliant legal career, but soon began to oppose the Hitler regime, which he regarded as a disgrace for his Fatherland. He gave surreptitious aid to the victims of Hitler, including legal assistance and help in leaving the country. He was founder and head of the Kreisau Circle, an informal association of young Germans concerned about the future of their country. Moltke favored a moral rejuvenation based on Christian principles. As an expert on international law for the German High Command, he communicated with the enemy and used his office to help hostages, prisoners of war and victims of forced labor. Arrested in January 1944, he was tried for treason. Condemned to death, he was executed at Plötzensee Prison on 23 January 1945.

120. BENTLEY, James. *Martin Niemoeller* New York: The Free Press (Macmillan), 1984.

A short biography of Martin Niemoeller (1892-1984), German pastor of the Protestant Evangelical Church, outspoken critic of Hitler and Nazism, and former U-boat commander, who survived Dachau and became a founder of the world peace movement. The author, an Anglican Vicar and senior chaplain of Eton College, presents a sympathetic portrait of the U-boat commander turned pastor and his extraordinary odyssey. Niemoeller's "Confessional Church" presented a coherent protest against Hitler's religious and racial policies. Discusses the political and moral struggles inside the German Protestant Church, a story of faith and suffering, of commitment and courage, of unusual transformation. Presents Niemoeller as a modern man of God searching for spiritual redemption.

121. *BETHGE, Eberhard. *Dietrich Bonhoeffer: Man of Vision, Man of Courage.* Translated from the German by Eric Mosbacher and others. New York: Harper & Row, 1970.
A biography of Dietrich Bonhoeffer (1906-45), evangelical theologian executed because of his opposition to Hitler and Nazism. Written by a close friend of the Bonhoeffer family, the book details the career of a man regarded in theological circles and elsewhere as a contemporary martyr. Traces the early life of Bonhoeffer, his career in academic theology and his gradual move from early critic of Hitler and Nazism to outright conspiracy. All who came in contact with the young pastor while he was in custody spoke of his noble bearing and cheerfulness under painful conditions.

122. BEWLEY, Charles. *Hermann Goering and the Third Reich: A Biography Based on Family and Official Records.* New York: Devin-Adair, 1962.
A biography of Hermann Goering (1893-1946), No. 2 Nazi and Hitler's heir apparent, head of the *Luftwaffe* and economics dictator in World War II. Like other biographers, the author is fascinated by the eccentricities and personality of Germany's Falstaff. Bewley, a retired Irish diplomat who served in Berlin during the Nazi era, and was on friendly terms with the Goering family, presents Goering as a man of honor, innocent of crime, a gentleman and a lovable leader with human weaknesses.

123. BEZYMENSKI, Lev. *The Death of Adolf Hitler: Unknown Documents from Soviet Archives.* New York: Harcourt, Brace & World, 1968.

This book by Soviet journalist Lev Bezymenski offers the Soviet version of Hitler's death. Reveals that Russian troops found the bodies of Hitler and his wife Eva outside the bunker on 4 May 1945. Includes an autopsy report by the Forensic Medical Commission of the Red Army, which revealed that splinters of a poisoned capsule had been found in Hitler's mouth and that there was no bullet hole in the skull. The implication was that the *Führer* had died a coward's death. In addition, the report added that he had but one testicle, despite doctors' notes to the contrary. The book was received with some skepticism by critics, who asked why the "evidence" was withheld for twenty-three years.

124. BLACK, Peter S. *Ernst Kaltenbrunner: Ideological Soldier of the Third Reich.* Princeton, NJ: Princeton University Press, 1984.
A study of the life of Ernst Kaltenbrunner (1903-46), Austrian National Socialist, lawyer and police official, and successor to Reinhard Heydrich as chief of the SD, the Security Service. Brought before the International Military Tribunal at Nuremberg, he was charged with war crimes and crimes against humanity, and was hanged at Nuremberg Prison on 16 October 1946. Offers massive documentation, including a twenty-page bibliography. Describes Kaltenbrunner as unswervingly devoted to Hitler, and gives special attention to his role in the persecution of Jews, churches and foreign labor from eastern Europe. Considers Kaltenbrunner's conviction at Nuremberg as fully justified.

125. BLUMENTRITT, Günther. *Von Rundstedt, the Soldier and the Man.* Translated from the German by Cuthbert Reavely. London: Oldhams, 1952.
Gerd von Rundstedt (1875-1953) was a General Field Marshal and one of the highest-ranking officers in the Third Reich. On the invasion of Soviet Russia in 1941, he was given command of Army Group South, with instructions to clear the Black Sea Coast, take Rostov, seize the Maikop oil fields and then press on to Stalingrad on the Volga to sever Stalin's last link with the Caucasus. Coming into conflict with Hitler on matters of strategy, he was relieved from duty on 12 December 1941. On 1 March 1942, he was placed in command of Army Group West to replace General Erwin von Witzleben. On 2 July 1944, angered by the failure at Normandy, Hitler dismissed Rundstedt temporarily. As early as 1942 Rundstedt knew about the

Resistance movement, but failed to commit himself to the conspiracy. After the July 1944 Plot he presided over the military court which found the conspirators guilty.

126. BOLDT, Gerhard. *Hitler: The Last Ten Days.* Translated from the German by Sandra Bancy. New York: Coward, McCann & Geoghegan, 1973.
    Translated from the German *Die letzten Tage der Reichskanzlei* (1947), this book records the final days of Hitler and his Third Reich. Like Hugh R. Trevor-Roper's *The Last Days of Hitler* (1947), Boldt's study describes the chaotic conditions in the Berlin bunker as a half-mad *Führer* faced the end as master of Germany. While great clouds of smoke hovered over doomed Berlin, while Russian artillery shells exploded incessantly, Hitler was deploying imaginary battalions and disposing of formations that existed only in his mind. It was the *Götterdämmerung*, the Twilight of the Gods, for the Third Reich, played to the bombastic accompaniment of Richard Wagner, Hitler's favorite composer.

127. BOSANQUET, Mary. *The Life and Death of Dietrich Bonhoeffer.* London: Hodder & Stoughton, 1968; New York: Harper & Row, 1969.
    A sympathetic biography of Dietrich Bonhoeffer (1906-45), Protestant theologian and pastor, who was a leading figure in the German Resistance movement. Insisting on freedom to preach the Gospel without National Socialist interference, Bonhoeffer was willing to risk his life for his beliefs. He resisted Hitler and the Nazis in every way possible, including his work in helping Jews escape from Nazi Germany. Arrested by the *Gestapo*, he was imprisoned and executed on 9 April 1945, only weeks before the end of the war. Pays tribute to Bonhoeffer as a Christian martyr, who sacrificed his life for his principles.

128. BUBENDEN, Friedrich, ed. *Deutschland muss leben* (Germany Must Live). Berlin: Paul Steegemann Verlag, 1934.
    The collected letters of Albert Leo Schlageter (1894-1923), one of the most important martyrs in the Nazi lexicon. As a young *Freikorps* officer in the Ruhr in the immediate post-World-War-I years, Schlageter was arrested by the French, tried for espionage and sabotage, and executed on 26 May 1923. In the early days of the Nazi movement, he was elevated to the level of a folk hero, as a patriot who had given his life for his country. Nazi propaganda promoted him as the perfect specimen of "the

new man." This special edition of his letters was published soon after Hitler acceded to the chancellorship.

129. *BULLOCK, Alan. *Hitler: A Study in Tyranny.* New York: Harper & Row, 1964.
A new edition of a biography published originally in 1953. British historian Alan Bullock tells the extraordinary story of the rise and fall of a blood-drenched, power-drunk charlatan, the supreme hater, from his early days as a starving rabble-rouser to the final Holocaust against the Jews and his own holocaust in his hidden Berlin bunker. Bullock seeks to answer two questions: (1) was the Nazi regime the will of one man and one man alone? and (2) what were the gifts Hitler possessed which enabled him to obtain and then maintain such power? Concentrates on Hitler's record, thoughts and policies, diplomatic conquests and role in World War II.

130. CARR, William. *Hitler: A Study in Personality and Politics.* New York: St. Martin's Press, 1979.
Is concerned with the interrelationship betwen the personality of Hitler and those social forces which made National Socialism possible. Aims to place his subject within the context of the times. Concentrates on Hitler the politician, dictator and military commander.

131. CIANO, Galeazzo. *The Ciano Diaries, 1939-1943.* Garden City, NY: Doubleday, 1946.
Italian politician, Fascist diplomat and son-in-law of Mussolini, Galeazzo Ciano (1903-44) kept personal diaries from the beginning of the war until 1943. Ciano took part in the coup of 25 July 1943, as a result of which Mussolini was overthrown and Italian Fascism collapsed. Found guilty of treason after a mock trial, he was shot in the back while tied to a chair, despite his wife's pleas for his life. His diaries were published after the war from notes kept by his spouse Edda, Mussolini's daughter.

132. COLVIN, Ian. *Admiral Canaris: Chief of Intelligence.* London: Gollancz, 1951.
Traces the career of Admiral Wilhelm Canaris, Chief of the *Abwehr*, the military intelligence service of the High Command of the Armed Forces (OKW), from 1 January 1935 until February 1944. Canaris played a dual role in the *Abwehr*: he praised Hitler's political and military achievements and at the same time indicated his disgust with Nazi brutalities and the

crimes of the *Gestapo*. He worked with the Resistance in its efforts to strike Hitler down and at the same time was a patriot who worried about Germany's impending defeat. He was eventually arrested and executed for treason on 9 April 1945, along with Dietrich Bonhoeffer and Hans Oster at Flossenburg concentration camp with the sound of Allied bombing in the distance. Gives much attention to Canaris' Hamlet-like character.

133.   CROSS, Colin. *Adolf Hitler*. London: Hodder & Stoughton, 1974.
Describes Hitler as an unsophisticated, self-taught thinker who fastened on to prejudices quite common among the ordinary people in Germany and in Europe generally in the early twentieth century. "He was earnestly patriotic and believed his own people to be better than others." He suffered acutely from "the politicians' occupational disease, megalomania."

134.   *DAVIDSON, Eugene. *The Making of Adolf Hitler*. New York: Macmillan, 1977.
Eugene Davidson, whose book on the Nuremberg Trial (1966) received much attention, describes the birth and rise of Nazism. Contends that Hitler's coming to power had no single cause, but that the *Führer* was a moving part in a series of events that shook German society to its roots. Shows how a highly successful state (a mixture of pioneering social democracy and ultraconservative forces) was transformed into an unstable, malfunctioning, radicalized society overburdened with problems for which it had no solution other than the promises of a demigod. The Nazi movement absorbed psychopaths, fanatics, criminals and representatives of the counterculture, who multiplied under abnormal conditions. An army of mutually warring factions was united only in a will to destroy the old order.

135.   DESCHNER, Günther. *Heydrich, The Pursuit of Total Power*. Translated from the German by Sandra Bance, Brenda Woods and David Ball. London: Orbis, 1981.
A biography of Reinhard Heydrich (1904-42), head of the Reich Security Service, Deputy Reich Protector of Bohemia and Moravia, administrator of concentration camps, and a specialist in Nazi terror. Architect of Hitler's "Final Solution," Heydrich died on 2 June 1942, of wounds inflicted by two Free Czech agents of the Resistance. Describes Heydrich's sadism.

136. DIMITROV, Georgi. *Letters from Prison.* Edited by Alfred
     Kurella. Translated by Dona Torr and Michael Davidson.
     New York: International Publishers, 1936.
     Georgi Dimitrov was a Bulgarian Communist who with four
     others was placed on trial after the *Reichstag* fire of 27 February
     1933. Dimitrov won the attention of a worldwide audience
     when he confronted Hermann Goering in a dramatic courtroom
     scene. "You are a Communist crook, who came to Germany to
     set the *Reichstag* on fire. In my eyes you are nothing but a
     scoundrel, a crook, who belongs on the gallows." Dimitrov
     turned the debate into a challenge to Goering and into a trial
     of the Nazis themselves. In this book, written from Moscow
     after his acquittal, Dimitrov relates his political defense, his
     imprisonment, the trial itself, his acquittal and his deportation
     from Germany. Also features articles and interviews published
     after his release.

137. *DODD, Martha. *Through Embassy Eyes.* New York:
     Harcourt, Brace, 1939.
     When Professor William E. Dodd went to Berlin in 1933 as
     American Ambassador to Germany, he was accompanied by his
     daughter, Martha. Dodd, liberal historian, democrat and
     humanitarian, soon proved to be a thorn in the side of Nazi
     officialdom. His daughter was even more annoying to the
     humorless Nazi hierarchy. This is Martha Dodd's story of
     disillusionment and growing fury.

138. *DODD, Martha, ed. *Ambassador Dodd's Diaries, 1933-1935.*
     New York: Harcourt, Brace, 1941.
     William E. Dodd (1889-1940) was United States Ambassador
     to the Third Reich from 1933 to 1937. By study, training and
     disposition, he was within the tradition of other American
     historians sent to the embassy in Berlin, including George
     Bancroft, and such journalists as Bayard Taylor. His diaries,
     kept during the first two years of Hitler's regime, show con-
     tempt for the excesses of the Nazis. He refused to attend the
     Nuremberg rallies, and tried to stop the persecution of Jews
     with notable lack of success. He was unable to effect the col-
     lection of debts due American creditors, and was unsuccessful
     in trying to break the deadlock in German-American business
     relations. He opposed appeasement and made efforts to stop it.
     He saw Hitler as a badly educated romantic, with a semicriminal
     record.

139. DOENITZ, Karl. *Memoirs: Ten Years and Twenty Days.* Translated by R. H. Stevens and D. Woodward. London: Weidenfeld & Nicolson, 1959.

     The memoirs of Karl Doenitz (1891-1980), Grand Admiral, builder of German U-boats and political successor to Hitler for a few days. Doenitz was astonished when he was indicted, with twenty-one other Nazi leaders, by the International Military Tribunal at Nuremberg. "None of these charges concerns me in the least. Typical American humor!" His judges decided that, although he constructed Hitler's U-boat arm, he was not privy to the conspiracy to wage war, and sentenced him to ten years' imprisonment for crimes against peace and war crimes. Doenitz's memoirs concern those ten years (plus an additional twenty days) of imprisonment. He pleads innocence of all charges and refers to the file of letters from Allied naval officers who had written to him expressing their sympathy and understanding.

140. DOUGLAS-HOME, Charles. *Rommel.* New York: Saturday Review Press, 1973.

     A biography of the German field marshal, the famous Desert Fox of World War II. Rommel was the only German general during World War II who aroused the admiration of his counterparts in the Allied military commands. This biography, as well as others written about Rommel, reveals him as an honorable officer well outside the Nazi mold.

141. DROBISCH, Klaus. "Der Freundeskreis Himmler" (Himmler's Circle of Friends). *Zeitschrift für Geschichtswissenschaft*, VIII (1960), 304-28.

     Studies the immediate entourage of Heinrich Himmler (1900-45), *Reichsführer-SS*, head of the *Gestapo* and the *Waffen-SS*, and Minister of the Interior from 1943 to 1945. The second most powerful man in the Third Reich, Himmler was surrounded by a special circle of friends (*Freundeskreis Heinrich Himmler*), consisting of wealthy patrons drawn from the top echelons of industry, banking and insurance. The group played a major role in financing the 1932-33 election campaigns as well as supplying Himmler's *Waffen-SS* units with arms and uniforms during World War II. Himmler saw to it that his friends were allocated scarce labor from concentration camps. The circle met every second Monday in Berlin and all members were expected to contribute to a special fund for expenses which

Himmler could not meet from his own budget, such as cultural activities and medical experiments in concentration camps.

142. ENGEL, Gerhard. *Heeresadjutant bei Hitler* (Hitler's Army Adjutant). Stuttgart: Deutsche Verlagsanstalt, 1974.
For several decades after World War II there was a flood of memoirs by those who observed the *Führer* at first hand, including secretaries, servants, acquaintances and friends in his early years, co-workers and political associates. Among these books are the reminiscences of Gerhard Engel, who served as Hitler's army adjutant from 1938 to 1943. Seeks to explain the mysteries of the *Führer's* character.

143. ERFURTH, Waldemar. "Generaloberst a.D. Halder zum 70. Geburtstag" (Retired Colonel-General Halder on his 70th Birthday). *Wehrwissenschaftliche Rundschau*, IV (1954), 241-51.
Contributes a *Festschrift* on the 70th birthday of Franz Halder (1884-1972), Chief of the General Staff of the German Army from 1938 to 1942. Praises Halder, leader of the Halder Plot, the first Resistance movement in the officers' corps seeking to remove Hitler from power. Halder insisted that Germany had been stabbed in the back not by Social Democrats but by Hitler.

144. ESCHENBURG, Theodor. "Franz von Papen." *Vierteljahrshefte für Zeitgeschichte*, I (1953), 153-69.
An essay on Franz von Papen (1879-1969), politician and statesman during the late Weimar Republic, explains the career of an eccentric character who played so important a role in the rise to power of Hitler and the Nazis.

145. FABRICIUS, Hans. *Reichsinnenminister Dr. Frick: Der revolutionäre Staatsmann* (Reich Minister of the Interior Dr. Frick: The Revolutionary Statesman). Berlin: Verlag Kultur-Wacht, 1939.
Wilhelm Frick (1877-1946), one of Hitler's closest advisers during the early years of the Nazi movement and Reich Minister of the Interior from 1933 to 1943, was directly responsible for harsh measures taken against Jews and dissenters whom he denounced as "traitors and destroyers." Presents Frick as a "revolutionary statesman." After the war Frick was hanged at Nuremberg.

146. FEST, Joachim C. *Hitler.* Translated from the German by
      Richard and Clara Winston. New York: Harcourt Brace
      Jovanovich, 1974.
      Journalist Joachim C. Fest is more concerned with Hitler and
      his times than with Hitler the man. Combines the main narra-
      tive with "intermediate reflections," analyzing the historical
      meaning of the event just described. Although not impressed
      by the work of psychohistorians, he considers the three most
      traumatic events in the life of Hitler: the death of his mother,
      his wounds and Germany's defeat in World War I, and the sui-
      cide of his niece in 1932.

147. FORSTER, Wolfgang. *Generaloberst Ludwig Beck* (Colonel-
      General Ludwig Beck). Munich: Isar Verlag, 1953.
      Examines the career of General Ludwig Beck (1880-1940), chief
      of the armed forces from 1933 to 1938 and a central figure in the
      Resistance movement. Devotes major attention to Beck's
      struggle to avoid the outbreak of World War II. In 1938 Beck
      protested against Hitler's intention of conquering
      Czechoslovakia and insisted that the Army was unprepared for
      war. He tried to get the Chiefs of Staff to oppose Hitler's policy
      of aggression but failed. He resigned his post as Chief of Staff
      on 18 August 1938.

148. FRANÇOIS-PONCET, André. *The Fateful Years: Memoirs
      of a French Ambassador in Berlin, 1931-1938.* Translated
      from the French by Jacques LeClercq. London: Gollancz,
      1949; New York: Harcourt, 1949.
      A study by a French diplomat and scholar, a trained observer
      who from the vantage point of Berlin was able to witness the rise
      of Hitler to political power and the prewar years after 1934, as
      the *Führer* geared his country for war. Draws brief portraits of
      the leading Nazis from Goering to Ribbentrop, and analyzes
      German and French official views, some of which differed
      strongly from his own. From his background as a longtime
      student of German culture and politics, describes what he saw
      and experienced in a critical era, especially reports of his
      conversations with Hitler.

149. *FRANK, Anne. *The Diary of a Young Girl.* Garden City, NY:
      Doubleday, 1952.
      Anne Frank (1929-45) was a German-Jewish girl who with her
      family hid from the *Gestapo* in Amsterdam for two years and
      died in Belsen concentration camp. An immediate sensation,

her diary was translated eventually into thirty-two languages and later became a successful stage play and motion picture. The young girl described the vicissitudes of people living together under dangerous circumstances, facing hunger and the ever-present threat of discovery, boredom, misunderstandings – all the cruelties and kindnesses of human behavior. In her opening lines she expresses the hope that the reader would support and comfort her. In the final passage she states that if she were watched she first became snappy, then unhappy and finally twisted her heart around again "so that the bad is on the outside and the good on the inside." She would keep on seeking a way to become what she would like to be and what she could be "if there weren't any other people living in the world." Despite all, she found good in the world. The conscience of readers everywhere was aroused by this story of a sensitive and warm-spirited young girl passing through the critical years of adolescence until her early tragic death.

150. FRANK, Hans. *Im Angesicht des Galgen* (In the Presence of the Gallows). Munich: Beck, 1953.
Hans Frank (1900-46), National Socialist jurist and Governor-General of Poland during World War II, was placed on trial before the International Military Tribunal at Nuremberg and executed as a war criminal on 16 October 1946. He treated the Poles as slaves in a Greater German Reich and exploited them ruthlessly. His policy toward Jews was especially brutal: "I ask nothing of Jews except that they should disappear." In prison he wrote these memoirs "in the presence of the gallows," in which he claims that as early as 1942 he had called for a return to constitutional government and that he had been stripped of all Party honors and legal posts, although he remained as Governor-General in Poland. Renders an apologia for his career and actions as a Nazi jurist.

151. FRISCHAUER, Willi. *Himmler: The Evil Genius of the Third Reich.* London: Oldhams, 1953.
A biography of Hitler's Grand Inquisitor and master of destruction. As early as 17 June 1936, the *Führer* designated Himmler head of the unified police system in the Third Reich as *Reichsführer* of the SS and leader of the *Gestapo*. The former poultry farmer controlled the vast machinery of political oppression as well as the extermination of "racial degenerates." Shows how Himmler typified the extreme mysticism of the National Socialist movement and how he sought to implement

Hitler's concepts of race and hostility to the Jews. Behind the colorless exterior was a fanatical, sadistic nature, a rigid authoritarian who developed a passion for unlimited control over his fellow Germans.

152. GEHLEN, Reinhard. *The Service: Memoirs of General Reinhardt Gehlen.* Translated from the German by David Irving. New York: World Publishing, 1972.
First published in a shorter edition in 1971 by von Hase & Koehler Verlag, Mainz, this book offers the memoirs of a legendary spy-master-in-chief. Gehlen was head of German military espionage in Soviet Russia during World War II. When the war ended, he transferred his mammoth files and network of spies to the service of the United States. Ultimately he became chief of the official West German intelligence agency. States that Martin Bormann, Hitler's right-hand man, was a Soviet agent throughout the war.

153. GELLICHSHEIMER, Ivy Hilda (Ivy Carl, pseud.). *From the South Seas to Hitler.* New York: Dutton, 1936.
Autobiography of the daughter of a famous German World War I spy. As an infant she was sent to live with an uncle on a South Seas island. Later she settled in Munich during the early years of Hitler's rise to political prominence. Her memoirs, written at the age of nineteen, reveal the power of German nationalism and Hitler's control over the German mind.

154. *GILBERT, G. M. *Nuremberg Diary.* New York: Farrar, Straus, 1947.
Captain G. M. Gilbert, a military intelligence officer with the U.S. 20th Armored Division, assigned as prison psychologist for the Nuremberg trial, checked the I.Q. of the Nazi overlords on trial, listened in the cells to their excuses and explanations, observed their threats, curses, taunts and double crosses common to Nazism, noted their personal disintegration and collected a mass of information on the leaders and prophets of the Third Reich and National Socialism. In the silence of their cells, the top Nazis, grasping at any means to save their lives, confessed their bewilderment and confusion to the American captain.

155. *GISEVIUS, Hans Bernd. *To the Bitter End.* Translated from the German by Richard and Clara Winston. Boston: Houghton Mifflin, 1947.

Hans Bernd Gisevius (1904-54), diplomat and writer, was German Vice-Consul in Zürich during World War II and liaison between the U.S. Office of Strategic Services (OSS) and the Resistance movement within the *Abwehr*, the foreign and counterintelligence department of the High Command of the Armed Forces. Describes the leading Third Reich personalities and notes the inhumanities of the Nazi regime. Absolves the overwhelming majority of Germans who had no part in the hideous affairs of the Nazi state. "The cowed middle class stared at the Nazi monster like a rabbit at a snake." Points to the silent acquiescence of millions of Germans "who played hide-and-seek with themselves, feigning ignorance of Nazi excesses and never seeking to learn the fate of its victims." Gisevius was a privileged prosecution witness at the Nuremberg Trial, testifying against Goering and for Schacht. His book offers an inside account of what transpired in the Third Reich.

156. GOEBBELS, Joseph. *The Goebbels Diaries, 1939-1941.* Translated from the German by Fred Taylor. New York: Putnam, 1983.
The diaries of Joseph Goebbels (1897-1945), Hitler's Reich Minister for Public Enlightenment and Propaganda, were published piecemeal for the years 1925-26 [1963], 1942-43 [1948], and 1945 [1978]. This volume covers the years 1939-41. As all the volumes, this is a deeply personal account of the man second in command to Hitler himself, with intimate and almost daily access to the *Führer*. The diaries reveal how the diminutive propaganda expert sought to keep tight rein on all German media. His vituparation against the Jews is relentless. Presents himself as a glowing patriot, absolutely loyal to the man he regards as the greatest German of all time.

157. GOERING, Emmy. *My Life with Goering.* London: David Bruce & Watson, 1972.
Emmy Goering (1893-1973) was the second wife of Hermann Goering, No. 2 Nazi. The statuesque Swedish actress married Goering on 20 April 1935, in a semi-royal celebration. Because Hitler was unmarried, she played a leading role in the social life of the Nazi élite. Her memoirs are adulatory: "My husband was the greatest love of my life: I love him and will always love him until I draw my last breath."

158. GRABER, G. S. *Stauffenberg.* New York: Ballantine, 1973.

This story of the Resistance movement within the German General Staff emphasizes the role played by Claus Schenk Count von Stauffenberg (1907-44), Chief of Staff to the Commander of the Reserve (Army) and main conspirator in the attempted murder of Hitler on 20 July 1944.

159.   GUDERIAN, Heinz. *Panzer Leader.* Translated from the German by Constantine FitzGibbon. London: Michael Joseph, 1952; New York, Dutton, 1952.
Heinz Guderian (1888-1954), German tank expert, is regarded along with General Charles De Gaulle and General A. F. C. Fuller as one of the founders of modern mechanized warfare. Explains how after World War I he specialized in developing the *Panzer Korps.* Hitler quickly promoted him up the military ladder. The conspirators of the July 1944 Plot on Hitler's life tried to obtain Guderian's support, but they were unsuccessful. On 22 July 1944, two days after the assassination attempt, Guderian was appointed to the General Staff of the Armed Forces, whereupon he denounced the conspirators as cowards and weaklings who had preferred disgrace to "the road of duty and honor."

160.   GUN, Nerin E. *Eva Braun: Hitler's Mistress.* Translated from the German. London: Frewin, 1969; New York: Meredith Press, 1969.
Eva Braun (1912-45) was the mistress of Hitler from 1932 and his wife during the last few hours of his life. Born in Munich, the daughter of Bavarian peasants, she was employed in her late teens by Heinrich Hoffmann, Hitler's photographer, who introduced her to the *Führer.* Though considerably older, Hitler exerted a strong influence over the girl. During a stormy courtship Eva attempted suicide and eventually became mistress of the man who was the German dictator. She was Hitler's official hostess at Berchtesgaden and was present at most important gatherings. She joined her doomed lover in Berlin, where he finally made her his wife. They perished together during the Russian assault. The author of this book received reluctant cooperation from those who knew both Hitler and Eva Braun. There are many anecdotes.

161.   HANFSTAENGL, Ernst. *Hitler: The Missing Years.* London: Eyre & Spottiswoode, 1957.
Ernst Franz Sedgwick Hanfstaengl (1887-1975) was Hitler's unofficial jester in the early days of the Nazi movement. Born

in Munich of mixed German-American heritage, he was grad-
uated from Harvard in 1909. A towering 6-foot 4-inch giant
with enormous head, pugnacious jaw and thick hair, he endured
the name Putzi throughout his career. He formed an attachment to Hitler, then an aspiring agitator, in the early 1920s and
later became a favorite of the Austrian politician. With his
practical jokes and broad sense of humor, the tall Bavarian was
gay and amusing, a kind of Shakespearean jester whose main
task was to provide relaxation for the harried *Führer*. He often
played Wagnerian music for Hitler. Relations cooled in 1934.
In March 1937, sensing that he was in danger, Hanfstaengl fled
from Germany. Later he was told of a plot to liquidate him by
dropping him from a plane. Offers full details of his relationship with Hitler and many descriptions of the personality
and character of the German dictator.

162. *HEIDEN, Konrad. *Der Fuehrer: Hitler's Rise to Power*.
Translated from the German by Ralph Manheim. London:
Gollancz, 1944; Boston: Houghton Mifflin, 1944.
Heiden's book was one of the early accounts of Hitler's struggle
to win the Chancellorship of Germany. In 1923, as the leader
of a small democratic organization at the University of Munich,
Heiden tried, with all the earnestness of youth and with complete lack of success, to "annihilate Hitler by means of protest
parades, mass meetings and giant posters." His account of
Hitler's rise emphasizes the fact that behind all the nonsense was
unrivaled political cunning. Bases the book on documentary
evidence as well as personal observations.

163. *HEIDEN, Konrad. *Adolf Hitler: Eine Biographie* (Adolf Hitler:
A Biography). Zürich: Europa Verlag, 1937, 2 vols.
Describes Hitler as a leader whose acts would be dominant in
the immediate future in Europe. Hitler was destroying the
principles of freedom and democracy and was seeking to institute the leadership of the strong over the weaker masses. He
represented the socially dissatisfied middle class. Examines
each of the *Führer's* boasted accomplishments and explodes
them one by one – how the unemployed were absorbed into the
army, how living costs and taxes had risen, all in addition to loss
of freedom for the German people, the lowering of German
culture, persecution of the Jews and hatred and fear of the entire
world. Offers inside stories of political events and many revealing anecdotes about Hitler. The second volume is titled *Ein
Mann gegen Europa* (One Man against Europe).

164. HEINEMAN, John L.   *Hitler's First Foreign Minister Constantin Freiherr von Neurath, Diplomat and Statesman.* Berkeley and Los Angeles, CA: University of California Press, 1979.
A biography of Constantin Freiherr von Neurath (1873-1956), German Foreign Minister from 1932 to 1938 and later Reich Protector of Bohemia and Moravia. Neurath was found guilty at Nuremberg of war crimes, crimes against peace, and crimes against humanity. He served eight years of a fifteen-year sentence. Describes Neurath as an intensely private man, more at home on his estate than in the world of politics. The diplomat lived by the code of the civil servant. He was too inhibited by temperament to protest against Hitler's excesses. He clung to his post, accepting and covering measures of which he disapproved.

165. HESS, Rudolf. *Reden* (Talks). Munich: Eher Verlag, 1937.
A collection of the speeches of Rudolf Hess (1894-   ), Deputy to the *Führer* at a time when Hitler was in the heyday of his power, issued by the official Nazi publishing house.

166. *HILLGRUBER, Andreas, ed.   *Staatsmänner und Diplomaten bei Hitler: Vertrauliche Aufzeichnungen über Unterredungen des Auslandes, 1939-1941* (Statesmen and Diplomats Surrounding Hitler: Confidential Notes on Conferences Concerning Foreign Countries, 1939-1941).   Frankfurt am Main: Bernard & Graefe Verlag für Wehrwesen, 1967.
A report by German historian Andreas Hillgruber on confidential conversations between Hitler and a number of representatives of foreign countries in the Third Reich.   Each document is preceded by a brief, pertinent explanatory introduction.   Records ninety-eight conversations in all, eighty-six of which have been already published in the *Akten zur deutschen auswärtigen Politik.* The conversations reveal the personality of Hitler in the years of his astonishing triumphs – he was vain, arrogant, confident, omniscient and insufferable.

167. HITLER, Adolf.   *Hitler's Secret Book.*   Translated from the German by Salvator Attanasio. New York: Grove Press, 1962.
This long-suppressed book was discovered by a U.S. Army captain in Munich, then it was lost among the maze of captured German documents, and finally relocated by a young American professor, Gerhard L. Weinberg, who later became known for

his studies on Nazi foreign policy. The "secret" book is a rehash of *Mein Kampf*, with its turgid prose and ideas of a badly educated Austrian. Presents his own versions of the ideas of Darwin and Nietzsche, attacks "World Jewry," gives his views on racialism and issues polemics about all the forces he detested. Elaborates his ideas on foreign policy as described in his first book. Calls again and again for *Lebensraum*, or living space, as necessary for Germany, while at the same time denying complicity of any desire for aggression.

168. HOESS, Rudolf. *Commandant of Auschwitz.* New York: Popular Library, 1961.
Rudolf Franz Hoess (1900-47), commandant of the extermination camp at Auschwitz, was said to be responsible for the execution of 2.5 million inmates, not counting a half million who were allowed to starve to death. A 1944 SS report called him "a true pioneer in this area because of his new ideas and educational methods." In this autobiography, written in a Polish jail before his execution, Hoess presents an apologia for his life. Regards himself as a perfectly normal man who led an uneventful family life while carrying out orders to the best of his ability. Sees himself as a sensitive human being who tried to hide the defect by an icy exterior. Was convinced that anti-Semitism was a form of pest control. To him the business of exterminating Jews was strictly an impersonal, mechanical system with the precision of modern industry. Regards his work as hygienic and clinically clean. He was condemned to death in 1947 and executed at Auschwitz.

169. HOFFMANN, Heinrich. *Hitler Was My Friend.* Translated from the German by R. H. Stevens. London: Burke, 1955.
Heinrich Hoffmann (1885-1957) was court photographer for Hitler and the National Socialist Party and, with Max Amann, the man responsible for the *Führer's* wealth. His personal and political relations with Hitler began in Munich in the early days of the Nazi movement and he later became the *Führer's* close companion. For some time he belonged to Hitler's inner circle, and introduced Hitler to Eva Braun, who worked in his photography shop and who later became the wife of Hitler for one day before his suicide. Hoffmann and Martin Bormann insisted that the *Führer's* photograph be placed on postage stamps of different denominations, a decision that led to an enormous accumulation of funds. The photographer himself became a millionaire. In 1947 Hoffmann was tried before a

West German court and sentenced to ten years' imprisonment.
Most of his wealth was confiscated. He served five years.

170.   HUTTON, Joseph Bernard. *Hess: The Man and His Mission.*
       New York: Macmillan, 1970.
       The life story of Rudolf Hess (1894-   ), Deputy *Führer* of the
       Nazi Party and after Hermann Goering the No. 3 Nazi in the
       Third Reich. Devotes special attention to Hess's secret flight
       from Germany to Scotland on 10 May 1941, when Hess bailed
       out and hoped through proposed intermediary the Duke of
       Hamilton to convince Britons that Hitler did not wish to destroy
       a fellow Nordic nation and that he only wanted a free hand to
       pursue his drive for living space in eastern Europe. He said that
       if Great Britain did not collaborate, she would be destroyed.
       Much to his surprise, Hess was arrested and treated as a pris-
       oner of war. The author believes that Hitler knew all about
       Hess's flight. Also offers the reminiscences of Frau Hess, and
       presents a plea for the release of the wizened old prisoner at
       Spandau.

171.   INFIELD, Glenn B. *Eva and Adolf.* New York: Grosset &
       Dunlap, 1974.
       A chronological account of the relations between Hitler and his
       mistress Eva Braun ending with their suicides the day after their
       wedding in the Berlin bunker. Uses the so-called Musmanno
       Archives, named after Michael A. Musmanno, naval aide to
       General Mark W. Clark and later a judge at the Nuremberg
       Trials. Presents Eva as an attractive all-cosmopolitan girl.

172.   IRVING, David. *The Rise and Fall of the Luftwaffe: The Life
       of Field Marshal Erhard Milch.* Boston: Little, Brown,
       1974.
       The author, a prolific English writer on subjects concerning
       Hitler and the Third Reich, uses this biography of Field Mar-
       shal Erhard Milch as a means of telling the story of the rise and
       fall of the *Luftwaffe*, the German Air Force. In his early career
       Milch was instrumental in establishing *Lufthansa* as an interna-
       tional air line, and as Goering's State Secretary in the Air
       Ministry, played a central role in creating Nazi air power. Por-
       trays Milch as a politically naïve, loyal follower of Hitler, who
       did his very best for the German war effort despite the adminis-
       trative chaos in the leadership of the German Air Force.

173. IRVING, David. *The Trail of the Fox.* New York: Dutton, 1977.
A biography of General Irwin Rommel (1881-1944), the famed Desert Fox. Describes Rommel as both a defeatist and indomitable combat leader against strong odds. Presents the failures of Rommel as strategist and tactician, but also praises his chivalry, personal magnetism and courage. Claims that Rommel was never truly associated with the July 1944 plot on Hitler's life.

174. JACOBSEN, Hans Adolf, ed. *Kriegstagebuch: Tägliche Aufzeichnungen des Chefs des Generalstabes des Heeres, 1939-1942 (von) Generaloberst Halder* (War Diary: Daily Entries by the Chief of the General Staff of the Army, 1939-1942 (by) Colonel-General Halder). Stuttgart: Kohlhammer, 1962, 1964, 3 vols.
The text of the war diary of General Franz Halder (1884-1972), Chief of the Army Staff between 1938 and 1942. During the war Halder was torn between his dislike for Hitler and his loyalty oath to the *Führer.* He was dismissed on 24 September 1942 after a disagreement with Hitler on strategy at Stalingrad. Arrested after the July 1944 Plot, he was confined to a concentration camp, from which he was liberated by the Americans. A professional soldier, Halder believed that Hitler's activities as a war leader were catastrophic and that the *Führer* was responsible for Germany's defeat in the war by removing control of the army from professional generals.

175. JETZINGER, Franz. *Hitler's Youth.* Translated from the German by Lawrence Wilson. London: Hutchinson, 1958.
Dismisses all other accounts of Hitler's youth as filled with "fantasies and lies" and presents his version of the truth. Describes the early years of Hitler with attention to his birth in the small village of Braunau on the Inn River between Austria and Germany, his parents, his schooling in Linz, his friendship with August Kubizek and his move to Vienna in October 1907. This book was originally published in Vienna by Europa Verlag in 1956 under the title *Hitlers Jugend: Phantasien, Lügen — und die Wahrheit* (Hitler's Youth: Fantasies, Lies — and the Truth).

176. JOHN, Otto. *Twice through the Lines: Autobiography.* Translated from the German by Richard Barry. New York: Harper & Row, 1972.

The former head of West Germany's internal secret service who won global attention in 1954 when he disappeared in Berlin, denies that he had defected to the Russians. Claims that the Soviets abducted him as a cover for their arrest of agents in East Germany. In postwar Germany, John was the last survivor of the conspiracy to assassinate Hitler. For allegedly "defecting" to the East, he was sentenced to four years of hard labor when he returned to West Germany. He served the full term in solitary confinement and spent the time preparing his book. British historian Hugh R. Trevor-Roper wrote the introduction, labeling the book "a record of a life of conspiracy, danger, frustration and failure."

177. KALLENBACH, Hans. *Mit Adolf Hitler auf Festung Landsberg* (With Adolf Hitler in Landsberg Prison). Munich: Kress & Hornung, 1939.
Landsberg-am-Lech was a fortress prison in Bavaria to which Hitler was sent after the 1923 Munich Beer-Hall *Putsch*. Found guilty of conspiracy to commit high treason, he was sentenced to five years' detention, but he served only nine months. This book by a fellow-prisoner reveals how Hitler was pampered, how he read voraciously and received visitors. Conveys the impression that the Austrian politician regarded his incarceration as no more than an uncomfortable interruption in his career. The book is designed to give a flattering picture of the *Führer* during the early days of his career.

178. KERSTEN, Felix. *The Kersten Memoirs, 1940-1945*. Translated from the German by Constantine FitzGibbon and James Oliver. London: Hutchinson, 1956.
Memoirs of Dr. Felix Kersten, a physician who treated Himmler, Ribbentrop, Ley, Hess and other Nazi leaders. In his conversations with these important figures of the Third Reich he learned of Hitler's plans for aggression. There is much scandalmongering, including the claim that Hess was impotent, Ley a drunk and lecher and Ribbentrop a syphilitic. Writes that the medical report on Hitler which he got from Himmler showed the *Führer* to be suffering from an uncured syphilis, as well as mental unbalance.

179. KESSELRING, Albert. *A Soldier's Record*. Translated from the German by Lynton Hudson. New York: Morrow, 1954.

Memoirs of Albert Kesselring (1885-1960), German Field Marshal in the *Luftwaffe*. On 6 May 1947, a British court-martial convicted Kesselring on a charge of having allowed the shooting of 335 Italian civilians in reprisal for an attack by Italian Partisans on a German company. He was sentenced to death, but the penalty was commuted to life imprisonment. He was pardoned and freed in 1952. Defends his record as a soldier. Indeed, Allied commanders regarded him as one of the most able of World War II generals.

180. KLOTZ, Helmut, ed. *The Berlin Diaries, May 30, 1932-January 30, 1933.* Translated from the German. New York: Morrow, 1934.
    The editor identifies the author of these diaries as a German War Office general closely associated with the political leaders of the day. Covers the ground from 30 May 1932, the day of Chancellor Brüning's dismissal, to the accession of Hitler on 30 January 1933. Describes the corruption, cabals and jealousies among politicians at the time, and how Germany was delivered into the hands of political gangsters. Exculpates the military class from the betrayals and secret negotiations which delivered the Weimar Republic into Nazi hands.

181. KOEVES, Tibor. *Satan in Top Hat: The Biography of Franz von Papen.* New York: Alliance, 1941.
    Offers a devastating portrait of Franz von Papen (1879-1969), politician and statesman who played a major role in Hitler's drive for power. Describes how von Papen, the wealthy scion of a noble family, served in Washington, DC, as military attaché during World War I. There he became notorious for clumsy secret service activities and was expelled as *persona non grata*. Scarcely a technically proficient professional, he was never taken seriously in German politics because of his indifference and happy-go-lucky career. But this "Satan in top hat" always seemed to survive seemingly catastrophic defeats. In 1932, despite lack of experience, he was appointed to the Chancellorship to succeed Heinrich Brüning. Angered by machinations of his enemies, he advised the elderly President Paul von Hindenburg to appoint Hitler as Chancellor. Von Papen was acquitted at Nuremberg of war crimes.

182. KUBIZEK, August. *The Young Hitler I Knew.* Translated from the German by E. V. Anderson. Boston: Houghton Mifflin, 1955.

August Kubizek was Hitler's closest friend when they were in their teens. An upholsterer's helper in Linz on the Danube in Upper Austria, Kubizek met young Hitler in 1904 at the local opera house. The two subsequently became roommates, took frequent walks through the town and went on local excursions. The tense, meticulous Adolf dominated his friend, who served as a kind of private audience. "His speeches," Kubizek writes, "seemed like a volcano erupting. It was as though something quite apart from him was bursting out of him." In Vienna, "Gustl" studied viola at the Academy of Music. His roommate, Adolf, was turned down by the Academy of Fine Arts, a blow from which he never recovered. "He choked on his catalogue of hates. He was at odds with the world. I had the impression that Adolf Hitler had become unbalanced."

183. LAACK-MICHEL, Ursula.   *Albrecht Haushofer und der Nationalsozialismus: Ein Beitrag zur Zeitgeschichte* (Albrecht Haushofer and National Socialism: A Contribution to Contemporary History).   Stuttgart: Klein Verlag, 1974.

Albrecht Haushofer (1903-43), teacher, poet, dramatist and member of the Resistance movement against Hitler, was son of the former general and founder of geopolitics, Professor Kurt Haushofer. The writer of several dramatic works, he became a co-worker in his father's specialty and was appointed Professor of Political Geography at the University of Berlin in 1940. From then on, he worked at the Foreign Office. This study concerns his relations with National Socialism. He regarded Nazism as a calamity for the German people and joined in the Resistance movement to oppose it. His *Moabiter Sonette*, written in prison, preserved by accident and published later, described the spirit of the conspirators. He was shot on 24 April 1945, while being transferred from Berlin-Moabit Prison, just a few days before the end of the war in Europe.

184. *LEIBHOLZ-BONHOEFFER, Sabine.   *The Bonhoeffers: Portrait of a Family*.   Translated from the German.   New York: St. Martin's Press, 1971.

An account of the life of Sabine Leibholz-Bonhoeffer and her remarkable family. Sabine was the twin sister of Pastor Dietrich Bonhoeffer, the theologian who was a leading figure in the German Resistance movement. This close-knit family sacrificed four of its men, Dietrich himself, but also Klaus Bonhoeffer and two brothers-in-law, Hans von Dohnanyi and Rüdiger

Schleicher.   As the wife of Gerhard Leibholz, a Professor of
Constitutional Law, Sabine and her family lived in England
during the National Socialist era.

185.   LEY, Robert.   *Wir alle helfen den Führer* (We All Help the
       Führer).   Munich: Eher Verlag, 1940.
       A propaganda book by Robert Ley (1890-1945), Nazi politician
       and head of the German Labor Front.   Published in Nazi
       Germany during the early months of the war, the book was de-
       signed to promote public morale because "we all help the
       Führer."

186.   LOCHNER, Louis P., ed.   *The Goebbels Diaries*.   Translated
       from the German and edited by Louis P. Lochner.
       London: Hamilton, 1948; Garden City, NY: Doubleday,
       1948.
       An American foreign correspondent edits excerpts from the
       diaries of Dr. Joseph Goebbels, Minister for Public Enlight-
       enment and Propaganda in the Third Reich.   The years covered
       are in the midst of World War II, when Goebbels was respon-
       sible for stimulating and maintaining the morale of the German
       people.   The entries are designed to shed light on the personality
       and character of Hitler's publicist.

187.   LUDECKE, Kurt Georg W.   *I Knew Hitler: The Story of a Nazi
       Who Escaped the Blood Purge*.   New York: Scribner, 1937.
       The author, who knew Hitler for a while, was one of the first to
       give the outside world a character sketch of the *Führer*.   Por-
       trays Hitler as a master of the art of propaganda: "He has a
       matchless instinct of taking advantage of every breeze to raise
       a political whirlwind."   He was a Jekyll and Hyde: "There were
       times when he gave the impression of unhappiness, of loneliness,
       of inward searching.   But in a moment he would turn again to
       whatever frenzied task with the swift command of a man born
       for action."   His mind jumped from subject to subject: "It was
       almost impossible to keep Hitler concentrated on one point."
       He was aloof: "He always maintained a considerable distance
       from other people."   He was disorderly: "He had a typical
       Austrian *Schlamperei* (slovenliness)."   Ludecke survived Hitler's
       1934 Blood Purge.   Dedicates his book to Ernst Roehm and
       Gregor Strasser "and many other Nazis who were betrayed,
       murdered and traduced in their graves."

188. MANSTEIN, Erich von. *Lost Victories.* Translated from the German by Anthony G. Powell. Chicago: Regnery, 1958.
Memoirs of Friedrich Erich von Lewinson von Manstein (1887-1973), armored warfare strategist, the mastermind behind the *Blitzkrieg* against France in 1940. Approached by officers of the Resistance in 1942, Manstein at first intimated that he was not averse to their goal, but he was so disgusted with the behavior of General Friedrich von Paulus at Stalingrad that he reaffirmed his allegiance to Hitler. After the war he was sentenced to eighteen years' imprisonment, of which he served four years.

189. *MANVELL, Roger and Heinrich FRAENKEL. *Doctor Goebbels: His Life and Death.* New York: Simon & Schuster, 1960.
A biography of Dr. Joseph Goebbels (1897-1945), master propagandist of the Hitler regime, relates the story of how the little man with a deformed foot dictated the cultural life of the Third Reich for twelve years. Hitler had cause to be grateful to Goebbels, the creator and promoter of the *Führer* myth, the Messiah-redeemer. The Reich Minister for Public Enlightenment and Propaganda was highly successful in winning the German masses for National Socialism through his stage-management and manipulation of the media. The authors stress his deep-rooted contempt for humanity as well as his astute combination of propaganda, bribery and terrorism. They end with an account of the suicide of Goebbels and the deaths of his wife Magda and their six children (because Goebbels did not want them to grow up in a non-Nazi Germany).

190. *MANVELL, Roger and Heinrich FRAENKEL. *Goering.* New York: Simon & Schuster, 1962.
A biography of Hermann Goering (1893-1946) describes the No. 2 Nazi as an arrogant, vain and cruel human being overcome by his lust for power. The authors note utter subservience to Hitler until the final days of the Third Reich. During their research they gained the confidence of members of the Goering family who survived, as well as many intimates who knew him well. They present enough material to prove, despite Goering's denials at the Nuremberg Trial, that he did know of the exterminations and the Nazi regime's other atrocities.

191. *MANVELL, Roger and Heinrich FRAENKEL. *Hess: A Biography.* London: MacGibbon & Kee, 1971.

Manvell and Fraenkel, collaborators on biographies of Goebbels (1960), Goering (1962), and Himmler (1964), present their version of the life of Rudolf Hess (1894-   ), Deputy Leader of the Nazi Party and No. 3 Nazi in the Third Reich after Goering. The authors tell the story of Hess's flight to Scotland on 10 May 1941, when he hoped to convince the British that Hitler had no desire to destroy a fellow Nordic nation, but that he only wanted living space in eastern Europe.

192. *MANVELL, Roger and Heinrich FRAENKEL. *Himmler.* New York: Putnam, 1964.
    The authors describe Heinrich Himmler (1900-45) as "an idealist without ideals" and as one of the most pitiless mass murderers in history. They recount Himmler's work as *Reichsführer-SS,* as head of the *Gestapo* and the *Waffen-SS* and as the supreme overseer of the "Final Solution," by which he was determined to cleanse Germany of "inferior races," including above all the country's Jews.

193. MARTON, Kati. *Wallenberg.* New York: Random House, 1982.
    An account of the young Swede, acting for the War Refugee Board, who helped save many Hungarian Jews from extermination by the Nazis. Using his Swedish diplomatic status, Wallenberg rescued thousands of Jews from certain death. The author, a Hungarian journalist, pays tribute to the Swedish diplomat and believes that he may still be alive in a Soviet prison.

194. MASER, Werner. *Hitler: Legend, Myth, and Reality.* Translated from the German by Peter and Betty Ross. New York: Harper & Row, 1973.
    German author Werner Maser, whose books have gone through more than one-hundred editions and translations, claims to present a picture of the *Führer* "as never seen before" by other writers. Offers evidence to show that Hitler was an ineffective administrator and that his regime lacked any coherent political, economic or social theory. In other words, the Hitler regime was an altogether inefficient jumble of competing jurisdictions. At the same time argues that Hitler was a basically normal, well-meaning and misguided political leader.

195. McGOVERN, James. *Martin Bormann.* New York: Morrow, 1968.

A biography of Martin Bormann (1900-?45), Hitler's private secretary, close associate and trusted confidant after Rudolf Hess's flight to England in May 1941. Employed by the CIA and in charge of the search for Bormann after he disappeared from the Berlin bunker, McGovern attempts to determine what happened to Bormann and provides his life story. Also describes the corrupt ways in which National Socialism pushed its way to political power, the ruthless means of Hitler's expansion policy and its guilt in the horrible Holocaust. Concludes that Bormann is dead, probably buried by the Soviets in an unmarked grave.

196. MEISSNER, Otto. *Als Staatssekretär unter Ebert, Hindenburg und Hitler* (As Secretary of State under Ebert, Hindenburg and Hitler). Hamburg: Hoffmann & Campe, 1950.
Memoirs of Otto Meissner (1880-1953), Chief of the Reich Chancellery under Socialist Friedrich Ebert, first President Paul von Hindenburg, and the National Socialist dictator Hitler. Along with Oskar von Hindenburg, Meissner was an intimate member of the camarilla that convinced President von Hindenburg to name Hitler Chancellor. As a reward for his services, Meissner was retained by Hitler as State Secretary at the Presidential Chancellery. In 1949 he was acquitted of war crimes at Nuremberg. Presents a defense of his career and denies that he had committed criminal offences of any kind.

197. MORELL, Theodore Gilbert. *The Secret Diaries of Hitler's Doctor*. New York: Macmillan, 1983.
Edited by historian David Irving, these diaries are devoted to Hitler's health from July 1941 to Morell's dismissal in April 1945. Dr. Morell (1886-1948) was the physician who treated his hypochondriacal patient with a bewildering variety of drugs to cure his gastric and other health problems. Editor Irving regards Morell as less of a quack doctor than a careless one. Hitler himself was so convinced of Morell's genius that he denounced anyone who dared criticize his doctor. Other Nazis, notably Ribbentrop and Ley, were as eager as Hitler to receive Morell's pills and injections. In these secret diaries Morell seeks to justify his status as a responsible physician.

198. MÜLLER, Klaus-Jürgen. *General Ludwig Beck*. Boppard: Boldt Verlag, 1980.
A sympathetic portrait of Ludwig Beck (1890-1944), a general who served as Chief of Staff of the Armed Forces from 1935 to

1938. Beck was the only high officer who consistently did what he could to thwart Hitler's plans for war. He attempted to organize resistance inside the General Staff, but ultimately failed. Later, he became the recognized military leader of the Resistance movement. He was forced to commit suicide after the failure of the 20 July 1944 attempt on the life of Hitler.

199. NEUMANN, Peter, pseud. *The Black March: The Personal Story of an SS Man.* Translated from the French by Constantine FitzGibbon. New York: Sloane, 1959.
A narrative in the form of a journal of the career of an SS man, including his indoctrination in the Hitler Youth, his training as an SS officer and his capture on the Russian front in 1945.

200. *NIEMOELLER, Martin. *Here Stand I.* Translated from the German by Jane Lymburn. Chicago: Willet, Clark, 1937.
Martin Niemoeller (1882-1984) was a German pastor of the Protestant Evangelical Church and an outspoken anti-Nazi. In World War I he had won honors as a U-boat commander, but after the war he turned to a life of pacifism and religious service. Originally welcoming the rise of the Nazis to power, he later became disillusioned as Hitler tried to "coordinate" the Evangelical Church. He became leader of what he termed the legitimate Protestant Church of Germany. Arrested in 1937, he was found guilty of subversive attacks against the state and sentenced to seven months' imprisonment, the same year this book, stating the principles of his life, was published in Chicago. Niemoeller wrote that he refused to remain silent at man's behest when God commanded him to speak. His title was taken from Luther's speech "Here Stand I." Niemoeller spent the next seven years in Hitler's concentration camps.

201. *OLDEN, Rudolf. *Hitler.* Translated from the German by Walter Ettinghausen. New York: Covici, Friede, 1936.
A biography of Hitler published originally in Amsterdam. Like other biographers, Olden sought to explain psychological motivations of a complex character. Example: he tells how, when Hitler sensed opposition in an audience he was to address, he would run out of the meeting without saying a word: "This is a trick which the *Führer* will use often; when the situation becomes embarrassing, he hides." Offers details of Hitler's early life, analyzes the ideology in *Mein Kampf* and discusses political tactics. Olden, the biographer of Stresemann, was an editor of the *Berliner Tageblatt* when he watched the rise of National

Socialism, and later left his homeland. His portrait of Hitler is filled with contempt and detestation, as he shows his disgust for the brutality and vulgarity of Nazism.

202. PADFIELD, Peter. *Dönitz; the Last Führer, Portrait of a Nazi Leader.* New York: Harper & Row, 1984.
A study of Karl Dönitz (1891-1980), Grand Admiral and Commander-in-Chief of the German Navy after 1943 and successor to Hitler as the *Führer* of the Third Reich during its last few days. Utilizes memoirs, interviews, primary sources and standard secondary materials. Dönitz received the lightest sentence at Nuremberg — ten years. The author maintains that Dönitz was guilty by association of the horrors of the Holocaust as were other Nazis.

203. PAGET, R. T. *Manstein: His Campaigns and His Trial.* London: Collins, 1951.
This biography of Field Marshal Erich von Manstein (1887-1973), armored-war strategist and tactician, presents Manstein as one of the ablest and most talented German commanders of World War II. Traces the campaigns from France to the Eastern Front, where he conquered the Crimea for the Third Reich and later headed the Army Group South from 14 February 1943 to 30 March 1944. For a time he seemed to support General Ludwig Beck in the Resistance movement, but later reaffirmed his allegiance to Hitler.

204. PAPEN, Franz von. *Memoirs.* New York: Dutton, 1953.
Franz von Papen (1879-1969), politician active in the late days of the Weimar Republic and throughout the Nazi regime, seeks to justify his bizarre career. Paints himself as a man of impeccable social grace. Identifies his own interests as an upper-class nobleman with those of the state and shows his support for the anti-republican, anti-parliamentarian right. Makes it a point of disassociating himself from Nazi guilt, and attributes the Hitler regime to paganism. Clothes his monarchism and nationalism in a kind of pseudo-Christian vocabulary. Denounces Hitler, the man he helped bring to power in 1933, as a pathological liar.

205. PAYNE, Robert. *The Life and Death of Adolf Hitler.* New York: Praeger, 1973.
Presents what the author contends is all that is known about the life of the solitary schoolboy who became dictator of an empire

greater than that of Alexander the Great or Napoleon. A prolific writer, Payne claims that Hitler was mad "almost from the
very beginning." Cites the Blood Purge of 20 June 1934 as the
work of an insane man.

206. PEUSCHEL, Harald. *Die Männer um Hitler* (The Men Who
 Surrounded Hitler). Düsseldorf: Droste, 1982.
 "Brown biographies" of leading Nazis, including Bormann,
 Goebbels, Goering, Heydrich, Himmler and others.

207. PRYCE-JONES, David. *Unity Mitford: A Quest.* London:
 Weidenfeld & Nicolson, 1976.
 A biography of Unity Valkyrie-Mitford (1914-48), English
 aristocrat and friend of Hitler. One of seven children in the
 eccentric Redesdale family, Unity was a statuesque blonde,
 lively and active. From 1933 on, she was a member of the
 Führer's salon in Munich, where she was regarded as an outstanding example of Nordic beauty. She fell deeply in love with
 Hitler and probably hoped to become his wife. On 3 September
 1939, the day on which Great Britain and France declared war
 on Germany, Unity tried to kill herself with a small-caliber pis-
 tol in the *Englischer Garten* in Munich. Hitler sent his best
 medical specialists to help her. As soon as she was able to
 travel, she was sent home to England via a special train to
 Switzerland. She died unmarried on 28 May 1948.

208. PUCCETTI, Roland. *The Death of the Fuehrer.* New York: St.
 Martin's Press, 1972.
 An account of the last days of Hitler in his Berlin bunker. With
 the war hopelessly lost, the *Führer*, now on the verge of
 madness, played out the final act of his life. He spent hours
 before giant war maps, shifting colored pins about to locate
 units that no longer existed. In the early hours of 29 April 1945,
 he married Eva Braun, and immediately afterward dictated his
 last will and political testament, in which he sought to justify his
 life and work. The next day he retreated to his suite and killed
 himself.

209. RABITSCH, Hugo. *Aus Adolf Hitlers Jugendzeit* (On Hitler's
 Days of Youth). Munich: Deutscher Volksverlag, 1938.
 A Nazi publication designed to show Hitler as an enormously
 attractive youth who revealed in his actions the seeds of future
 greatness. There were many publications of this kind in prewar
 Germany. Presents the youthful reminiscences of a fellow stu-

dent of Hitler's at the *Realschule* (non-classical secondary school) at Linz.   Although Hitler's performance as a student was less than mediocre, the author found leadership qualities in his friend at school.

210.   RAEDER, Erich. *My Life*. Translated from the German by Henry W. Drexel. Annapolis: U.S. Naval Institute, 1961.
Erich Raeder (1878-1960), Grand Admiral and Commander-in-Chief of the German Navy, a post he held until his retirement in 1943, played a central role in building and directing Hitler's new navy.   Placed on trial at Nuremberg after the war, he admitted that the German Navy had violated the Treaty of Versailles "as a matter of honor."   Sentenced to life imprisonment, he was released in 1955 because of ill-health. This biography, published in translation by the U.S. Naval Institute, pays attention to differences with Hitler which led to Raeder's retirement in 1943.   It also emphasizes the Admiral's role in naval rearmament.   In the second volume of the original memoirs in German, *Mein Leben: Von 1935 bis Spandau* (1957), Raeder apologizes for Hitler's expansionist policies and describes the *Führer* as "an extraordinary man worthy of becoming Germany's leader."

211.   RAUSCHNING, Hermann. *Men of Chaos*. Translated from the German by E. W. Dickes. New York: Putnam, 1942.
The American version of a book published in England as *Makers of Destruction*.   Hermann Rauschning, born 1887, former president of the Danzig Senate and National Socialist politician, who fled from Germany to Switzerland in 1936, wrote a number of books criticizing Hitler and the Nazi regime.   Describes his meetings and talks with Nazi leaders in the Third Reich, recollects conversations and offers character analyses of the men surrounding Hitler.   Relates the ruthless planning and the scientific precision of Nazi propaganda from 1933 to the outbreak of war in 1939.

212.   REES, J. R., ed. *The Case of Rudolf Hess: A Problem in Diagnosis and Forensic Psychiatry*. London: Heinemann, 1947.
A collection of essays describing the case of Rudolf Hess (1894-   ), Deputy Leader of the Nazi Party, known for his doglike devotion to Hitler, as a problem in diagnosis and forensic psychiatry.   Most of the contributors seek to explain Hess's extraordinary flight to Scotland on 10 May 1941, when he hoped to convince the British that the considerate *Führer* had

no intention of destroying Great Britain but would combine
with the British to smash the Russian Communists. The flight
transformed the beetle-browed worshipper of his leader into one
of the most famous psychiatric cases of the century.

213. REITSCH, Hanna. *The Sky My Kingdom.* Translated from the
      German by Lawrence Wilson. London: Bodley Head,
      1955. Also published under the title *Flying Is My Life.*
      New York: Putnam, 1954.
      Memoirs of Hanna Reitsch (1912-79), leading German aviatrix
      and one of the last visitors to the bunker in Berlin during
      Hitler's final days. Her country's outstanding stunt pilot and
      flier, Reitsch set many European records. Claims that, as an
      enthusiastic admirer of Hitler, she begged to be allowed to die
      with him in the bunker. British historian Hugh R. Trevor-
      Roper described Fräulein Reitsch's character as "well suited to
      the atmosphere in that last subterranean madhouse in Berlin."

214. RIBBENTROP, Joachim von.   *The Ribbentrop Memoirs.*
      Translated from the German by Oliver Watson. London:
      Weidenfeld & Nicolson, 1954.
      The memoirs of Hitler's Minister of Foreign Affairs from 1938
      to 1945 reveal the character of a vain and humorless man who
      aroused almost universal dislike and criticism for his incompe-
      tence. A former champagne salesman, he was accepted by
      Hitler as a man of the world. His rival, Dr. Goebbels, was
      contemptuous: "He bought his name, he married his money,
      and he swindled his way into office." In 1937, as Ambassador
      to Great Britain, he alienated nearly everyone by his awkward
      behavior and diplomatic bungling, including the *faux pas* of
      greeting the King with a Nazi salute. His pompousness and
      arrogance were gone in the dock at Nuremberg, where he ap-
      peared pathetic, pale, stooped and beaten. Ribbentrop was the
      first defendant to be hanged in Nuremberg prison.

215. *RIESS, Curt. *Joseph Goebbels.* Garden City, NY: Doubleday,
      1948.
      Dr. Joseph Goebbels (1897-1945) was a high-ranking Nazi
      politician, close friend of Hitler and propaganda expert of the
      Third Reich. Depicts Goebbels as the most outstanding expo-
      nent of an amoral nihilism. Without his propaganda image,
      Hitler certainly would never have become a world menace.
      Tremendous power was given to Goebbels without which he
      could never have carried out his propaganda experiments.

"Goebbels created a new reality woven entirely out of lies."
Includes Goebbels in the category of such chauvinistic petty
bourgeois as Hitler and Himmler or of the great gangsters as
Goering. The book utilized the many speeches, articles and
books by Goebbels, as well as talks with people who had known
and worked with him.

216.   RÖHM, Ernst. *Die Geschichte eines Hochverräters* (History of
       One Guilty of High Treason). Munich: Eher Verlag, 1928,
       1934.
Autobiography of Ernst Röhm (1887-1934), Nazi politician,
early friend of Hitler's and chief of the SA, the Brown Shirts, the
private army which fought the battle of the streets against the
Communists. After the Nazis came to power in 1933, Röhm
attempted to promote a "second revolution" on behalf of the
socialist side of National Socialism. He was liquidated in the
Blood Purge of 1934. In his autobiography published in 1928,
ironically titled *History of One Guilty of High Treason*, Röhm
presents his personal philosophy. "The Germans have forgotten to hate. Virile hate has been replaced by feminine
lamentation....To hell with peace and prudence."

217.   ROMMEL, Erwin. *Rommel's Papers*. London: Collins, 1953.
The papers of General Erwin Rommel (1891-1944), Field Marshal and the popular German commander known as the Desert
Fox, shed light on his extraordinary successes in the North
African campaigns, including the recall from his hospital bed in
Germany just two days after the battle of El Alamein had begun. Rommel also reveals his strategy for countering the expected Allied invasion of France. Carefully avoids writing
anything about his possible implication in the conspiracy
against Hitler.

218.   ROSENBERG, Alfred. *Memoirs*. With commentaries by Serge
       Lang and Ernst von Schenck and translated from the
       German by Eric Posselt. Chicago: Ziff-Davis, 1949.
In his cell at Nuremberg, Alfred Rosenberg (1893-1946), leading
ideologist of National Socialism, penned his memoirs. They
were intended to help him in his defense and to justify himself
in his own eyes and in those of the world. Presents what he calls
the great achievements of Hitler and Nazism, reveals a deep-
rooted hatred for the Slavic East as well as for Jews and offers
an insight into the bitter internecine rivalries of Nazi leaders.

219. ROSENBERG, Alfred, ed. *Dietrich Eckart: Ein Vermächtnis* (Dietrich Eckart: A Testimony). Munich: Eher Verlag, 1928.
Dietrich Eckart (1868-1923) was a nationalist poet and member of Hitler's personal entourage in the early post-World-War-I years in Munich. His poem *Jeurjo* (1919) used the words "*Deutschland erwache*" ("Germany Awake!"), which became the battle cry of the Nazi movement. From the beginning he was a notorious Jew-baiter. Together with his young protegé, Alfred Rosenberg, who later became the official ideologist of the Nazi movement, Eckart edited the *Völkischer Beobachter*, the party organ. Eckart was a heavy drinker and a morphine addict who spent some time in an asylum for the mentally diseased. This book, edited by Alfred Rosenberg and issued by a publisher specializing in Nazi works, was an effort to rehabilitate Eckart and promote him as a Nazi martyr. The text asserts that his fatal illness was due to mistreatment in a Bavarian prison. It accuses Jews of being arch-materialists who wanted to strip mankind of its soul.

220. RUDEL, Hans Ulrich. *Stuka Pilot.* Translated by Lynton Hudson. Dublin: Euphorion Books, 1952.
Memoirs of Nazi Germany's most highly decorated soldier, the only holder of the Knight's Cross, Swords and Diamonds. In 1938 Rudel (b. 1912) was posted to a *Stuka* formation as an engineering officer. In September 1941 he sank an Allied cruiser and the battleship *Marat*. Caught by the Russians in March 1944, he escaped. Shot down in February 1945, he lost a leg. By the end of the war he was a colonel, officially credited with 2,539 operations and 532 tank kills. His book, originally published in Buenos Aires, where he had fled to become a member of the Nazi community there, expresses continued admiration for Hitler and glorifies the Nazi role in World War II. Rudel became an idolized hero of rightist circles in postwar Germany.

221. SCHELLENBERG, Walter. *The Schellenberg Memoirs.* Edited and translated from the German by Louis Hagen. London: Deutsch, 1956.
Walter Schellenberg (1910-52) was the supreme head of Hitler's espionage service and Heinrich Himmler's right-hand man toward the end of World War II. In 1944 he was head of the united SS and *Wehrmacht*, military intelligence. Tried by the American military tribunal at Nuremberg, he was acquitted of the charge of genocide. He claimed successfully that he had

nothing to do with the "Final Solution." However, he was found guilty of complicity in the murder of Russian prisoners of war and sentenced to six years' imprisonment, but served fewer than two years. Describes his career in active espionage, how he counteracted Soviet intelligence, how he expanded the Nazi Swedish network, his work for a united intelligence service and his rivalry with Foreign Minister Joachim von Ribbentrop.

222. *SCHIEDER, Theodor. *Hermann Rauschnings "Gespräche mit Hitler" als Geschichtsquelle* (Hermann Rauschning's Talks with Hitler as Historical Source Material). Opladen: Westdeutscher Verlag, 1972.
    Hermann Rauschning, a Nazi politician, later exposed the corruption and ruthlessness of Hitler and his Nazi regime. After writing a denunciation of Nazism (*The Revolution of Nihilism* [1939]), he published an account of his conversations with Hitler (*Hitler Speaks* [1939]), as a warning to the free world that the *Führer* would stop at nothing to satisfy his lust for power. This volume by the distinguished late historian Theodor Schieder of the University of Cologne examines Rauschning's *Gespräche mit Hitler* to establish its validity after many other German historians raised serious questions about it. Vindicates Rauschning and concludes that his account of his talks with Hitler fitted well into the evidence of documentary knowledge about the personality and character of the *Führer*.

223. SCHIRACH, Baldur von. *Ich glaubte an Hitler* (I Believed in Hitler). Hamburg: Mosaik Verlag, 1967.
    Baldur von Schirach (1907-74), Leader of German Youth, ranked at the top level of the Nazi hierarchy. He was presented to the German public as a kind of demigod embodying all that was fine among youngsters in the Third Reich. His pictures were second only to Hitler's in displays throughout Nazi Germany. His enemies ridiculed him for his girlish behavior, especially his bedroom in white. At Nuremberg the Tribunal found Schirach guilty of participating in the persecution of Jews: bulletins advocating the extermination of Jews were found in his office. Sentenced to twenty years' imprisonment, he served the full term. In his memoirs, *I Believed in Hitler*, published a year after his release, Schirach attempts to explain the fatal fascination Hitler exerted on him and the younger German generation. He now condemns Nazism and calls for opposition to its rebirth in any form. Blames himself for not having done more to oppose the policy of concentration camps.

224. SCHMIDT, Matthias. *Albert Speer: The End of A Myth.* Translated from the German by Joachim Neugroschel. New York: St. Martin's Press, 1984.
In his memoirs, *Inside the Third Reich* (1970), Albert Speer, Hitler's favorite architect and Minister for War Production from 1942 to 1945, sought to show that he was a man of honor and integrity in comparison with his criminal Nazi colleagues. His effort impressed many historians. In this book Matthias Schmidt, an associate professor at the Friedrich-Meinecke-Institute for Historical Research in West Berlin, presents new documents and his own interviews with Speer's former colleagues to show that Speer created "the most carefully crafted falsification in modern history," that his memoirs dangerously polluted history. Attacks the image of Speer as "an apolitical technocrat," and unsparingly accuses Speer of excelling in the machinations of Nazi politics, a man who was well aware of the "Final Solution" and who actually tried to succeed Hitler as *Führer*.

225. SCHMIDT, Paul. *Hitler's Interpreter: The Secret History of German Diplomacy.* Edited by R. H. C. Steed. New York: Macmillan, 1951.
A linguist with an extraordinary memory, Dr. Paul Schmidt was Hitler's chief interpreter for some ten years after 1935. At times he was the only third party present at meetings of critical importance. Offers a first-hand account of Prime Minister Neville Chamberlain's tragic failures at Munich and Bad Godesberg at the time of the Czechoslovak crisis. Relates many anecdotes, such as Lloyd George falling prey to Hitler's charms; Mussolini's insistence, to the consternation of the Germans, that Italy wanted to enter the war; Molotov sparring with the Nazis; how Mussolini suffered while Hitler did all the talking; and Goering showing off his model train. Insists that he never was a Nazi sympathizer and is often contemptuous of them. Claims that he merely did his job as a civil servant and expert technician.

226. SCHUSCHNIGG, Kurt von. *My Austria.* Translated from the German by John Segrue. New York: Knopf, 1938.
Kurt von Schuschnigg (1897-1977), last Chancellor of independent Austria, tells the story of his unfortunate country. Part autobiography, part political history, the book is a detailed study of the years in which the author played so important a part. Records in diary form his stewardship, domestic and for-

eign policies, building of the army, economic program and aims and hopes for Austria. Relates his struggle against Hitler before being forced from office. Offers a character sketch of Engelbert Dollfuss, the Austrian Chancellor slain by the Nazis on 25 July 1934.

227. SCHWARTZ, Paul. *This Man Ribbentrop: His Life and Times.* New York: Messner, 1943.
A biography of Joachim von Ribbentrop (1893-1946), National Socialist statesman and Hitler's Minister of Foreign Affairs. Describes Ribbentrop's misleading advice to Hitler that Britons were so lethargic and paralyzed that they would accept without complaint any aggressive moves by Nazi Germany. It was a critical misstatement of fact which led the *Führer* to his reckless course in Poland in an effort to implement his concept of *Lebensraum*, or living space.

228. SERAPHIM, Hans-Günther. *Das politische Tagebuch Alfred Rosenbergs* (The Political Diary of Alfred Rosenberg). Munich: Deutscher Taschenbuch Verlag, 1984.
The political diary of Alfred Rosenberg (1893-1946), the semi-official philosopher of the Third Reich. In charge of the Foreign Affairs Department from 1933 to 1945, Rosenberg was responsible for Nazi Parties in other countries. Relates his close relations with Hitler during a succession of campaigns. For example, at the end of September 1939, during the invasion of Poland, Rosenberg records how the *Führer* informed him that he wished to remove all German-controlled Jewry into an area between the Vistula and Bug Rivers. Rosenberg was aware of Hitler's extreme anti-Semitism and often commented on it.

229. *SHIRER, William L. *Berlin Diary: The Journal of a Foreign Correspondent, 1934-1941.* New York: Knopf, 1941, 1942, 1943.
The 1934 to 1941 journal of the well-known foreign correspondent. A reporter of long and steadfast memory, Shirer learned much in the frenzied Nazi capital beyond the Elbe — about the sinister plots, the fateful decisions and the Germans gripped in an iron dictatorship. At the time Hitler was at the zenith of his power. His "master race" had conquered most of Europe and enslaved its stunned inhabitants. Hitler was determined to turn on the Soviet Union and conquer Great Britain.

230. *SHIRER, William L. *End of a Berlin Diary*. New York: Knopf, 1947.
Continuation and conclusion of *Berlin Diary* (1941) by reporter-historian Shirer. His first diary ended in December 1940 when he left Berlin to return to the United States. He had no intention of going back to Germany, but when the news of the war's end flashed over the wires, he was again in Berlin to find out what had happened since he left. In entries from 1945 to 1947 he tracked down as many Nazi secrets as he could – the true story of the Munich appeasement, Franco's relations with Hitler, the invasion of Norway, the attempt to conquer Great Britain, the war in Russia, the collapse of the *Wehrmacht* and the secret documents revealing Hitler's decisions on America's destiny.

231. *SHIRER, William L. *The Nightmare Years, 1930-1940*. Boston: Little, Brown, 1984.
Journalist-historian William L. Shirer published another volume of his memoirs, *20th Century Journey*, in 1976. In this volume he covers the decade from 1930 to 1940. Initially as a newspaperman and then as one of the first overseas radio correspondents, Shirer gives an eyewitness account of the crucible out of which Hitler appeared. Writes how, with increasing horror and fascination, he watched Hitler crush freedom and the human spirit in Germany, persecute the Jews and prepare to massacre them, destroy all who opposed him and drag a great nation toward conquest and destruction. Observes to his consternation that most Germans joined joyously "in this Nazi barbarism." Details his first impressions of Hitler (1934-35), life in the Third Reich (1934-38), the men around Hitler, the road to Armageddon (1935-38) and the coming of the war (1939-40). He left Germany in December 1940, "fifteen months after Hitler plunged Europe into war."

232. SMITH, Bradley F. *Adolf Hitler: His Family, Childhood, and Youth*. Stanford, CA: Stanford University Press, 1967, 1979.
Originally published in 1967 in The Netherlands, this study was later reprinted in several editions by the Hoover Institution of War, Revolution and Peace. Reviews most of the published and unpublished material from Nazi archives, concentrating on the events and conditions in Hitler's formative years which left marks on the *Führer*'s personality and character. Prefers the techniques of the historian rather than those of psychoanalysts

or sociologists. Finds in the boy the man whose career was to shake the very foundations of Western civilization.

233.   SMITH, Howard K.   *Last Train from Berlin.*   New York: Popular Library, 1962.
A reprint of the original 1942 publication by Knopf of foreign correspondent Howard K. Smith's last days in Berlin before the United States and Germany went to war in late 1941.   The well-known reporter describes life in Berlin during the early critical war days.

234.   SMITH, Stanley F.   *Heinrich Himmler: A Nazi in the Making. 1900-1926.*   Stanford, CA: Hoover Institution Press, 1971.
A study of the formative years of Heinrich Himmler (1900-45), *Reichsführer-SS*, head of the *Gestapo* and *Waffen-SS*, and the second most powerful man in Nazi Germany.   Uses the Himmler family's personal papers and other captured German records to offer a portrait of an awkward, talkative boy who later turned into a prudish intrigue-artist and mass murderer. Shows how Himmler tried to integrate for himself the contradictory values of his background and his later propulsion to the top of the Nazi heap.

235.   SNYDER, Louis L.   *Hitler and Nazism.*   New York: Bantam Books, 1976.
A compact version of Hitler's life, politics and meteoric career. Uses a psychohistorical approach to describe the Nazi phenomenon.

236.   SPEER, Albert.   *Infiltration.*   Translated from the German by Joachim Neugroschel.   New York: Macmillan, 1981.
Albert Speer again seeks to defend himself against charges of being a war criminal.   Discusses several major topics: (1) Heinrich Himmler's ambition to create an SS industrial empire and the author's decision to rely primarily on private management; (2) a summary of Himmler's machinations, threats, deceits and other nefarious activities; and (3) the conflict between those (including Speer) who merely wanted to use Jews as a source of skilled labor and those who were hardline exterminators.   Insists that he had nothing to do with the "Final Solution."

237. SPEER, Albert. *Inside the Third Reich: Memoirs of Albert Speer.* Translated from the German by Richard and Clara Winston. New York: Macmillan, 1970.

Memoirs of Albert Speer (1905-81), Hitler's personal architect and city planner and Reich Minister for Armaments and War Production from 1942 to 1945. Wrote the first draft in Spandau prison in Berlin where he was serving a twenty-year sentence as a war criminal, smuggled out the pages bit by bit and then organized the material into a publishable manuscript. Offers a detailed account of his years at Hitler's side and the many rivalries inside the Nazi hierarchy. Reveals how Hitler's unlimited power was combined with new devices of modern technology. The Third Reich, far from being a monolithic state, was allegedly a patchwork of local fiefdoms, each one jealously guarded. Denies participation in atrocities; claims that he had inadvertently "made a pact with the devil."

238. SPEER, Albert. *Spandau: The Secret Diaries.* Translated from the German by Richard and Clara Winston. New York: Macmillan, 1976.

After the success of his *Inside the Third Reich* (1970), Albert Speer decided to publish his secret diaries kept during imprisonment in Spandau Prison, Berlin. From more than 20,000 pages which his family had kept in a trunk after he sent them from Nuremberg and Spandau, he published this book of diary notes and smuggled letters. Divided into twenty chapters (for twenty years at Spandau), the book offers recollections of Hitler, Speer's own ingenuity in finding means to mitigate the boredom of confinement and sketches of other Nazi leaders. Speer also analyzes his own guilt.

239. STACHURA, Peter D. *Gregor Strasser and the Rise of Nazism.* London: Allen & Unwin, 1983.

Nazi populist Gregor Strasser (1892-1934) was a leader of the social-revolutionary wing of the early Nazi Party and Hitler's most dangerous rival at that time. The author analyzes the role of Strasser in the rise of the National Socialist movement. Strasser challenged Hitler's supposed abandonment of socialist ideals. On 30 June 1934, the night of the Blood Purge, he was murdered on Hitler's orders by the *Gestapo.* This meant the destruction of the left-wing of the Nazi Party.

240. STARHEMBERG, Ernst Rudiger Prince. *Between Hitler and Mussolini: The Memoirs of Prince Starhemberg.* New York: Harper, 1942.
Memoirs of Prince Ernst Rudiger Starhemberg (1899-1956), member of one of Austria's oldest aristocratic families, wealthy landowner and onetime Fascist leader of Austria. After World War I he joined the German *Freikorps*, an illegal paramilitary organization responsible for many political assassinations. In 1923 he accompanied Hitler on the famous Munich Beer-Hall *Putsch*, organized the Fascist movement in Austria, and as Minister of Interior, Vice-Chancellor and leader of the *Heimwehr* movement contributed to the destruction of parliamentarianism and democracy in his homeland. After Hitler's *Anschluss* joined Germany and Austria, Starhemberg deserted Hitler, lost his Austrian nationality and saw all his properties confiscated. Early in World War II he joined General Charles De Gaulle's Free French Air Force. His memoirs were written to show the world the incredible hypocrisy of the Hitler-Mussolini alliance.

241. STAUDINGER, Hans. *The Inner Nazi: A Critical Analysis of Mein Kampf.* Baton Rouge, LA: Louisiana State University Press, 1981.
After a distinguished career in government service in high posts, including membership in the German *Reichstag* from 1932 to 1933, Dr. Hans Staudinger fled his homeland in 1933 and later became Professor of Economics and Dean of the Graduate Faculty at The New School for Social Research in New York City. Presents a critical analysis of Hitler's autobiography *Mein Kampf*. Like other readers, Staudinger was astonished by the crude thinking and accumulated hatreds of the Austrian politician.

242. *STEIN, George H., ed.   *Hitler.*   Englewood Cliffs, NJ: Prentice-Hall, 1968.
This paperback book, published in the *Great Lives Observed* series under the general editorship of Gerald Emanuel Stearn, is divided into three parts: Hitler Looks at the World, The World Looks at Hitler, and Hitler in History. Part 1 presents selections from Hitler's public and personal materials; Part 2 explains how Hitler was perceived by his followers and by foreign diplomats and journalists; and Part 3 offers estimates by such commentators as Alan Bullock, Ernst Nolte, A. J. P. Taylor and Hugh R. Trevor-Roper.

243. STEVENSON, William. *The Bormann Brotherhood.* New
York: Harcourt Brace Jovanovich, 1973.
A study concerning the men surrounding Martin Bormann,
Hitler's designated successor, in 1945 the second most powerful
man in the Third Reich, who was tried *in absentia* and sentenced
to death at Nuremberg in 1945. (See entry 255).

244. STOCKHORST, Erich. *Fünftausend Köpfe: Wer war was im
Dritten Reich* (Five Thousand Heads. Who Was What in
the Third Reich). (Velbert & Kettwig): Blick & Bild
Verlag, 1967.
Succinct biographies of "who was what" in the Third Reich.

245. STRASSER, Otto. *Hitler and I.* Translated from the German
by Gwenda David and Eric Mosbacher. Boston:
Houghton Mifflin, 1940.
Otto Strasser (1897-1974) was a brother of Gregor Strasser,
Nazi populist and Hitler's early rival for leadership of the National Socialist Party, killed in the Blood Purge of 1934. Otto,
also a leader of the left wing of the NSDAP, was denounced by
Hitler as a "parlor Bolshevik," as a victim of the "cardinal sins
of democracy and liberalism" and expelled from the party in
1930. Claiming to be the true National Socialist, he formed a
splinter group, the Black Front, and continued to attack Hitler
as "the betrayer of the revolution." He left Germany and
moved first to Prague and then to Canada. Describes his relationship with Hitler and the bitter struggle between them. It is
part autobiography, part accusation, part self-defense.

246. *TOLAND, John. *Adolf Hitler.* Garden City, NY: Doubleday,
1976.
A giant biography of more than one-thousand pages, this is a
popular account of Hitler's life. Toland conducted some 250
interviews with those who knew Hitler intimately — adjutants,
secretaries, his pilot, doctors, architects, military leaders and
women Hitler admired. All but a dozen of these interviews are
stored in the Library of Congress for safekeeping. Presents
Hitler as the greatest mover and shaker of the 20th century, a
man who disrupted millions of lives and stirred grinding hatred
as "a knight of the *Hakenkreuz*, a warped archangel, a hybrid
of Prometheus and Lucifer." Sees Hitler as far more complex
and contradictory than he had ever imagined, and regards him
as a half-madman, as a political and military bungler and as an
evil murderer beyond redemption.

247. *TREVOR-ROPER, H. R. *The Last Days of Hitler.* New York: Macmillan, 1947.

Hugh R. Trevor-Roper, who became Regius Professor of Modern History at Oxford University, was a British Intelligence Officer at the time he was sent, under official orders, to collect the material for this book. This is a narrative of the so-called *Götterdämmerung*, the final days in the *Führerbunker* under the Chancellery in Berlin, a detailed account of what happened in the bomb shelter, with accent on the mounting hysteria, the wishful thinking, the blood lust and the general air of lunacy in "a cloud-cuckoo land."

248. TREVOR-ROPER, Hugh R., ed. *The Bormann Letters.* London: Weidenfeld & Nicolson, 1954.

British historian Trevor-Roper, author of *The Last Days of Hitler* (1947), edited the Bormann letters. Martin Bormann (1900-?45) was head of the Party Chancellery and private secretary of Hitler. By the end of World War II, Bormann had become second only to the *Führer* in political power. At the Nuremberg Trial in 1946, he was sentenced to death *in absentia.* In April 1973, a German court formally pronounced him dead, but controversy remains as to whether or not he died after escaping from Hitler's bunker in the last days of the war.

249. TRUE TO TYPE. London: Hutchinson, n.d.

Letters and diaries of German soldiers and civilians on the Soviet front. Excerpts describe what it was like for German troops at Stalingrad. "God almighty! Put an end to this torture!"

250. TURNER, Henry Ashby, Jr., ed. *Hitler: Memoirs of a Confidant.* Translated from the German by Ruth Hein. New Haven: Yale University Press, 1985.

A first-hand account of Hitler's rise to political power by a member of the Nazi inner circle. Reveals intimate details concerning the *Führer*, with special attention to his personality and character. Describes the *Führer* as a windy, cunning, fanatical, pretentious and predatory human being, vegetarian, celibate and insomniac, a spellbinder. At the same time, seeks to deodorize the memory of Hitler.

251. VANSITTART, Robert Gilbert. *Lessons of My Life.* New York: Knopf, 1943.

Lord Vansittart, former British Under-Secretary of State for Foreign Affairs was the center of a stormy international controversy during World War II. Sums up what his lifetime of diplomatic service had taught him about Germany and its relations with the rest of the world. Deals critically not only with the Nazis and the Prussian officer caste but also with industrialists, intelligentsia and parties of the Left. The strongly anti-German text is filled with thundering maledictions and many personal opinions. During the war, Vansittart's strictures of the German people were so intense that the point of view he propounded became generally known as Vansittartism.

252. VINKE, Hermann. *The Short Life of Sophie Scholl.* Translated from the German by Hedwig Pachter. New York: Harper & Row, 1984.
A children's book published in Germany about the life of Sophie Scholl (1921-43), who with her brother Hans was at the heart of the White Rose, the underground organization of Munich students opposed to Hitler. Profusely illustrated, the book was the recipient of the Buxtehuder Bulle, awarded in Germany to an outstanding children's book promoting peace. Portrays a dreamy but utterly fearless young woman who sacrificed her life for a belief in a decent Germany. "With all those people dying for the regime, it is high time that someone died against it."

253. WEIZSÄCKER, Ernst von. *Memoirs of Ernst von Weizsäcker.* Translated from the German by John Andrews, pseud. Chicago: Regnery, 1951.
Ernst Freiherr von Weizsäcker (1882-1951) was a Foreign Office diplomat who served the Third Reich as State Secretary and later as Ambassador to the Holy See. Arrested by the Allies as a war criminal, he was sentenced in 1949 to five years' imprisonment, but eighteen months after his conviction he was released under a general amnesty. His memoirs are, in effect, a brief for his defense as well as an *apologia pro vita sua.* Insists that he had made every effort to keep Nazis out of the Foreign Office. Claims that he repeatedly offered to resign to return to the Navy, but that he was forced to give up in disgust and abandon his hopeless cause. Writes that he became a member of the Nazi party only for "decorative reasons" and had accepted only "honorary" rank in the SS.

254. WHITING, Charles. *Otto Skorzeny*. New York: Ballantine, 1972.
      This biography of Otto Skorzeny (1908-75), the most publicized adventurer and soldier of fortune in Nazi Germany, devotes special attention to Skorzeny's role in the rescue of Italian dictator Mussolini at the Gran Sasso d'Italia, high in the Abruzzi Apennines. On 13 September 1943 Skorzeny led an airborne commando force by glider in a dangerous landing to snatch Mussolini from a mountainside hotel and carry him to Germany. The daring rescue won Skorzeny instant fame throughout the world. His daring exploits served to raise German morale during World War II. Presents Skorzeny as the most dangerous man in Europe.

255. WHITING, Charles. *The Hunt for Martin Bormann*. New York: Ballantine, 1973.
      Martin Bormann (1900-?45) was Hitler's private secretary and close associate, the most powerful man next to the *Führer* during the declining years of the Third Reich. His Party comrades dubbed him "the Brown Eminence," and his enemies called him "the Machiavelli behind the office desk." At a time in the Berlin bunker when others deserted the raging *Führer*, Bormann remained faithful to Hitler, who called him "my most loyal Party comrade." The paladin signed Hitler's political testament and witnessed the wedding ceremony uniting Hitler and Eva Braun. Bormann watched the flames devour Hitler's body in the courtyard of the Reich Chancellery. For a few hours he tried to negotiate with the Allies, then he vanished. Describes his own vain search for Bormann over two continents and in six countries.

256. WIGTON, Charles. *Heydrich: Hitler's Most Evil Henchman*. London: Oldhams, 1962.
      Reinhard Heydrich (1904-42) was head of the Reich Security Service, Deputy Reich Protector of Bohemia and Moravia, administrator of concentration camps and a specialist in Nazi terror. Considers Heydrich the most evil rogue in the coterie of the *Führer's* collection of bully boys and scoundrels. Heydrich's father, musician Bruno Heydrich, was described in Hugh Riemann's *Musiklexikon* as "Heydrich, Bruno, real name Süss." This entry, intimating that the elder Heydrich was Jewish, was to haunt Reinhard Heydrich for the rest of his life. At the core of his character was the haunting suspicion that his body was tainted by Jewish blood. Shows how Heydrich was

chosen to administer the "Final Solution," the liquidation of Jews. On 29 May 1942 Heydrich was assassinated by two young men of the Czech Resistance. Infuriated by the loss of his "man with the iron heart," Hitler struck back by obliterating the entire village of Lidice on the charge that its inhabitants had harbored the assassins.

257. WINTERBOTHAM, Frederick William. *The Nazi Connection*. New York: Harper & Row, 1978.
Memoirs about the author's activities for the British as a gatherer of intelligence on growing German air power after 1934. Aided by his "Aryan" good looks, Winterbotham managed to establish a friendly relationship with Nazi ideologist Alfred Rosenberg, through whom he met many Nazi leaders. Reveals Hitler's aggressive ambitions.

258. *WISTRICH, Robert. *Who's Who in Nazi Germany*. London: Weidenfeld & Nicolson, 1982.
A reference book presenting over 350 succinct biographies of the most prominent and significant individuals who influenced every aspect of life in Nazi Germany. Covers a wide range of occupations, social and political roles, including high Nazi Party leaders, *Gestapo* personalities, diplomatic personnel, industrialists, churchmen, academics, artists, writers, entertainers and resistance workers. Offers a representative cross-section of German society under Hitler. Each minibiography is linked to a facet of the Third Reich.

259. *YOUNG, Desmond. *Rommel: The Desert Fox*. New York: Harper, 1950.
A biography of Erwin Rommel (1891-1944), the "Desert Fox" of World War II, who won a reputation not only as Germany's most popular general but also as a respected tactician by the Allied military. Many Allied officers saw him as a master of desert warfare and also as a fair-minded military professional. Increasingly disillusioned by Hitler's unrealistic strategy, as well as by the global reaction to Nazi atrocities, Rommel eventually turned to the Resistance movement, although he personally opposed projected attempts on Hitler's life. The conspirators regarded him as their new Chief of Staff after the elimination of Hitler. After the failure of the 20 July 1944 plot on Hitler's life, one of the conspirators, before he died in agony on a meat hook, blurted out Rommel's name to his tormentors. Hitler gave the general the choice of suicide or trial. Rommel took poison.

CHAPTER 4

POLITICS AND GOVERNMENT

Nazi Party, Rise to Power, Administration, Organization, Coordination

Hitler's political stance was nihilistic in tone — *nothing* was to be left unchanged. It was dominantly negative — anti-Semitic, anti-Catholic, anti-Protestant, anti-Seventh Day Adventist, anti-Masonic, anti-Communist, anti-Socialist, anti-liberal, anti-democratic, anti-parliamentarian, anti-Gypsy, anti-Russian, anti-French, anti-British and anti-American. The very name "National Socialist" was a contradiction in terms — it represented two opposing themes — nationalism and internationalism. It was a fraudulent political phenomenon designed to attract all elements of German society, from bored aristocrat down to disgruntled worker. A highly civilized but apolitical public was taken in by Nazi propaganda. Seldom in history has so cultured a people as the Germans succumbed so completely to the political wiles of a dangerous charlatan.

All this was recorded in study after study on the political aspects of Hitlerism and the Third Reich. Scholars differ on the reasons for the decline of the Weimar Republic and the subsequent rise to power of Hitler and the Nazi Party. Most tend to judge the Hitler regime not by the rhetoric of its *Führer* but by his actions and those of his subordinates. Agreement is virtually unanimous, including among postwar German historians, that the Nazi state was an abomination, a political monstrosity which marked a descent into vulgarity such as the world had seldom seen. Historians and journalists alike write about a half-demented *Führer*, who proclaimed himself to be the greatest German of all time, and how he presided over a court of ambitious ruffians and rogues. Here was the kind of politician who would be rejected in a decent society. He promoted a bizarre era lasting twelve years in which such men of ability as Hjalmar Schacht and Albert Speer gave their talents to a totalitarian regime.

Entries in this chapter include titles on various aspects of political development in the Third Reich, including party matters, the rise of Hitler to power as Chancellor, conflicts in the governmental apparatus, organizational units and the policy of *Gleichschaltung* (coordination).

BIBLIOGRAPHY

260.   ABEL, Theodore. *The Nazi Movement.* New York: Atherton Press, 1965.
       This book was originally published in 1938 by Prentice-Hall as *Why Hitler Came to Power.* Describes the nature of Hitler's appeal to average Germans and why so many of them, including former Communists, turned to the *Führer* and supported his movement. The Nazi leader shrewdly offered something to everyone. A miserable people after the catastrophe of World War I eagerly joined the mass surge to Hitler's political control.

261.   ABSOLON, Rudolf. *Die Wehrmacht im Dritten Reich* (The *Wehrmacht* in the Third Reich). Boppard am Rhein: Boldt Verlag, 1961, 1971, 1975, 3 vols.
       A study of the *Wehrmacht*, the official name of the Third Reich's combined army, navy and air forces. Under the *Wehrgesetz* (defense law) of 21 May 1935, the *Reichswehr*, the 100,000-man army of the Weimar Republic permitted by the Treaty of Versailles, was replaced by the *Wehrmacht*. Traces the remilitarization, whereby Hitler hoped to end the Versailles system.

262.   ALQUEN, Gunter d'. *Die SS* (The SS). Berlin: Junker & Dünnhaupt, 1939.
       A history of the organization and tasks of the *Schutzstaffel*, the SS or Elite Guard of the National Socialist German Workers' Party, told from the National Socialist point of view.

263.   ARONSON, Shlomo. *Reinhard Heydrich und die Frühgeschichte von Gestapo und SS* (Reinhard Heydrich and the Early History of the *Gestapo* and SS). Stuttgart: Deutsche Verlagsanstalt, 1971.
       Analyzes Reinhard Heydrich (1904-42), head of the Reich Security Service. Shows how the ultimate character of the Nazi state emerged, how aspects of the Nazi ideology prevailed and

how the "Final Solution" was promoted. Discusses the SS, the *Gestapo* and the political police of the Third Reich. Rejects the rumor of Heydrich's Jewish ancestry.

264. BAUMBACH, Werner. *The Life and Death of the Luftwaffe.* New York: Coward, McCann, 1960.
The story of the building of the German Air Force by Hermann Goering and its utilization in World War II includes accounts of triumphant Nazi victories in Poland and France, the loss of the Battle of Britain, deterioration and final inability to control the air anywhere in Europe. Discusses political aspects of German air power and gives attention to the mistakes made by Hitler and Goering in utilizing the *Luftwaffe*.

265. BENNECKE, Heinrich. *Hitler und die SA* (Hitler and the SA). Munich and Vienna: Olzog, 1962.
An account of the relations between the *Führer* and the SA, the *Sturmabteilung*, or Storm Detachment. The early private army of the Nazi party was designed originally to protect National Socialist mass meetings and oppose rival political parties, especially the Communists. From its early days, Hitler regarded it as a political and not a military force; he resented Röhm's efforts to promote a Second Revolution stressing the socialist side of National Socialism. Hitler eliminated Röhm and tamed the SA in the Blood Purge of 1934.

266. BERGHAHN, Völker Rolf. *Der Stahlhelm* (The Steel Helmets). Düsseldorf: Droste, 1966.
A study concerned with the Steel Helmets, a nationalist ex-servicemen's organization formed in 1918 to oppose the German socialist revolution. The veterans' group played a prominent role in German politics in the early 1930s. Once in power, Hitler wanted no opposition of any kind in his coordinated Third Reich and accordingly incorporated all members up to the age of 35 in the SA, the Storm Troopers. This was not a popular decision, because there was antagonism betwen *Stahlhelm* members and the SA. In 1934, the *Stahlhelm* was given a new name — National Socialist League of Ex-Servicemen.

267. BESSELL, Richard. *Political Violence and the Rise of Nazism.* New Haven, CT: Yale University Press, 1985.
Explores the factors that led to the rise and fall of the *Sturmabteilungen* (SA), while also seeking to explain the Storm

Troopers' violent behavior in the Nazi movement and the early years in power. Concentrates on the SA in Eastern Germany from 1925 to 1934.

268. BILLUNG, R. *N.S.D.A.P. Die Geschichte einer Bewegung* (N.S.D.A.P. The History of the Movement). Munich: Bernhard Funck Verlag, 1931.
This German history of the National Socialist Party offers valuable information about the nature of the new Nazi movement. Unfortunately, it was never translated into English, and the American and British public remained unaware of Hitler's political designs and the revolutionary nature of National Socialism.

269. BRACHER, Karl Dietrich. "Stufen totalitärer Gleichschaltung: Die Befestigung der nationalsozialistischen Herrschaft, 1933/34" (Stages in Totalitarian Coordination: The Establishing of National Socialist Rule, 1933/34). *Vierteljahrshefte für Zeitgeschichte*, IV (1956), 31-42.
A study by German historian Karl Dietrich Bracher of the steps taken by Hitler in his goal of *Gleichschaltung* (coordination), as a means of consolidating and maintaining his dictatorship.

270. BRACHER, Karl Dietrich, Wolfgang SAUER and Gerhard SCHULZ. *Die nationalsozialistische Machtergreifung: Studien zur Errichtung des totalitären Herrschaftsystems in Deutschland, 1933/34* (The National Socialist Power Seizure: Studies on the Erection of the Totalitarian System in Germany, 1933/34). Cologne: Westdeutscher Verlag, 1960.
The authors analyze the National Socialist drive for power with accounts of the political infighting preceding Hitler's assumption of the chancellorship. They also discuss the means used to consolidate the dictatorship.

271. BRISSAUD, André. *The Nazi Secret Service*. Translated from the French by Milton Waldman. New York: Norton, 1974.
Discusses the machinations of the Nazi secret service. Describes the *Reichssicherheitshauptamt*, the RSHA, or Reich Main Security Office, the main security department of the Reich government, formed in 1939 to combine all the existing police forces, including the *Gestapo*, the secret police, the criminal police (*Kriminalpolizei*) and the SD, the Security Service. Writes about

the "real boss," Reinhard Heydrich (1904-42), who served until his death. The RSHA was responsible for taking into custody all enemies of the state.

272. BROSZAT, Martin, ed. *Internationale Konferenz zur nationalsozialistischen Macht Uebernahme* (International Conference on the National Socialist Taking of Power). Berlin: Siedler, 1983.
Papers and discussion at the International Conference on the Nationalist Socialist Taking of Power, sponsored by the Historical Commission in Berlin and the *Institut für Zeitgeschichte* in Munich.

273. *BROWN BOOK OF THE HITLER TERROR: THE BURN-ING OF THE REICHSTAG.* London: Gollancz, 1933; New York: Knopf, 1933.
Published only months after the *Reichstag* fire of 27 February 1933, this book was prepared by the World Committee for the Victims of German Fascism. The "real incendiaries" are identified as the Nazis themselves: "Captain Goering was the organizer of the *Reichstag* fire. His party comrade Goebbels invented the plan. Goering carried it through." Emphasizes the Oberfohren memorandum, which accused the Nazis of having started the fire. Also treats Hitler's power seizure, the destruction of workers' organizations, persecution of Jews, the campaign against culture, atrocities of the Hitler terror and conditions in the concentration camps.

274. BUCHHEIM, Hans. "Die SS in der Verfassung des Dritten Reiches" (The SS in the Constitution of the Third Reich). *Vierteljahrshefte für Zeitgeschichte*, III (1955), 127-57.
Examines the role of the SS, originally Hitler's personal guard, but later transformed into a mass army by Heinrich Himmler, in the constitution of the Third Reich. The SS served as a political police and was later assigned to duty in the concentration and extermination camps. The *Waffen-SS*, its military army and the largest of its major branches, was one of the most important units of the German military establishment during World War II.

275. CALIC, Edouard. *Himmler et son empire* (Himmler and His Empire). Paris: Stock, 1966.

Discusses Heinrich Himmler and the SS, the *Schutzstaffel*, or Elite Guard, which he commanded and which played a powerful role in the political and military history of the Third Reich.

276.   COOPER, Matthew.   *The German Air Force, 1933-1945: An Anatomy of Failure.* London: Jane's, 1981.
Discusses the failure of Hitler's *Luftwaffe*. Recounts its loss of command of the air over England in 1940, over the Atlantic in 1941, over the Mediterranean in 1942 and how by the middle of 1943 it was unable to take the initiative in the air anywhere over Europe. Blames this deterioration on Hitler and Goering. Relates mistakes in manufacturing of aircraft, including dive bombers, heavy bombers and jet aircraft, and errors in strategy.

277.   CRANKSHAW, E.   *Gestapo: Instrument of Tyranny.*   New York: Viking, 1956.
Recounts every conceivable facet of the *Geheime Staats Polizei*, the secret state police, dedicated to the task of maintaining the National Socialist regime.   Its aim was to track down and eliminate all dissidents, complainers and opponents. Any individual, no matter what his status, was suspected by the *Gestapo*, which became a symbol of the Nazi reign of terror. This study, originally published in England, shows how the *Gestapo* played a major role in virtually all the developments of the Nazi movement and regime.   It extended its activities throughout Europe, and even to distant parts of the world. It followed the German armed forces into occupied countries and used its methods of terror to destroy all political opposition to Nazi rule.

278.   DEIST, Wilhelm.   *The Wehrmacht and German Rearmament.* Toronto: University of Toronto Press, 1981.
Presents the thesis that Hitler's rearmament program from 1934 to 1939 was based on the *Führer*'s idea for *Blitzkrieg* or lightning war.   It was apparently highly successful on the surface, but actually it was burdened by improvisations and especially by bitter infighting among jealous subordinates. There were early victories, but eventually the program broke down because of inner contradictions among contending forces.

279.   DEUERLEIN, Ernst.   "Hitlers Eintritt in die Politik und die Reichswehr" (Hitler's Entrance into Politics and the *Reichswehr*).   *Vierteljahrshefte für Zeitgeschichte*, VII (1959), 177-227.

After Germany's humiliation in World War I, Hitler returned to Munich. Angered by the revolution in Germany and the emergence of the Weimar Republic, he turned to politics to work against the Treaty of Versailles. Remaining on the roster of his old regiment, he was assigned to spy on political parties. Explores his relations at the time with the *Reichswehr*, the armed forces of the early Weimar Republic.

280. DIAMOND, Sander A. *The Nazi Movement in the United States, 1924-1941*. Ithaca, NY: Cornell University Press, 1974.
Explores the Nazi movement in the United States, with special attention to Fritz Kuhn and his German-American *Bund*. Mass rallies were held, including one at Madison Square Garden in New York from which journalist Dorothy Thompson was ejected for laughing. Although the German-American population was large in the country, the Nazi effort to win broad support in the United States was unsuccessful.

281. DIMITROV, Georgi. *Der Reichstagbrandprozess* (The Reichstag Fire Trial). Berlin: Verlag Neuer Weg, 1946.
Georgi M. Dimitrov (1882-1949) was a Bulgarian Communist arrested directly after the *Reichstag* fire of 27 February 1933, along with two other Bulgarian Communists, Blagoi Popov and Vassili Tanev. Dimitrov was the central figure at the sensational trial, which attracted world attention. No threats of silence or expulsion could intimidate the angry defendant. He provided one side of a dramatic confrontation with Hermann Goering. Obviously not guilty of having helped set the fire, he was acquitted. From that moment on, he became a hero to Communists everywhere. Presents Dimitrov's version of the trial.

282. EDINGER, J. "German Social Democracy and Hitler's National Revolution." *World Politics*, V (1953), 330-67.
Explains that in his drive for power and during the "coordination" era of his early regime, Hitler made no distinction among Social Democrats, Communists and Jews, all of whom he intended to eliminate from German political life. He dropped the "socialist" part of his own program when on 30 June 1934 he eliminated Ernst Röhm and the projected "Second Revolution," which stressed the socialist side of National Socialism. Within a few months after winning political power,

Hitler banned all political parties in favor of his NSDAP.
German social democracy disappeared from 1933 to 1945.

283.   FEDER, Gottfried. *Hitler's Official Programme and Its Funda-
       mental Ideas.* London: Allen & Unwin, 1934.
       Gottfried Feder (1883-1941) was a National Socialist Party
       ideologist and economics adviser to Hitler. Although influential
       in the early days of the movement, he remained a peripheral
       figure in the Third Reich.   The idea of *Zinsknechtschaft*
       (interest-slavery) became the central core of his teaching.
       Feder, assisted by Anton Drexler and Dietrich Eckart, wrote the
       Twenty-five Points of the German Workers' Party, which later
       became the program of the *Nationalsozialistische Deutsche
       Arbeiterpartei* (the NSDAP, or National Socialist German
       Workers' Party).

284.   FEST, Joachim C. *The Face of the Third Reich: Portraits of the
       Nazi Leadership.* Translated from the German by Michael
       Bullock. New York: Pantheon Books (Random House),
       1970.
       Analyzes National Socialism in the Third Reich, with attention
       to its political, economic and social conditions.   The author
       later published a biography of Hitler (1974), which became a
       best seller in the literature on National Socialism.

285.   FISCHER, Conan.   *Stormtroopers; A Social, Economic, and
       Ideological Analysis, 1929-35.*   London: Allen & Unwin,
       1983.
       A study of the *Sturmabteilung*, the SA, the brown-shirted
       battalions which acted as Hitler's private army in the early days
       of the movement.   Sees the SA as composed of losers incapable
       of adjusting adequately to an everyday routine.   These were
       unreliable radical activists led by Ernst Röhm (1887-1934), who
       was purged with many of his followers on 30 June 1934, because
       they advocated a second, socialist-orientated, revolution.
       Challenges the myth of National Socialism as a bourgeois
       movement, claiming instead that its rank and file came over-
       whelmingly from the working class.   Asserts that the SA
       activism and violence were a response to the political and eco-
       nomic failings of the Weimar government.

286.   FOERTSCH, Hermann.   *Schuld und Verhängnis* (Guilt and
       Destiny).   Stuttgart: Deutsche Verlagsanstalt, 1951.

Considers the "guilt and destiny" of the Fritsch crisis in the spring of 1938, when General Werner Freiherr von Fritsch (1880-1939), Commander-in-Chief of the German army, was dismissed by Hitler on charges of homosexuality. Forced to resign, Fritsch was acquitted by an honor court of officers. Recalled to the Army just before the outbreak of World War II, he died near Warsaw on 22 September 1939. He was believed to have deliberately sought death on the battlefield because of the deep depression caused by the charges against him.

287.   FRANZ, Georg. "Munich: Birthplace and Center of the National Socialist German Workers' Party." *Journal of Modern History*, XXIX (1957), 319-34.
Describes the early stages of the NSDAP centered in Munich, where Hitler had come to make his way in a political career.

288.   FRESCAROLI, Antonio. *La Gestapo*. Milan: Giovanni De Vecchi, 1967.
Investigates the atrocities and secrets of "the Nazi Inquisition."

289.   GALLO, Max. *The Night of Long Knives*. Translated from the French by Lily Emmet. New York: Harper, 1972.
Narrates the events which led to the assassination of Ernst Röhm and other leaders of the SA Brown Shirts in Hitler's determination to break with the leaders of a Second Revolution devoted to the socialist side of National Socialism. Describes the events leading to the purge and the night of murder.

290.   GEORG, Franz-Willing. *Die Hitlerbewegung* (The Hitler Movement). Hamburg: Decker, 1962.
Recounts the National Socialist political movement with attention to the early period from 1919 to 1922. Those were the days when the World War I veteran Hitler, convinced that he possessed political genius, began the formation of the party which was to take over control of Germany in 1933.

291.   GERTH, Hans H. "The Nazi Party." *American Journal of Sociology*, XLV (1940), 517-41.
Explores the leadership and composition of the National Socialist German Workers' Party, the Nazi Party, with attention to Hitler's dominant role in its formation and progress. The theme is politically and socially oriented.

292. *GORDON, Harold J.   *Hitler and the Beer-Hall Putsch.*
     Princeton, NJ: Princeton University Press, 1972.
     Recounts the Nazi Beer-Hall *Putsch* in Munich on 8-9 November 1923, an unsuccessful attempt by Hitler and his new Nazi Party to seize power at an early stage of the Nazi movement. Describes the background of the event and traces its step-by-step development. On the surface, the Beer-Hall *Putsch* seemed to be a failure, but actually it was a brilliant achievement for a political unknown.

293. GÖRING, Hermann.   *Aufbau einer Nation* (The Building of a Nation). Berlin: Mittler, 1934.
     An account by No. 2 Nazi Hermann Goering of how the Nazi Party won its way to triumph. Defends Hitler's ideology and the Nazi revolution and praises the *Führer*'s political instincts.

294. *GRUNBERGER, Richard.   *Hitler's SS.* New York: Dell, 1973.
     A brief account of the "Order of the Death's Head," Hitler's *Schutzstaffel*, Elite Guard. Describes the origins of the order and analyzes the type of persons attracted to its ranks. Goes beyond this goal by exposing the basic inconsistencies of Nazi ideology. Explains SS practices which included everything from pagan rituals to the most bestial forms of torture and destruction. Describes SS interests from eugenics to euthanasia, from procreation assistance to genocide.

295. *HALPERIN, S. William.   *Germany Tried Democracy.* New York: Crowell, 1965.
     A new and revised editon of Halperin's political history of the Weimar Republic, originally published by Crowell in 1946. Describes the rise and fall of a "venture in democracy." "Had this venture succeeded, World War II might never have taken place. Its failure plunged a nation into slavery." In 1919 the Republic seemed to have the support of most Germans. Fourteen years later, it was dead. Devotes the final ten chapters to Hitler's rise to power. Sees the Weimar Republic as a noble experiment, sabotaged by friend and foe alike. Judges the great economic depression of 1929 to have made possible the phenomenal growth of National Socialism. The conservative authoritarianism of Hindenburg, Schleicher and Papen was succeeded by the nihilist totalitarianism of Hitler and his brown-shirted cohorts in one of the great political revolutions of the 20th century.

296. *HALPERIN, S. William. *Mussolini and Italian Fascism.* Princeton, NJ: Van Nostrand, 1964.
This study, No. 67 in the Van Nostrand-Krieger series of original paperbacks in history, is concerned primarily with the Italian dictatorship under Benito Mussolini in politics and government, but two final chapters of Part I are devoted to Mussolini's relationship with Hitler and National Socialism. Describes how the *Duce* used Hitler for purposes of blackmail from 1933 to 1935, the genesis of the Rome-Berlin Axis, *Anschluss*, Munich, the Pact of Steel and Italo-German relations during World War II.

297. *HERZ, John H. "The Fiasco of Denazification in Germany." *Political Science Quarterly*, LXIII (1948), 569-94.
Highly critical article on the unsatisfactory process of denazification in postwar Germany. Since then, other scholars have added more evidence to support Herz's early charges.

298. HIGHAM, Charles. *American Swastika.* Garden City, NY: Doubleday, 1985.
Analyzes Nazi collaborators in the United States from 1933 to the present day, based on research in FBI, CIA and State Department and Department of the Army files, assembled from thirty-thousand pages of declassified materials. Offers an exposé of the long-standing, long-hidden involvement of Americans with Nazism by documenting the covert activities of Nazi collaborators in the United States Senate and in the hierarchy of the Roman Catholic Church.

299. HILDEBRAND, Klaus. "Hitlers Ort in der Geschichte des Preussisch-Deutschen Nationalstaates" (Hitler's Place in the History of the Prussian-German National State). *Historische Zeitschrift*, CCXVII (1973), 584-632.
Historians differ on the concept of the Bismarck-to-Hitler continuity. Some see a direct line from Bismarckian authoritarianism to the National Socialist dictatorship. Klaus Hildebrand, like other German historians, perceives fundamental differences between the two. At the same time, concedes some similar features in their conceptions of the nation-state.

300. HIRSCHFELD, Gerhard, *et al. Der "Führerstaat": Mythos und Realität* (The Leader-State: Myth and Reality). Stuttgart: Klett-Cotta, 1981.

A collection of essays on a recent controversy among historians. One side describes the anarchic administration in the Third Reich as bureaucratic chaos, a constant struggle among officers and agencies, with the result that this "polycracy" did not allow Hitler, a weak dictator, to determine the course of policy. The opposing group of historians maintains that Hitler had a definite program and carried it out by regularly making the appropriate decisions. Tim Mason designates the two groups as functionalists and intentionalists, with two entirely different interpretations of the Third Reich. The historical argument continues.

301. HOETTL, Wilhelm. *Secret Front: The Story of Nazi Political Espionage.* Translated from the German by R.H. Stevens. New York: Praeger, 1954.
An account of the *Sicherheitsdienst*, SD, or Secret Service, its development out of the Secret Police and the National Socialist Party, how it absorbed the Military Intelligence Service of the *Wehrmacht*, its main rival, how it furthered Hitler's war efforts, and how it was finally liquidated by the Allies. The author joined the German Secret Service in 1938 and had access to the innermost workings of the organization. The translator, who vouches for the accuracy of the book, was a British agent who was captured early in the war and received some painful treatment from the *Gestapo*.

302. HOFMANN, Hanns Hubert. *Der Hitlerputsch* (The Hitler Putsch). Munich: Nymphenburger Verlagshandlung, 1961.
An account of "a critical year of German history." Factually relates the unsuccessful Beer-Hall *Putsch* 8-9 November 1923. On the surface, the *Putsch* seemed to be a failure, but many historians see it as an extraordinary achievement at the time.

303. JONZA, K. "Aux origines juridiques de la Grand Allemagne" (On the Juridical Origins of Greater Germany). *Revue d'histoire de la deuxième guerre mondiale*, XXIV (1974), 1-12.
Considers the juridical arguments offered for Hitler's idea of *Lebensraum*, or living space. Hitler presented his concept of expansionism as necessary for the life of Germany. Discusses the legal justifications offered by Nazis for German expansion and places them in the context of international law, including the law on minorities.

304. *KEEGAN, John. *Waffen-SS: The Asphalt Soldiers.* London: Macdonald, 1968.
British military historian John Keegan shows how the SS-man's basic attitude had to be that of a fighter for fighting's sake, unquestionably obedient, emotionally hard and filled with contempt for "racial inferiors." These soldiers, addicted to stupefying ruthlessness, were a law unto themselves during World War II.

305. *KEYSERLINGK, Robert H. "Hitler and German Nationalism Before 1933." *Canadian Review of Studies in Nationalism,* V (1978), 24-44.
Maintains that it was not German nationalism but mystical radicalism which formed the basis of Hitler's ideology. The German *Führer*, however, made it a point to exploit German nationalism in his leadership of the Third Reich. Presents the view that Hitler's racialism, judged by its massive scale, was the antithesis of German nationalism. The Nazi leader attempted to go far beyond specific German nationalism of the 19th-century variety and actually sought to mold a new system for all Europe.

306. KIPPHAN, Klaus. "Julius Streicher unter den 9. November, 1923" (Julius Streicher on 9 November 1923). *Zeitschrift für Bayerische Landesgeschichte,* XXIX (1976), 277-88.
Julius Streicher (1885-1946), Nazi Germany's leading Jew-baiter, managed to ingratiate himself with Hitler during the early days of the Nazi movement. An intimate friend of Hitler when he joined the NSDAP in 1921, he was one of the earliest Nazis in northern Bavaria. Details the role Streicher played in the Hitler Munich *Putsch* on 8-9 November 1923.

307. KIRST, Hans Helmut. *The Night of the Long Knives.* Translated from the German by J. Maxwell Brownjohn. Greenwich, CT: Fawcett, 1976.
Recounts the assassination campaign unleashed by Hitler on the night of 30 June 1934, to strike against the growing power of the SA, the brown-shirted Storm Troopers. The *Führer's* goal was to prevent a Second Revolution. From its beginning, the Nazi movement was pulled in two directions. The very name of the party spelled trouble – *National Socialism* indicated two opposing movements – nationalism and internationalism. Eventually Hitler was forced to choose between them and

inaugurated a blood purge which took the lives of Ernst Röhm and other leaders of the SA.

308. KRAUSNICK, Helmut, *et al.* *Anatomy of the SS State.* Translated from the German by Richard Barry, Marian Jackson and Dorothy Long. London: Collins, 1968.
In late December 1963, some twenty-two former members of the SS were brought to trial before a German court in Franfurt am Main. Four historians of the German Institute of Contemporary History wrote depositions to help the court understand the political, organizational and moral background of SS crimes. These included persecution of Jews, command and compliance, concentration camps and mass executions of Russian prisoners. The defendants pleaded "superior orders."

309. LEVINE, Herbert S. *Hitler's Free City: A History of the Nazi Party in Danzig, 1925-1939.* Chicago: University of Chicago Press, 1973.
Analyzes the progress of the Nazi movement in pre-World War II Danzig and the subsequent erosion of the city's international status. Uses archival material in Germany and elsewhere as well as interviews, giving an account of how the Nazis managed to take over the free city. The political struggle resembled events in the Reich itself.

310. LÜDDE-NEURATH, Walter. *Regierung Dönitz: Die letzten Tage des Dritten Reiches* (The Dönitz Government: The Last Days of the Third Reich). Leoni am Starnberger See: Druffel Verlag, 1981.
Karl Dönitz (1891-1980), Grand Admiral, who was Commander-in-Chief of the German Navy after 1943, was named in the second part of Hitler's political testament on 29 April 1945 as President of the Reich and Commander of the Armed Forces. The Dönitz government lasted from 1 to 23 May 1945, when the new Head of State was captured by the British.

311. MANVELL, Roger and Heinrich FRAENKEL. *The Hundred Days to Hitler.* New York: St. Martin's Press, 1974.
The authors present a day-by-day account of how Hitler came to political power in Germay, from the downfall of Gregor Strasser, a key Nazi leader who stressed the socialist side of National Socialism, on 7 December 1932, to the Enabling Act on 23 March 1933 which gave Hitler dictatorial power. They

analyze the political, economic and social conditions which encouraged the rapid growth of the Nazi Party. They acknowledge that much of their material came from many volumes of the proceedings of the International Military Tribunal at Nuremberg, as well as from the participants' books written in the postwar period. In the ongoing debate about how the *Reichstag* fire was set, the authors insist that the Dutchman van der Lubbe could not possibly have done it by himself.

312. MASER, Werner. *Die Frühgeschichte der NSDAP* (The Early History of the NSDAP). Frankfurt am Main: Athenäum Verlag, 1965.
A German specialist on Hitler and the Nazi movement presents the early history of the National Socialist German Workers' Party until 1924. Emphasizes the methods Hitler used to take over control of the German Workers' Party for himself, and explains how he fashioned his own political party in its fledgling days.

313. McKALE, Donald M. *The Nazi Party Courts: Hitler's Management of Conflict in His Movement, 1921-1945.* Lawrence, KN: University of Kansas Press, 1974.
Discusses how Hitler managed conflicts in his movement. Describes the party tribunals which made up the elaborate judicial system. The legal setup made it plain that anyone who did not accept National Socialism would be eliminated or destroyed. The structure was supposed to be legally objective, but it was always subordinated to Nazi control.

314. McKALE, Donald M. *The Swastika Outside Germany.* Kent, OH: Kent State University Press, 1977.
Studies several hundred Nazi organizations outside Germany, directed by the *Auslandsorganisation, A.O.,* or Organization for Foreigners, the special branch of the National Socialist party responsible for the supervision of Germans abroad: "A German day in Buenos Aires or Chicago concerns us just as deeply as the struggle for our brethren near our frontiers." Concludes that these organizations were badly managed.

315. MERKL, Peter H. *Political Violence under the Swastika: 581 Early Nazis.* Princeton, NJ: Princeton University Press, 1975.
Using new technological advances, analyzes 581 autobiographical accounts of early adherents to Nazism. Calls

into question several previously accepted assumptions regarding National Socialism – that it was a revolt of the lower middle class, that it was a rebellion against modernity, that there was a particular variety of "authoritarian personality" and that the ideological motivation was of primary importance in determining action.   Downgrades the role of ideology in National Socialism, but maintains the importance of anti-Semitism.

316.   MOMMSEN, Hans.   "Der Reichstagsbrand und seine politischen Folgen" (The *Reichstag* Fire and Its Political Consequences).   *Vierteljahrshefte für Zeitgeschichte*, XII (1964), 351-413.

In 1960 a controversy began among German historians and journalists about the origins of the *Reichstag* fire on 27 February 1933, at a time when the Germany of the Weimar Constitution went up in flames and from the ashes rose the Third Reich. It was widely believed at the time that the Nazis were the real incendiaries.   In 1960 a German investigator, Dr. Fritz Tobias, published in the news magazine *Der Spiegel* his view that a half-witted young Dutchman named Marinus van der Lubbe, who carried an identification card of the Dutch Communist Party, had acted alone in setting the fire. His thesis was supported by Professor Hans Mommsen, historian at the Ruhr University of Bochum.   Both agreed that there was no Nazi participation whatever.   Later, in March 1973, Professor Walter Hofer, on the Swiss University of Berne, accused Tobias and Mommsen of resorting to "non-scientific methods" in supporting the lone arsonist theory.   Mommsen refused to retreat: "Professor Hofer's rather helpless statement that the accomplices of van der Lubbe could only have been Nazis is tacit admission that [his] committee did not actually obtain any positive evidence in regard to the alleged accomplice's identity." This article presents Mommsen's case.

317.   MOWRER, Edgar Ansell.   *Germany Puts the Clock Back.* London: Penguin, 1938.

A decidedly unfavorable report on Nazi Germany written by a distinguished foreign correspondent.   Mowrer's accent on the deplorable aspects of National Socialism was substantiated by many books published after the appearance of this volume. Mowrer was troubled by political and military trends in the Third Reich, which he felt would lead to dangerous crises and perhaps war.

318. *NAMIER, Lewis Bernstein. *In the Nazi Era.* New York: St.
     Martin's Press, 1952.
     Lewis Namier, British historian then at Manchester University,
     presents a collection of essays on the political, diplomatic and
     military moves and countermoves of the decade between 1936
     and 1945. Deals with "The Men Who Served Hitler," as well
     as with German soldiers and diplomats who in the immediate
     postwar period attempted to exculpate themselves and their na-
     tion. Pays special attention to the 1938 crisis inside Germany
     as seen in published official documents.

319. NEUBERGER, Helmut. *Freimauerei und Nationalsozialismus*
     (Freemasonry and National Socialism). Hamburg:
     Bauhutten, 1980.
     Freemasonry concerns the teachings and practices of the secret
     and fraternal Order of Free and Accepted Masons, the largest
     worldwide secret society. In Germany the advance of
     Freemasonry was furthered by the intellectual support of such
     men as Lessing, Herder, Fichte and Goethe. But because he
     believed that Freemasonry was involved in politics, Hitler
     determined to bring every institution under his control and in-
     cluded Freemasons in his category of enemies of the state. De-
     scribes the persecution of Freemasons by Hitler's *völkisch*
     movement and by National Socialism.

320. NICHOLLS, Anthony and Erich MATTHIAS, eds. *German
     Democracy and the Triumph of Hitler.* New York: St.
     Martin's Press, 1971.
     This collection of essays concerning the political pathology of
     Weimar Germany and the rise of Hitler includes a study of the
     Bavarian background of National Socialism, essays on the im-
     pact of the Treaty of Versailles and Article 48 of the Weimar
     Constitution, studies on Hitler's ideas about the Western pow-
     ers and the legacy of 1918 for National Socialism, and German
     women's participation in professional life during the 1930s.

321. NOAKES, Jeremy. *The Nazi Party in Lower Saxony,
     1921-1933.* London: Oxford University Press, 1971.
     A regional treatment of the NSDAP from 1921 to 1933, con-
     fined to an area of Lower Saxony. Denigrates the self-serving
     image of rigid centralization promoted by the functionaries of
     the party's Munich headquarters. Explains the differences be-
     tween the northern *völkisch* movement and its southern
     counterparts.

322. NYOMARKAY, Joseph. *Charisma and Factionalism in the
      Nazi Party.* Minneapolis, MN: University of Minnesota
      Press, 1967.
      A study of the internal disputes of the National Socialist
      German Workers' Party from its early days to the Blood Purge
      of June 1934. Contends that the sole source of legitimacy in the
      Nazi Party was the charisma of Hitler, which led to the accept-
      ance of his leadership. The contending factions for the most
      part did not dare challenge him but instead vied for his favor
      during confrontations. The *Führer* acted as an arbiter, holding
      off decisions as long as possible, rather than as a condemning
      judge.

323. OBBERGEN, Paulus van (Johann von Leers). *The Oberfohren
      Memorandum.*   London: German Information Bureau,
      1933.
      The Oberfohren memorandum, supposedly written and circu-
      lated by Dr. Ernst Oberfohren, accused the Nazis of having
      started the *Reichstag* fire on the evening of 27 February 1933.
      It contended that Dr. Joseph Goebbels, who the next month was
      to become Reich Minister for Public Enlightenment and
      Propaganda, and then Captain Hermann Goering, acting
      Prussian Minister of the Interior, supervised the arson. In the
      ensuing debate the London-based German Information Library
      denounced the memorandum as a figment of the imagination
      and absolved the Nazi government of any blame for the fire.
      The memorandum was first published in the *Manchester
      Guardian* on 27 April 1933. On 7 May, Oberfohren, former
      parliamentary leader of the German People's Party, was re-
      ported to have committed suicide.

324. O'NEILL, Robert J. *The German Army and the Nazi Party,
      1933-1939.* London: Cassell, 1966.
      An account of the relations between Hitler's National Socialist
      Party and the German Army. For Hitler it was of prime
      importance to subjugate the military to the Nazi Party and his
      own will. Those generals who objected were sacked, as was the
      case in the Fritsch-Blomberg affairs of 1938, when the *Führer*
      dismissed two of his top generals and took over control of the
      armed forces himself.

325. ORLOW, Dietrich. "The Conversion of Myths into Political
      Power: The Case of the Nazi Party, 1925-1926." *The
      American Historical Review*, LXXII (1967), 906-24.

This study of the early history of the National Socialist German Workers' Party emphasizes the means by which Nazi ideological myths began to impress the German public and paved the way for Hitler's assumption of political power in 1933.

326. *ORLOW, Dietrich. *The History of the Nazi Party, 1919-1933*. Pittsburgh: University of Pittsburgh Press, 1969.
This study, based on captured documents, offers a brief survey of the development of the NSDAP from its infancy to the attainment of power in 1933. Concentrates upon the position of Hitler within the party, its organizational development and propaganda program through the years. Discusses the labyrinth of currents and cross-currents in the wake of Hitler, with comments on his ability to solve the crises that arose within the party and turn imminent political disaster into success.

327. *ORLOW, Dietrich. *The History of the Nazi Party, 1933-1945*. Pittsburgh: University of Pittsburgh Press, 1973.
Continues the narrative of his earlier *The History of the Nazi Party, 1919-1933* (1969). The first volume told the story of ultimate Nazi success, whereas this book recounts a dismal failure. The NSDAP never became the instrument of power which its leaders intended it to be. Describes its problems in great detail. Far from being a monolithic body, the Nazi Party was split into numerous factions, each at war with the others and held together only by common allegiance to the *Führer*.

328. PETERSON, Edward N. *The Limits of Hitler's Power*. Princeton, NJ: Princeton University Press, 1969.
Contends that the personal power of Hitler, as well as that of Stalin, has been exaggerated by most historians. Bases his conclusion on an analysis of the Interior Ministry, the state of Bavaria, the cities of Nuremberg and Augsburg, and several smaller communities. Maintains that Hitler's reluctance to become involved in day-to-day operations of the government and party gave civil servants and political appointees almost free rein to pursue their own purposes. Claims that Hitler did not possess unlimited power and his party was not able to achieve complete control over the German people. Finds that the authoritarian political system was not more operationally efficient than the democratic process.

329. *PHELPS, Reginald H.   "Hitler   and   the   Deutsche
     Arbeiterpartei" (Hitler and the German Workers' Party).
     The American Historical Review, LXVIII (1963), 974-86.
     In September 1919 Hitler, working as a spy for the *Reichswehr*,
     was assigned to investigate a small group of nationalistic veter-
     ans called the German Workers' Party. The party had no real
     program and little money, but Hitler was impressed by its ideas,
     which coincided with his own. He joined the party as member
     No. 5 and was made No. 7 on its Executive Committee. Relates
     how Hitler within two years advanced to leadership of the small
     party, whose name he decided to change to the National
     Socialist German Workers' Party, later to be known everywhere
     as the NSDAP.

330. POLIAKOV, Lèon and Josef WULF. *Das Dritte Reich und
     seine Diener: Dokumente* (The Third Reich and Its Serv-
     ants: Documents). Berlin: Arani Verlag, 1959.
     The authors, who wrote several books on the Third Reich, pre-
     sent text and documents concerning the more important
     underlings who served Hitler and did their level best to imple-
     ment his policies — from military rearmament to genocide. They
     also discuss Hitler's role in shaping Nazi philosophy.

331. PRIDHAM, Geoffrey.   *Hitler's Rise to Power: The Nazi
     Movement in Bavaria, 1923-1933*. New York: Harper &
     Row, 1973.
     A regional analysis of the Nazi movement in Bavaria during the
     decade 1923 to 1933 underscores the importance of Hitler as the
     personal embodiment of the Nazi program, and stresses the
     significance of the NSDAP's social and economic affiliate
     organizations after the onset of the Depression. The party was
     politically successful not because of its anti-Semitism but be-
     cause it was able to integrate anti-Semitic themes into its overall
     economic program. Confirms the centralized nature of the Nazi
     Party's operations.

332. REED, Douglas. *The Burning of the Reichstag*. New York:
     Covici-Friede, 1934.
     A report by Douglas Reed, special correspondent of *The Times*
     (London), concerning the *Reichstag* fire, includes verbatim dis-
     patches by the author to his newspaper. Suggests, even before
     the verdicts were announced, that the overwhelming weight of
     evidence was against the theory that van der Lubbe fired the
     edifice unaided. Claims not aspiring to defend or attack any-

body, but merely wants to tell the story of the events as known at that time.

333. REICHE, Eric G. *The Development of the S.A. in Nürnberg, 1922-34.* New York: Cambridge University Press, 1985.
This story of the SA (*Sturmabteilung*), the Nazi Storm Troopers, from its inception in 1922 until it was overthrown by Hitler in the Blood Purge of 1934 discusses marches and violent encounters, and analyzes how in a heavily industrialized city in which democracy initially enjoyed strong support, a growing number of men from virtually every stratum of German society decided to join the brown battalions.

334. *THE REICHSTAG FIRE TRIAL: THE SECOND BROWN BOOK OF THE HITLER TERROR.* London: John Lane The Bodley Head, 1934.
This "Second Brown Book of the Hitler Terror," published after the *Reichstag* fire, is based on material collected by the World Commission for the Relief of the Victims of German Fascism. In great detail and with what it presents as circumstantial evidence, the text surveys the proceedings and seeks to expose the conduct of the prosecution. Denounces the attempt to fasten the guilt of the fire on the Communist Party and presents evidence tending to implicate the National Socialists, "the one Party likely to gain in strength as a result of the fire." Presents the thesis that the trial was used for whitewashing the Nazis and blackening their enemies. An introductory chapter by Georgi Dimitrov, one of the Communist defendants found not guilty, is included, as well as an appendix introduced by novelist Lion Feuchtwanger on murder in Hitler Germany.

335. *REITLINGER, Gerald. *The SS: Alibi of a Nation.* London: Heinemann, 1957.
Hitler's power to a great extent was grounded on the SS, the *Schutzstaffel*, the original bodyguards distinguished by their black shirts. The *Führer* placed his trust in this special unit trained in Nazi ideology and certain to carry out his orders with blind obedience. Describes the organization, its origins and development, and discusses its importance in the Nazi state.

336. SCHULZ, Gerhard. *Aufstieg des Nationalsozialismus und Revolution in Deutschland* (Rise of National Socialism and Revolution in Germany). Berlin: Propyläen, 1975.

This account of the political rise of National Socialism sees Hitler's winning of power as a symptom of post-1890 European malaise and its special characteristics in Germany. Like other German historians, Schulz maintains that National Socialism and Fascism reflected the breakdown of the traditional inter-dependence of late-19th-century social classes.

337. *STEIN, George H. *The Waffen SS: Hitler's Elite Guard at War 1939-1945*. Ithaca, NY: Cornell University Press, 1966.
Discusses the story of Hitler's praetorian élite guard. Hitler set up the *Waffen-SS* as a part of the older SS guard under Heinrich Himmler. It became a major military force in World War II, eventually numbering thirty-nine divisions with one million men of fifteen nationalities. *Waffen-SS* troops took part in a dozen major battles and became noted for their fighting qualities. Elite units of the *Waffen-SS* were unquestionably of the highest military quality and compared favorably with the best of the *Wehrmacht*. *Waffen-SS* officers complained bitterly that they were accused of atrocities committed by regular SS units in concentration and extermination camps.

338. STRASSER, Otto. *Die deutsche Bartholomäusnacht* (The German Bartholomew Night). Zürich: Reso Verlag, 1935, 1940.
An account of Hitler's Blood Purge of 30 June 1934, the so-called Night of the Long Knives, when Hitler unleashed an assassination campaign against the growing power of the SA. Otto Strasser's brother, Gregor Strasser, was a victim of the purge, killed by bullets fired through the windows of his prison cell. Reveals the bitterness of the author at the death of his brother, Nazi populist and Hitler's early rival for leadership of the Nazi Party. Calls the slaughter "the German Bartholomew Night."

339. *SYDNOR, Charles W., Jr. *Soldiers of Destruction*. Princeton, NJ: Princeton University Press, 1977.
Describes the SS Death's Head Division from 1933 to 1945, with attention to the evolution and wartime activities of the notorious Nazi *Waffen-SS* division which eventually became the Third SS Panzer Division *Totenkopf*. Discusses its formation in the months between the conquest of Poland and the spring 1940 campaign in France. More than a divisional history, the study demonstrates the *Totenkopf*'s close association with the SS-run

mass-murder system, with roots deep into the Nazi underworld of mayhem and death.

340. TOBIAS, Fritz. *The Reichstag Fire Trial.* Translated from the German by Arnold J. Pomerantz. New York: Putnam, 1964.
Describes the *Reichstag* fire of 27 February 1933, which signified the beginning of the Nazi dictatorship, and concludes that Dutch Communist Marinus van der Lubbe was alone in setting the fire. This thesis contradicted the general belief that Nazis were the real incendiaries. Tobias' view was supported by Professor Hans Mommsen, historian at the Ruhr University of Bochum, and attacked by Professor Walter Hofer of Berne University, Switzerland, for Tobias' "non-scientific methods." In a brief introduction, British historian A. J. P. Taylor confesses past error and supports Tobias' thesis. The controversy lingers on.

341. TOLSTOY, Nikolai. *Night of the Long Knives.* London: Ballantine Books, 1972.
The night of 30 June 1934, also known as the Blood Purge, was Hitler's response to the call for a Second Revolution in the direction of socialism. Some seventy-seven leading Nazis and at least one hundred others, including General Kurt von Schleicher and his wife, were liquidated.

342. VOGELSANG, Thilo. *Reichswehr, Staat und NSDAP* (*Reichswehr*, State and NSDAP). Stuttgart: Deutsche Verlagsanstalt, 1962.
Traces the relationship among the *Reichswehr*, the state and the National Socialist German Workers' Party in its early days. The *Reichswehr* (Defense Forces) was the name of the standing army during the Weimar Republic era (1920-33), and the opening years of the Third Reich (1933-35). In 1935 Hitler changed its name from *Reichswehr* to *Wehrmacht*, the armed forces of the Third Reich.

343. WAGNER, Jonathan F. *Brothers Beyond the Sea: National Socialism in Canada.* New York: Humanities Press, 1981.
A brief study, based on archival material and interviews, on Nazism in Canada. Canadian Germans, mostly simple people, were bombarded with literature from Berlin designed to win their loyalty to Hitler. Many were interned in September 1939 at the beginning of the war. Analyzes the origins, organization,

aims and membership of Canadian National Socialism.   A
similar movement in the United States was smashed when
Germany declared war on the United States after Pearl Harbor.

344. *WAITE, Robert George Leeson. *Vanguard of Nazism: The Free
        Corps Movement in Postwar Germany, 1918-1923.*
        Cambridge, MA: Harvard University Press, 1952.
        Historian R. G. L. Waite gives an account of the *Freikorps*, or
        Free Corps movement, which after the defeat of Germany in
        1918 played an important role in the early history of the Weimar
        Republic.   Veterans, fanatical adventurers and unemployed
        youth, all rightist in philosophy, blamed Social Democrats and
        Jews for Germany's plight. Many of these freebooters became
        early advocates of Hitler and transferred their allegiance to his
        squads in the battle of the streets against Communists. Their
        rightist political philosophy and anti-Semitism became basic in
        the ideology of National Socialism.

345. WEINGARTNER, James J. *Hitler's Guard: The Story of the
        Leibstandarte   SS   and   Adolf   Hitler,   1933-1945.*
        Carbondale, IL: Southern Illinois University Press, 1974.
        Traces the evolution of the *Leibstandarte SS* from its formation
        in March 1933 to the end of World War II.   Gives special
        attention to its role and spectacular exploits in World War II.
        Devotes a large part of the text to biographical material on Josef
        (Sepp) Dietrich (1892-1966), one of Hitler's earliest supporters.

346. WIENER, Jan G. *The Assassination of Heydrich.* New York:
        Grossman, 1969.
        This detailed analysis of the assassination of Reinhard Heydrich
        (1904-42), head of the Main Reich Security Office, Deputy
        Reich Protector of Bohemia and Moravia, and specialist in the
        Nazi "Final Solution," explains how two Free Czech agents
        trained in England parachuted on 27 May 1942, into
        Czechoslovakia and gravely wounded Heydrich, who had
        spurned security arrangements and was driving in an open car
        without armed escort. Heydrich died a few days later. De-
        scribes the background of Heydrich's career and traces each step
        of the plot. An enraged Hitler ordered the destruction of the
        entire village of Lidice in reprisal.

CHAPTER 5

ECONOMICS AND THE NAZI REGIME

Industrialists, Financiers, Businessmen, Economy, Rearmament

In the early days of the Nazi Party, Hitler was much taken with the economic views of Gottfried Feder, leading ideologist of National Socialism and an adviser to the leader. An illiterate in economics, Hitler was much impressed by Feder's anti-industrialist view that the country's ruin near the end of World War I could be attributed to the manipulators of high finance. Feder favored retaining the capitalist system, especially such productive assets as factories, mines and machines, but he would abolish the idea of interest because it created no value. The idea of *Zinsknechtschaft* (interest-slavery) became the keynote of his teaching. In *Mein Kampf* Hitler wrote: "For the first time in my life I saw the meaning of international capitalism. After I had heard Feder's first lecture, the thought flashed through my head that I had found the essential suppositions for the founding of a new party."

After his prison sentence in 1924 for the abortive Beer-Hall *Putsch*, Hitler became convinced that Feder's populist and anti-industrial views were old-fashioned and would work against the success of the Nazi Party. Later, he turned to the brilliant economics expert Dr. Hjalmar Horace Greeley Schacht, who had warned him that Feder's bizarre economic policies would ruin the German economy. After coming to power, Hitler dismissed Feder from the Ministry of Economics in 1934 and turned instead to Schacht and to those who favored his policies. Schacht, indeed, presided over the financial end of Hitler's rearmament program and, in fact, made the German economy ready for war. Aware of his own ignorance of economics, Hitler was willing to place his trust in Schacht's traditional and tested views.

German finances were kept in good order during a politically revolutionary period.

The study of economic aspects of the Nazi regime led to a lively debate among economists and historians on the role of such industrialists as Gustav Krupp von Bohlen und Halbach and Fritz Thyssen not only in the early rise of National Socialism but also during the prewar and war years. One side sees the influence of industrialists and financiers as all-important, while the other contends that their role was exaggerated and was of lesser impact than the mass support Hitler received from Germans of every class — from élite to proletariat.

Among the highlights of this debate was the lively exchange between a senior and junior historian. In 1981 Princeton University Press published a study entitled *The Collapse of the Weimar Republic* by young historian David Abraham, not yet on tenure at Princeton University. Written from a Marxian point of view, the book contended that between 1925 and 1929 there was cooperation between the dynamic, export-oriented and liberal industrialists and the leaders of organized labor.   The text also claimed that the "Weimar System" politicized the economy, and that a part of the middle class, much of heavy industry and most of agriculture were, in fact, responsible for the rise of Hitler.   This thesis was strongly criticized by Henry Ashby Turner, Jr., Professor of History at Yale, who described the study as filled with "many dozens of errors" and called its central theme fallacious. Especially misleading, he charged, was Abraham's methods in dealing with evidence. The confrontation led to nearly 200 pages of debate in scholarly journals. Turner's views were defended by colleagues; other historians, notably several of Marxist persuasion, alleged political persecution and abuse of a junior colleague. In 1985, Turner published his *German Big Business and the Rise of Hitler*, with the thesis that, on balance, big business and industrialists gave only minor support to Hitler. Abraham did not win tenure at Princeton.

There are few studies concerning the economic aspects of National Socialism, at least in comparison with biographies and memoirs. Apparently, scholars and the general public are far more interested in the personalities and characters of the Third Reich, both the Nazi rogues and leading figures in the German Resistance movement. Economists offer involved statistical tables for their peers; armchair experts and history buffs prefer books on such subjects as the Night of the Long Knives or the medical history of Adolf Hitler.

BIBLIOGRAPHY

347. ABRAHAM, David. *The Collapse of the Weimar Republic: Political Economy and Crisis.* Princeton, NJ: Princeton University Press, 1981.
Using government publications, private papers and the contemporary press, the author, at the time of writing a professor at Princeton University, discusses the relationship of the industrial and agricultural sectors of capitalism, the working class and the German state. Is interested in conflicts between the economic sectors and the consequences for the Weimar Republic's multiparty political system. Contends that the dominant class of industrialists and large agricultural estate owners, traditional enemies of the Weimar Republic, attempted to subvert parliamentary democracy and in the long run helped Hitler's rise to political power. Also discusses the differences between the industrial and agricultural elements of pre-Nazi society.

348. ARMBRUSTER, Howard Watson. *German Dyes and American Dupes.* New York: Beechhurst Press, 1947.
A New Jersey chemical engineer tells the story of I. G. Farben, which he accuses of industrial conspiracy. Identifies individuals with evidence from official documents and court records. I. G. Farben, the world's most powerful chemical giant, a huge octopus of industry, provided Hitler with what he needed in his wars of conquest. During its wartime peak it controlled 900 German chemical factories, employed 250,000 people, supplied the *Wehrmacht* with 85% of its explosives, and presented an annual bill of one billion dollars. Accuses the chemical trust of unlimited bribery, and its foreign agents of forming the core of Nazi intrigue around the world.

349. BAUDIN, L. *L'économie française sous l'occupation allemand* (The French Economy under German Occupation). Paris: Editions Politiques, Economiques et Sociales, 1945.
A French scholar discusses the French economy under Nazi occupation. The country's economic system was rigidly controlled by Hitler's agents, who gave their special attention to food staples, industry and French products to be shipped to Germany.

350. BILLIG, Joseph. *Les camps de concentration dans l'economie du Reich hitlérien* (Concentration Camps in the Economy

of Hitler's Reich).   Paris: Presses Universitaires de France, 1973.
Studies the role of Hitler's concentration camps in the economy of the Third Reich.   Victims in the camps were used for the war effort until they either died or were exterminated.

351.   BIRKENFELD, W.   *Der synthetische Treibstoff, 1933-1945* (The Synthetic Dyes, 1933-1945).   Göttingen: Musterschmidt Wissenschaftlicher Verlag, 1964.
Because of the British blockade, Germany in both World Wars turned to the manufacture of synthetic goods to replace raw materials difficult to import.   Describes Hitler's attention to synthetic goods from the time he assumed the chancellorship to the final days of World War II.

352.   BORKIN, Joseph.   *The Crime and Punishment of I. G. Farben.* New York: Free Press, 1978.
An account of alleged corporate greed and ruthless disregard for lives.   Before World War I, Germany was the leading world producer of organic dyestuffs, pharmaceuticals and synthetic chemicals.   Charges that it was guilty of many crimes, and accuses its officials of exploitation and plunder of occupied territories as well as being indifferent to slavery and murder at its Auschwitz plant.   Also claims that I. G. Farben officials were given scandalously light sentences at their trials after the war.

353.   BRANDT, K., O. SCHILLER and F. AHLGRIMM. *Management of Agriculture and Food in the German Occupied and Other Areas of Fortress Europe.*   Stanford, CA: Stanford University Press, 1953.
Shows how Hitler saw to it that a steady stream of food supplies reached the Third Reich from the occupied territories of Europe.   The continent's food and art were plundered for the benefit of National Socialist Germany.

354.   BRAUN, R.   *Fascism, Make or Break?   German Experience Since the June Days.*   Translated from the German by Michael Davidson.   New York: International Publishers, 1935.
Presents the thesis that National Socialism did not lead to a corporate or guild state, but that its actions served to maintain finance-capitalism in preparation for a new world war.

355. CARROLL, Bernice A. *Design for Total War: Arms and Economics in the Third Reich.* The Hague: Mouton, 1968.
This study of arms and economics in the Third Reich, with special attention to policy and administration regarding economic mobilization for war, analyzes the relationship among economics and strategy, tactics and arms production.

356. CATHALA, P. *Face aux Réalités* (In the Face of Realities). Paris: Editions du Triolet, 1948.
Analyzes the public financial situation during the German occupation of France. Describes the iron grip held by the Nazis on the French economy.

357. CITRON, B. "Geldgeber der Nazis" (Contributors to the Nazis). *Weltbuehne*, II (1931), 72.
Discusses how the up-and-coming politician Hitler was supported financially by Rhineland industrialists and businessmen fearing Communist political strength.

358. DIE DEUTSCHE INDUSTRIE IM KRIEGE (German Industry in the War). Berlin: Duncker & Humblot, 1954.
Anonymous authors discuss the Nazi economy in World War II, and emphasize Hitler's measures taken to maintain the economy at an even level in difficult times.

359. *DROBISCH, Klaus. "Flick und die Nazis" (Flick and the Nazis). *Zeitschrift für Geschichtswissenschaft*, XIV (1966), 378-97.
Analyzes the relations between Friedrich Flick, industrialist and early supporter of the Nazi movement, and its officialdom. Flick joined the Nazi Party and contributed funds to it. He was also a member of the Circle of Friends of Heinrich Himmler, whose members gave money to the Nazis. He was tried at Nuremberg for complicity in helping Hitler rise to power and for promoting slave labor by having Jewish inmates of concentration camps sent to work in his various munitions plants. He was sentenced to serve seven years in prison but was released in January 1951 by an act of clemency. Flick died in 1972 at the age of eighty-nine, leaving a vast fortune in excess of one billion dollars.

360. *EINZIG, Paul. *Germany's Default: The Economics of Hitlerism.* New York: Macmillan, 1934.

Seeks to show that Germany was drifting toward a repudiation
of her foreign indebtedness, that this was a part of Hitler's economic program and that Hitler aimed to establish a super-
Empire that would rule Europe and the world. Believes that the
entire economic system of National Socialism made war highly
probable if pursued to its logical conclusion.

361. FEDER, Gottfried. *Kampf gegen Hochfinanz* (The Struggle
    Against High Finance). Munich: Eher Verlag, 1933.
    Gottfried Feder (1883-1941), Hitler's ideologist during the early
    days of the Nazi movement, stressed racist, populist and anti-
    industrialist views, including the expropriation of large landed
    estates and the property of Jews. He opposed *Zinsknechtschaft*
    (interest-slavery) and advocated a freeze in interest rates. This
    book bears the imprint of the official Nazi publishing house in
    Munich. When Feder's economic views caused a diminution
    of financial support for the Nazi Party from industrialists and
    businessmen, the *Führer* abandoned aggressive anti-capitalism.

362. *FLORINSKY, Michael T. *Fascism and National Socialism: A
    Study of the Economic and Social Policies of the
    Totalitarian State*. New York: Macmillan, 1936.
    Explains the roots of the convulsions of totalitarianism, and
    summarizes much that was then available on the economic sys-
    tems of Mussolini and Hitler. Bases many conclusions on what
    Italian and German officials told the author about their re-
    gimes. Gives special attention to the economics of dictatorship.

363. *GARRATY, John A. "The New Deal, National Socialism, and
    the Great Depression." *The American Historical Review*,
    LXXVIII (1973), 907-44.
    Compares the response to the Great Depression of the 1930s in
    the United States and Germany to about 1936 or 1937.
    Demonstrates that some Nazi and New Deal anti-depression
    measures were strikingly similar, although the two systems of
    government were fundamentally different.

364. GEORG, E. *Die wirtschaftlichen Unternehmungen der SS* (The
    Industrial Enterprises of the SS). Stuttgart: Deutsche
    Verlagsanstalt, 1963.
    Explains how Heinrich Himmler did all he could to extend the
    power of his SS into many different phases of German political,
    economic and social life. Describes the industrial enterprises of
    the SS during the National Socialist era.

365. GILLINGHAM, John. *Industry and Politics in the Third Reich: Ruhr Coal, Hitler and Europe.* New York: Columbia University Press, 1985.
Maintains that, contrary to widely held beliefs, the Ruhr industrialists were neither masterminds of the Third Reich's economic system nor helpless victims of dictator Hitler. Basing his conclusions on German and British archives, the author claims that the Ruhr operators refused to give the regime unqualified support, thereby annoying Hitler and his economic experts. The resultant chronic coal shortages hindered the German war effort. In this way the Ruhr industrialists preserved the traditional cooperation between Germany and the remainder of Europe that had developed between 1918 and 1939. That tradition helped provide the foundation for the postwar European Coal and Steel Community.

366. HARPER, Glenn T. *German Economic Policy in Spain.* The Hague: Mouton, 1967.
An account of Hitler's economic policy in Spain during the Spanish Civil War, 1936-39.

367. HOLT, John Bradshaw. *German Agricultural Policy, 1918-1934: The Development of a National Philosophy Toward Agriculture in Postwar Germany.* Chapel Hill, NC: University of North Carolina Press, 1936.
Traces the development of a national attitute toward agriculture from the end of World War I through the first year of the Nazi regime. Discusses the attitudes and policies of the different political parties and economic groups before the Third Reich and describes the emergence of National Socialist agrarianism. Analyzes taxation, tariff, price and production controls, farm labor and land settlement policies.

368. JÄGER, Jörg-Johannes. *Die wirtschaftliche Abhängigkeit des Dritten Reiches vom Ausland dargestellt am Beispiel der Stahlindustrie* (The Economic Independence of the Third Reich as Exemplified by the Steel Industry). Berlin: Berlin Verlag, 1969.
Analyzes the industrial independence of the Third Reich as seen from abroad with special attention to the steel industry. Describes Hitler's efforts to achieve industrial self-sufficiency in the event of war.

369. JANNSEN, Gregor. *Das Ministerium Speer: Deutschlands
      Rüstung im Krieg* (The Speer Ministry: Germany's Arma-
      ments in War). Berlin: Verlag Ullstein, 1968.
      Albert Speer (1905-81), Hitler's personal architect and city
      planner, was designated by Hitler in 1942 as Minister of Arma-
      ments and War Production, succeeding Dr. Fritz Todt, who had
      been killed in a plane accident. Describes Speer's ministry and
      its role in the arming of Germany during the war. With this
      appointment Speer changed from a master architect to a com-
      plete technocrat, the virtual dictator of the German war econ-
      omy. His production miracles, achieved despite opposition
      from other Nazi leaders and under heavy Allied bombing,
      undoubtedly prolonged the course of the war.

370. KLEIN, Burton. *Germany's Economic Preparations for War.*
      Cambridge, MA: Harvard University Press, 1959.
      Examines how Hitler geared Germany's economic system for
      the war of aggression he intended to fight. Demonstrates
      Hjalmar Schacht's role in preparing for confrontation on a ma-
      jor scale from 1933 to 1942.

371. KUCZYNSKI, Jürgen. *Germany: Economic and Labour
      Conditions Under Fascism.* New York: International Pub-
      lishers, 1945.
      The British economist and statistician analyzes the German
      Fascist movement in general and the development of German
      labor conditions specifically. Maintains that Fascism and mili-
      tary aggressiveness are synonymous. Stresses the war economy,
      especially labor conditions under German Fascist control.

372. MEIER-DÖRNBERG, Wilhelm. *Die Ölversorgung der
      Kriegsmarine 1935 bis 1945* (The Wartime Navy's Oil Sup-
      ply from 1935 to 1945). Freiburg: Verlag Rombach, 1973.
      Asserts that Hitler's Navy was confronted by two critical prob-
      lems: how to accumulate an oil reserve in anticipation of war,
      and how to keep the Navy afloat during the war. Traces the
      Navy's efforts to obtain sufficient oil supplies. Large quantities
      of American and Mexican oil found their way into the Third
      Reich via such neutrals as Japan, the Soviet Union, Sweden and
      Switzerland. The supply diminished after the summer of 1941,
      and especially following the Japanese attack on Pearl Harbor,
      which ended the American supply. Presents a familiar
      theme – the absolute necessity of an oil reserve for a modern
      navy.

373. MILWARD, Alan S. *The German Economy at War*. London: Athlone Press, 1965.
Discusses the German economy before and during World War II, with attention to Hitler's personal intervention in economic affairs. Criticizes A. J. P. Taylor, the British revisionist historian, who asserted that Germany's failure to mobilize the economy for total war meant that the *Führer's* intentions were not aggressive.

374. MISES, Ludwig Edler von. *Omnipotent Government: The Rise of the Total State and Total War*. New Haven, CT: Yale University Press, 1944.
Economist Ludwig von Mises explains the rise of Nazism by tracing Germany's development during the last century. Emphasizes economic changes, especially capitalism versus socialism.

375. POOL, James and Suzanne POOL. *Who Financed Hitler? The Secret Funding of Hitler's Rise to Power, 1919-1933*. New York: Dial Press, 1978.
This account of the Germans and foreigners, aristocrats and peasants, who brought Hitler to power through their contributions, explains the motives of such people as well as their methods.

376. POOLE, Kenyon E. *German Financial Policies, 1932-1939*. Cambridge, MA: Harvard University Press, 1940.
Examines German financial policies during the 1930s, when Hitler was rearming to challenge the Treaty of Versailles.

377. SASULY, Richard. *I. G. Farben*. New York: Boni & Gaer, 1947.
In a twenty-thousand word indictment, the twenty-four leading officers of I. G. Farben, the world's most powerful cartel, were brought to trial at Nuremberg for wilfully engaging in activities indispensable to Hitler's aggressive warfare. They were charged with enslavement and mass murder of foreign workers, and "the plunder and spoilation of public and private properties in the invaded coutries." Explains how, when and where I. G. Farben exercised its power, and stresses its army of scientists, spies, saboteurs and assorted conspirators. Accuses the cartel of serving Hitler well.

378.   SCHACHT, Hjalmar. *Confessions of an "Old Wizard."* Boston:
          Houghton Mifflin, 1956.
          Hjalmar Horace Greeley Schacht (1877-1970), financier, presi-
          dent of the *Reichsbank* and economic expert behind German
          rearmament in the mid-1930s, was generally regarded as an
          economic genius who worked diligently in the belief that Hitler's
          economic policies could be made consistent with his own. After
          the unsuccessful attempt on Hitler's life on 20 July 1944,
          Schacht was imprisoned in three concentration camps. Tried
          at Nuremberg, he was acquitted on the ground that, although
          he was active in organizing Germany for war, rearmament was
          not of itself a criminal act. Defends his career as an economist,
          and asserts that his greatest problem was to discourage inflation
          in the process of rearmament.

379.   SCHWEITZER, Arthur. *Big Business in the Third Reich.*
          London: Eyre & Spottiswoode, 1964.
          Studies large business corporations in Hitler's Germany. Ex-
          plains how Big Business, as every other institution in the Third
          Reich, was incorporated into the Nazi system.

380.   SCHWEITZER,   Arthur.   "Die   wirtschaftliche
          Wiederaufrüstung   Deutschlands   von   1934-1936"
          (Germany's Industrial Rearmament from 1934-1936).
          Zeitschrift für die gesammte Staatsgewissenschaft, CXIV
          (1958), 594-637.
          Analyzes Ge.many's industrial rearmament from 1934 to 1936,
          when Hitler initiated his program to challenge the provisions of
          the Treaty of Versailles.

381.   SCHWERIN VON KROSIGK, Lutz Graf von. *Es geschah in
          Deutschland* (It Happened in Germany). Tübingen:
          Wunderlich-Verlag, 1951.
          Lutz Graf Schwerin von Krosigk (1887-1952) was a member of
          Hitler's original Cabinet as Minister of Finance, a post he re-
          tained throughout the Third Reich era until its collapse in 1945.
          Hitler relied on him to finance the rearmament of Germany.
          During the next three years he denounced the "Mefo Bills," is-
          sued by Dr. Hjalmar Schacht to raise money for armaments, as
          merely another way of printing money. He regarded Hitler's
          anti-Semitic campaign as justified and called for "shoving Jews
          into other countries." Tried at Nuremberg in 1948, he was found
          guilty of war crimes and sentenced to ten years' imprisonment.

Released in 1951, he died the next year. Discusses his own work as Finance Minister and justifies his career.

382. SIMPSON, Amos E. *Hjalmar Schacht in Perspective.* The Hague: Mouton, 1969.
Explains the career of Hjalmar Schacht (1877-1970), financier, president of the *Reichsbank* and economics expert behind German rearmament. Claims to present an unbiased portrait of the financial wizard.

383. TENENBAUM, Edward Adam. *National Socialism vs. International Capitalism.* New Haven: Yale University Press, 1942.
Records the negation of free enterprise in the Third Reich after 1933. Surveys Nazi methods of economic warfare. Using the confidential files of the Joint Boycott Council, describes the Nazi challenge to international capitalism.

384. THYSSEN, Fritz. *I Paid Hitler.* Translated from the German by César Saerchinger. New York: Farrar & Rinehart, 1941.
Fritz Thyssen, industrialist and heir to the Thyssen fortune, deeply regrets that he had supported Hitler and Nazi activities in the early days of the National Socialist movement. Opposed to the Weimar Republic, a democracy "representing nothing," he was attracted in 1923 to a budding politician who convinced him that he would smash Communism in the streets. Also believed that Hitler would work for the restoration of the Hohenzollern monarchy. In the next decade Thyssen contributed more than one million marks to the National Socialist Party. In the presidential elections of 1932, he voted for Hitler: "I am convinced that he is the only man who can and will rescue Germany from ruin and disgrace." But after Hitler's assumption of power in 1933, Thyssen began to have serious doubts about the Nazi movement, and became more and more disillusioned. In 1939, he left Germany for Switzerland. From there he sent a long letter to Hitler. "My sole error is that I believed in you, Adolf Hitler, with all the ardor of one dispassionate German." He denounced "the brutal and cowardly attack on Jews." Hitler never replied.

385. TURNER, Henry Ashby, Jr. *Faschismus und Kapitalismus in Deutschland: Studien zum Verhältnis zwischen Nationalsozialismus und Wirtschaft* (Fascism and

Capitalism in Germany: Studies on the Relationship between National Socialism and Industry).   Göttingen:
Vandenhoeck & Ruprecht, 1972.
German translations of essays by Henry Ashby Turner, Jr.,
American authority on the economics of National Socialism,
concerning the general theme of Big Business and right-wing
politics in the Weimar Republic, and the relations between
industrialists and businessmen with National Socialism. Maintains that support for Hitler from business interests came after,
not before, the Nazis came to political power. The final essay
characterizes National Socialism as "a utopian form of anti-
modernism."

386.   TURNER, Henry Ashby, Jr. *German Big Business and the Rise
of Hitler.* New York: Oxford University Press, 1985.
Henry Ashby Turner, Jr., Professor of History at Yale University and the author of several works on German history, presents the thesis that Big Business did *not*, on balance, support
Hitler and his program. Conventional ideas on the economics
of Nazism hold that Big Business played a crucial role in Hitler's
rise to power, that German capitalists undermined the Weimar
Republic, that they financed the Nazi Party and that they exerted their influence on behalf of Hitler's appointment to the
chancellorship. Using the major corporate archives of Weimar
and Nazi Germany, the author examines the records of such gi-
ants of German industry as I. G. Farben, Flick, Siemens and
others, and concludes that the financial contributions of Big
Business and industrialists to the rise of Hitler were negligible.
Nazism, he asserts, was self-supporting thanks to internally-
organized funding devices.

CHAPTER 6

THE SOCIAL STRUCTURE

Classes, Masses, Social Values, Social Ethics, Sociology

One of the striking aspects of the social order in late Weimar Germany was the fact that virtually all elements of society were attracted to National Socialism. From top to bottom the social structure saw positive factors in Hitler's version of European fascism. There were dissidents from the beginning, but they were few in numbers and unsuccessful in the task of halting the Nazi steamroller.

The upper classes – aristocrats, monarchists, rightists, the military – saw in National Socialism a corrective for the Weimar Republic which they detested. The monarchists regarded the Nazi movement as a temporary phenomenon which would destroy the Weimar democracy and lead to a restoration of the Hohenzollern dynasty. The military, disgraced by the loss of World War I, seized the opportunity to win regeneration of its class. Dissatisfied rightists welcomed an effective leader who would smash the left.

Upper, middle and lower levels of the German middle class all were impressed by the ideology of National Socialism. Hit hard by inflation, disgruntled by the Treaty of Versailles, restive in harsh economic times, apolitical Germans saw a savior in the nervous little Austrian with his eloquent tongue. The man was fascinating and he seemed to speak sense to a harried bourgeoisie. Besides, National Socialism seemed to provide a bulwark against detested communism.

The Nazi movement also exerted tremendous appeal to the proletariat – workers and peasants. The massive displays of the Nuremberg rallies, the songs and marches, the rumble of boots on cobblestones, the extraordinary oratory of Hitler and Goebbels, all these managed to win increasing strength among the proletariat. Even Communists turned to the new movement. For a time the Nazi Party became known as the "Beefsteak Party, brown on the outside, red on the inside."

The studies of the Third Reich social structure are mostly scholarly in nature. Most interest is shown in the controversial subject of the role of the middle class in the rise of Hitler. There is equal attention devoted to the part played by industrialists, financiers and businessmen in Hitler's advent to the Chancellorship. Also, special studies investigated German youth who were attracted to National Socialism.

BIBLIOGRAPHY

387. ALLEN, William Sheridan. *The Nazi Seizure of Power: The Experience of a Single German Town, 1930-1935.* Chicago: Quandrangle Books, 1965.
      Examines the situation in the German town of Thalberg from 1930 to 1935. The author interviewed citizens from all levels of society and studied the local newspapers. Shows how the Nazi terror system succeeded primarily through the atomization of society and the disruption of normal human relationships. This was typical of a thousand similar towns throughout Germany. Nazi influence extended beyond the middle class. The pressures of conformity were always present. Devotes much attention to the powerful appeal of Nazi propaganda.

388. ARETZ, Jürgen. *Katholische Arbeiterbewegung und Nationalsozialismus* (The Catholic Workers' Movement and National Socialism). Mainz: Matthias-Grünewald-Verlag, 1978.
      Analyzes the Catholic Workers' movement and its relation to National Socialism, with special attention to the Association of Catholic Workers' and Miners' Clubs in Western Germany from 1923 to 1945. The clubs managed to escape destruction in 1933 because they were inscribed as religious rather than social or economic organizations, and therefore they could claim protection under the Concordat with the Roman Catholic Church.

389. *BECKER, Howard. *German Youth: Bond or Free.* New York: Oxford University Press, 1946.
    Howard Becker, then Professor of Sociology at the University of Wisconsin, analyzes the German youth movement from the *Wandervögel* (Roamers) of Kaiser Wilhelm II's era to the *Hitler Jugend.* Traces the "dear old days" of the *Biedermeier*, the revolt of German youth at the turn of the century against the bourgeois virtues of an industrial society, the sectarian splits in the Weimar Republic and the final turn to Hitler. Throughout, stresses the attraction of German youth to the leader's charisma, and to a strange combination of manliness, recklessness and intellectualism. Shows how Hitler carefully regulated education of the young to prepare them for military service.

390. BLUEL, Hans Peter. *Sex and Society in Nazi Germany.* Translated from the German by J. Maxwell Brownjohn. Philadelphia: Lippincott, 1973.
    A German reporter provides a sociological study of a regime based on inconsistency, contradiction and hypocrisy. Examines the role of sex in the Third Reich. Shows how, far from being demonic superhuman specimens of an emerging master race, Nazi leaders were lower middle-class men of trivial intellect and petty prejudice. This was revealed especially in their attitude toward sex. Their fanatical allegiance to national health, racial purity and "sound" genetics, added to their professed sexual puritanism, led to bizarre theories and grotesque practices. Discusses in detail how Nazi leaders reacted toward homosexuality and even entertainment and fashion, and how they came to sanction illegitimacy, sterilization and euthanasia.

391. *BRIDENTHAL, Renate, *et al.*, eds. *When Biology Became Destiny: Women in Weimar and Nazi Germany.* New York: Monthly Review, 1984.
    Fourteen essays showing the disastrous consequences for women's freedom and equality of the antifeminist policies adopted by the Nazis and already in operation to some extent in the Weimar Republic. The authors illustrate "the dangers implicit in a feminism that celebrates separate spheres and differences between the sexes, glorifies motherhood and women's bodies."

392. CHILDERS, Thomas. *The Nazi Voter: The Social Foundation of Fascism in Germany, 1919-1933.* Chapel Hill, NC: University of North Carolina Press, 1984.

Questions the traditional interpretation that Nazism was essentially a lower middle-class movement. Examines the Nazi constituency, how it was formed and its background of social groups. Concludes that electoral support for the NSDAP came from a much more diverse social milieu than was previously believed. Uses quantification methods with traditional literary and archival sources.

393. DEMETER, Karl. *The German Officer Corps in Society and State, 1650-1945.* Translated from the German by Angus Malcolm. New York: Praeger, 1965.
Originally published in 1930, this book was revised and reissued in 1965. Traces the development of the German officer-corps and the part it played in German history to the decade following the end of World War II. Addresses such questions as these: how, in an age of social fluidity, could anything as rigid as this officer-corps be created and preserved? How could it remain responsive to social and political developments, yet maintain its essential cohesion? What control did it have over its own recruitment? What were the relationships between the authorities and the military?

394. *DEUEL, Wallace. *People Under Hitler.* New York: Harcourt, Brace, 1942.
Investigates the lives of ordinary people living under the Nazi regime. Emphasizes the coordination of all parts of society in a rigid dictatorship. Describes a people brainwashed by propaganda and kept in line by a terroristic police force.

395. FRAENKEL, Heinrich. *The German People versus Hitler.* London: Allen & Unwin, 1940.
Contends that Hitler had gone to war against the wishes of the majority of German people. Two years later the author wrote a similar book titled *The Other Germany* (1942), in which he argued that there was another and decent Germany alongside the Nazi movement.

396. HAMILTON, Alice. "The Youth Who Are Hitler's Strength: A Study of the Nazi Followers and the Appeal That Has Aroused Them." *The New York Times Magazine*, 8 October 1933, 3, 16.
Describes the Nazi followers among German youth and the appeal that aroused them. This treatment of young people in Hitler's Third Reich was substantiated in subsequent studies.

397. HAMILTON, Richard F. *Who Voted for Hitler?* Princeton, NJ: Princeton University Press, 1982.
Questions the widely accepted proposition that the lower middle class of Weimar Germany responded to Nazi propaganda. Blames the collapse of Weimar Germany more on a struggle of parties than of classes. Explains why the people voted as they did. Attempts to clarify German voting habits during the late days of the Weimar Republic.

398. HAUSER, Heinrich. *Time Was: Death of a Junker.* Translated from the German by Barrows Mussey. New York: Reynal, 1942.
A German Junker describes his life over thirty years and the downfall of the Germany he knew. He eventually left his homeland for the United States, a hegira from German aristocratic landlordism to the liberty and equality of the American scene. Reveals how the Junkers, perhaps unwittingly, tried to counter democracy in Germany and thereby played into the hands of Hitler and his National Socialist ideology. A novelist himself, Hauser clinically diagnoses the chaotic minds of those young Germans who turned to Hitler. Seeks to shed light on how Hitler could bluff an entire nation into following the Nazi creed.

399. KATER, Michael H. *The Nazi Party: A Social Profile of Members and Leaders, 1919-1945.* Cambridge, MA: Harvard University Press, 1983.
Presents extensive data on Nazi Party members and leadership. The book is divided into two parts: the rank and file, and the leadership cadres. Provides statistical portraits as well as qualitative analyses of the causal factors operating during varied periods of the party's twenty-six years' existence. Seeks to identify and trace the proportions of the various socio-economic class groups in the leadership and rank and file of the Nazi Party. Finds the dominant value system as being essentially lower middle class, attracting also the old élite as well as the proletariat.

400. KELE, Max H. *Nazis and Workers.* Chapel Hill, NC: University of North Carolina Press, 1972.
Analyzes National Socialist appeal to German labor from 1919 to 1933. Contends that previous scholarship has unduly ignored the significance of the working-class element in the NSDAP's membership and voting appeal. Attributes this failure to a lib-

eral and Marxist bias among some historians. Discusses the bitter infighting within the Nazi Party over its stand on labor and socialism. Believes that Hitler's appeal to the workers was far more effective than has hitherto been realized.

401. *KIRKPATRICK, Clifford. *Nazi Germany: Its Women and Family Life.* Indianapolis, IN: Bobbs-Merrill, 1938.
An early sociological study of women and family life in Nazi Germany. Conducting his investigation inside Germany, the author, then Professor of Sociology at the University of Minnesota, found eager informants. Attempts to clarify the character of National Socialism at the time. Presents details about the conquest of women by the state, family life, "breeding for quality," the struggle for a higher birth-rate, and the renaissance of "*Kirche, Küche, Kinder*" (Kirk, Kitchen, Kids). "The Germans have become a nation of sleepwalkers who commit acts of hatred with words of love, who talk of peace and move toward war."

402. KLAUSENER, Erich. *Frauen in Fesseln* (Women in Chains). Berlin: Morus, 1982.
Dedicates this study of "Women in Chains" to "hope in darkness." Emphasizes the courage and sacrifice of Catholic women in the Third Reich.

403. KRÄMER, Gerhard F. *The Influence of National Socialism on the Courts of Justice and the Police of the Third Reich.* London: Weidenfeld & Nicolson, 1955.
Explains how Nazi ideology influenced the legal system and the police in Hitler's Germany. The strong police system was dedicated to the task of maintaining National Socialist political power against dissenters of all kinds, and the law courts were expected to promote the dictatorship.

404. *LAQUEUR, Walter Z. *Young Germany: A History of the German Youth Movement.* New York: Basic Books, 1963.
A study beginning in 1901 of the big-city movement of Protestant middle-class German youths who wanted to lead a life away from their stuffy parents' homes. Called *Wandervögel* (Roamers), they moved in small groups throughout the country. Most of the members of this youth movement eventually accepted National Socialism and became enthusiastic followers of Hitler. The early youth movement was non-

political, but under the Third Reich it became enmeshed in political Nazism.

405. MASON, Timothy W. *Sozialpolitik im Dritten Reich: Arbeiterklasse und Volksgemeinschaft* (Social Politics in the Third Reich: Working Class and National Community). Wiesbaden: Westdeutscher Verlag, 1977.
Based on intensive archival research and familiarity with Nazi literature, shows how the Third Reich attempted to win over the working class in order to help its own goal of expansion. This task was made difficult by Hitler's inclusion of labor in his program of *Gleichschaltung* (coordination), by which every element in the state was to be subordinated to Nazi ideology. The labor movement was effectively destroyed and brought under state control. The Nazi Labor Front was to draw workers away from "the illusion of class conflict."

406. MAYER, Milton. *They Thought They Were Free.* Chicago: University of Chicago Press, 1955.
An American journalist reports on his talks with ten average former Nazis in a small German town in an attempt to discover the basis of Nazi tyranny. He lived on intimate terms with the former Nazis, concealing the fact that he was a Jew. The men he selected belonged to the anti-labor, anti-capitalist and anti-democratic lower middle class, supposed to be the mainstay of the early National Socialist movement. Discovered that these "little men" looked back nostalgically on the Nazi regime, especially before 1939. The Nazi Party had given them a sense of belonging. The Allies' effort at enlightenment had failed to convince these men of the iniquity of anti-Semitism. Concludes that full justice has not caught up with Nazi crimes.

407. MITCHELL, Otis C. *Hitler Over Germany: The Establishment of the Nazi Dictatorship, 1918-1934.* Philadelphia: Institute for the Study of Human Issues, 1983.
Analyzes the relationship between Hitler as *Führer* and the German people as followers. Uses the year 1918 as the decisive turning point leading to the rise of Hitler and the Third Reich. Treats the political, socio-economic and cultural environment chronologically, and maintains that for the Germans only Hitler seemed to understand their problems to their satisfaction. Hitler's rise was the result of extreme discontinuity due to a lost war, the end of the monarchy, inflation and the Great Depression of 1929. Considers the Nazi Revolution not a culmi-

nation of German history but rather a "novelty" in the development of German society.

408.   MITSCHERLICH, Alexander and Fred MIELKE. *Doctors of Infamy: The Story of Nazi Medical Crimes.* Translated from the German by Heinz Norden. New York: Schuman, 1949.

This book is in part a translation of *Das Diktat der Menschenverachtung* (1947), published in Heidelberg by Lambert Schneider. Mitscherlich was head of the German Medical Commission to the U.S. Military Tribunal No. 1 at Nuremberg. The authors offer a documented report on Nazi medical crimes – the torture and killing of human beings under the guise of medical experimentation. They show how Nazi Germany's medical profession was harnessed to the apparatus guided by Heinrich Himmler's underlings. Dr. Mitscherlich won Nazi enmity when he was accused of harboring "illegal literature." He fled to Switzerland, where he studied medicine and returned in 1937 only to be arrested and jailed for eight months in a *Gestapo* prison in Nuremberg.

409.   PAUWELS, Jacques R. *Women, Nazis, and Universities: Female University Students in the Third Reich, 1933-1945.* Westport, CT: Greenwood, 1984.

Presents the thesis that, despite the misogyny of National Socialism, women were more successful in gaining admission to German universities in the Third Reich than at any other time. At first, Nazis tried to discourage women from studying by using restrictions and specious eugenic arguments. Women's enrollment declined less steeply than that of men. Female student leadership appointed by the Nazis faced continued problems.

410.   ROSE, Ramona M. *Position and Treatment of Women in Nazi Germany.* Vancouver: Tantalus Research, 1984.

Examines the role played by women in the Third Reich, as viewed from the perspective of the English-language press, 1933-45.

411.   *SCHOENBAUM, David S. *Hitler's Social Revolution: Class and State in Nazi Germany, 1933-1939.* Garden City, NY: Doubleday, 1966.

Emphasizes the impact of National Socialism on German society. Seeks to answer basic questions: why did so many Germans support Hitler in 1933 and why they continued to support him six years later when he led them into war? Analyzes Nazi appeal to farmers, workers, businessmen, industrialists, women and youth. The Nazi *Führer* improvised a program that offered something to everyone — above all the concept of a classless society with equality and equal opportunities for all Germans (excluding German Jews). Despite Hitler's efforts, the process of social disintegration accelerated to a point where the Third Reich headed straight for destruction.

412. SOSNOWSKI, Kiryl. *The Tragedy of Children Under Nazi Rule.* Edited by Wanda Machlejd. Translated from the Polish. Poznań: Zachodnia Agencja Prasowa, 1962.
The English edition of a Polish work on the fate of children in the occupied countries, especially Poland, discusses Jewish children in concentration and extermination camps as well as in ghettos. Offers statistics on birth and death rates, as well as on health and education.

413. STEINBERG, Michael Stephen. *Sabers and Brown Shirts: The German Students' Path to National Socialism, 1918-1935.* Chicago: University of Chicago Press, 1977.
Analyzes the German students' road to National Socialism from the Weimar Republic to the second year of the Third Reich. Shows how Weimar authorities were unable to deal with their problems and how the superior organization of the National Socialists exerted a tremendous appeal to German students. Emphasizes the politicizing of the universities and their coordination into the Nazi system. Offers much detail on vote tallies in university elections.

414. STEINER, John M. *Power Politics and Social Change in National Socialist Germany: A Process of Escalation into Mass Destruction.* New York: Humanities Press, 1977.
Examines the sociological and cultural dynamics that led to the creation of the Third Reich and made it evolve into a destructive authoritarian system. Describes the means of escalation into mass destruction: he himself was a victim of Nazism and spent several years in Hitler's concentration camps, including Auschwitz. Concludes that, because power comes from the people, the Germans were willing to give it to Hitler and his lieutenants. Gives special attention to the SS, its development and indoctrination with Nazi ideology.

415.   STEPHENSON, Jill.   *Women in Nazi Society.*   New York: Harper, 1976.
Presents her aim: "to describe and discuss some aspects of the status of, and opportunities for, women in Germany in one inter-war decade, the 1930s, and in so doing to explode some of the myths." A lecturer in history at the University of Edinburgh, Stephenson asserts that women, on the whole, benefited under the Nazi regime, but that they were given equal status with men only because of their functions as mothers, obligated to produce superior Aryan children as a racial duty. Offers details of the internal policies and disputes inside the NSF (Nazi Women's Group) during the critical first year of the Nazi regime from 1933 to 1934, when Hitler's policy of coordination shattered the liberal and socialist women's organizations.

416.   WALKER, Lawrence D.   *Hitler Youth and Catholic Youth, 1933-1936.*   Washington, DC: Catholic University Press, 1970.
Traces the conflict between State and Church authorities over existence of Catholic Youth organizations in the Third Reich. Discusses the history of the youth movement in Germany starting with the *Wandervögel* (Roamers) up to the establishment of the Hitler Youth in the 1920s, then investigates the origin and complexity of the Catholic Youth organizations. Recounts the restrictive measures imposed by the state and the countermeasures undertaken by the Church, and draws copiously on Gestapo microfilm reports.

417.   WINKLER, Dörte.   *Frauenarbeit im "Dritten Reich"* (Women's Work in the Third Reich).   Hamburg: Hoffmann & Campe Verlag, 1977.
Discusses Hitler's mobilization of women for war work. Because of the insatiable needs for the war economy, Nazi authorities insisted on using women of all classes for the war effort, amid much conflict behind the scenes about the proper procedures. Hitler, himself, allegedly held a personal prejudice against women: he regarded their proper place as mothers for racial breeding and he opposed mobilizing them fully for war work. Contends that women were manipulated shamelessly by Nazi ideology, which denied them a proper place in Nazi society.

CHAPTER 7

NATIONAL SOCIALIST CULTURE

Ideology, Intellectual Quality, Education, Literature, Art, Architecture

Scholars and journalists show intense interest in the quality of National Socialist culture and ideology. Much of it was so far out of the range of traditional German *Kultur* that it, indeed, called for special attention. The character of the Nazi intellect always reflected the thinking or lack of thinking of Hitler, the mastermind of the movement. Fawning subordinates listened meticulously for any sign of the *Führer's* wisdom, which they would immediately record or parrot to gain his favorable attention.

Most of Hitler's doctrines and opinions were presented, despite their irrational nature, in *Mein Kampf*, in its original edition an illiterate summary of his innermost thoughts. He derived his racialism from Germanized Englishman Houston Stewart Chamberlain and French Aryanist Baron Arthur de Gobineau, as well as the imitative work of Nazi philosopher Alfred Rosenberg. He took his bitter anti-Semitism, which remained with him to the last day of his life, from Austrian Pan-Germanist Georg Ritter von Schoenerer and anti-Semitic Mayor of Vienna Karl Lueger. He borrowed his idea of the Teutonic Superman from an erroneous interpretation of German philosopher Friedrich Nietzsche and English naturalist Charles Darwin.

An enthusiastic Wagnerian, Hitler was enthralled by the composer's slam-bang-cymbal music as specifically and totally German. He was even more delighted by Richard Wagner's crude anti-Semitism. He found justification for military aggression in the geopolitical theories of Karl Haushofer, derived second-hand from Rudolf Hess.

All this is described in the books on National Socialist culture. There is much unanimity among authors who write on the ideology of Nazism, although differences exist in explaining how such a combination of absurdities could appeal to virtually all elements of German society. The people who gave the world the music of Beethoven, Brahms and Bach, also contributed the machinations of Hitler, Himmler and Hess. Again, the Faust-Mephisto syndrome!

BIBLIOGRAPHY

418. ANGEBERT, Jean-Michel. *The Occult and the Third Reich.* Translated from the French by Lewis A. M. Sumberg. New York: McGraw-Hill, 1974.
A study by Jean-Michel Angebert, the joint pseudonym of Jean Angelin and Michel Bertrand, two French scholars who previously had extensively researched the role of mystical cults in European history. They argue that strange cults influenced Hitler and that National Socialism was linked to and sprang from medieval Catharist tradition. The Nazi movement, in their view, was not an isolated aberration of modern Germany, but merely the most recent of traditions that dominated Western society for centuries before Hitler's birth. They quote Hitler: "He who has seen National Socialism as only a political movement has seen nothing." They regard Nazism as only the most recent outcropping of militant paganism locked in a death struggle with its arch enemy, traditional Christianity.

419. BARNES, James J. and Patience P. BARNES. *Hitler's Mein Kampf in Britain and America: A Publishing History, 1930-39.* Cambridge (Eng.) and New York: Cambridge University Press, 1980.
The authors give an account of the publication of Hitler's autobiography in Great Britain and America. The text is an extended version of a scholarly article. Hitler's *Mein Kampf*, often judged to be one of the worst books ever written, received almost no attention at first in Great Britain and the United States. At the time it was regarded as being so bizarre that it merited little discussion. It took seven years for an English translation to appear of a book that was a best-seller in Germany, and even that was an abridgment. Only later did the world learn that *Mein Kampf* was of enormous historical importance and that it had to be taken seriously as a blueprint for Hitler's policy of *Lebensraum*, or living space.

420. BAUMGÄRTNER, Raimund. *Weltanschauungskampf im Dritten Reich* (The World-View Struggle in the Third Reich). Mainz: Matthias-Grünewald-Verlag, 1977.
Analyzes the struggle between the German churches and Alfred Rosenberg, National Socialist ideologist. To Hitler, Rosenberg was "the Church Father of National Socialism." Discusses the world-view of Rosenberg in his *Der Mythos des 20. Jahrhunderts* (1930), in which Rosenberg charged the German churches with being spiritually enslaved and thoroughly Judaized. Treats Rosenberg's intellectual and party development and influence on members of the Nazi Party.

421. BERBIG, Hans Joachim. "Zur Terminologie von Volk, Nation und Reich in der neueren deutschen Geschichte" (On the Terminology of *Volk*, Nation and Reich in Modern German History). *Zeitschrift für Religions- und Geistesgeschichte*, XXVIII (1976), 1-15.
Seeks to explain the terms *Volk*, *Nation* and *Reich* in German history, with special attention to their meaning in the Third Reich. Suggests that Germans never succeeded in the important task of finding a proper juxtaposition for these terms in German development.

422. BEYERSCHEN, Alan B. *Scientists under Hitler: Politics and the Physics Community in the Third Reich*. New Haven, CT: Yale University Press, 1977.
Presents the interaction between Nazis and the German physics community between 1933 and 1945. Describes academic life, and discusses the dismal impact of Nazi dismissal policy on the physics community in universities and research institutes. Uses the University of Göttingen as the focus of the study. Traces the development of "Aryan physics" and its ultimate failure.

423. BISCHOFF, Ralph Frederic. *Nazi Conquest Through German Culture*. Cambridge, MA: Harvard University Press, 1943.
The thesis of this study: the acceptance of National Socialism in Germany was "an outgrowth of the inborn cultural and blood nationalism of the German people, and the ability of their leaders to re-awaken, re-emphasize and reform certain characteristics, traditions and faith already existent in Germany and in other German communities."

424. BLACKBURN, Gilmer M. *Education in the Third Reich*. Albany, NY: State University of New York Press, 1985.

Examines textbooks used in Nazi Germany, with attention to the presentation of racial theory and the study of German history as perceived by Nazi educators.

425. *BOSSENBROOK, William John. *The German Mind.* Detroit, MI: Wayne State University Press, 1961.
Analyzes intellectual trends in Germany from the medieval era through the Nazi period. Because of the separation of state from nation, Germany moved from Western liberalism to a totalitarian state under a charismatic leader. Describes the Nazi regime as "a triumph of totalitarian nationalism." From the early 19th century on, the German mind tended to concentrate on race and soil, a concept far removed from the liberal-democratic developments of the century.

426. BROSZAT, Martin.   "Die völkische Ideologie unter den Nationalsozialismus" (*Völkisch* Ideology under National Socialism). *Deutsche Rundschau*, LXXXIV (1958), 53-68.
Analyzes the *völkisch*, or "ethnic," ideal which formed the basis of National Socialist ideology. The concept was based on the presumed superiority of the so-called Aryan "race," which Hitler depicted as being in deadly confrontation with the Semitic "race."

427. BROSZAT, Martin. *German National Socialism, 1919-1945.* Translated from the German by Kurt Rosenbaum and Inge Pauli Boehm. Santa Barbara, CA: Clio Press, 1966.
This brief study, which appeared originally in Germany in 1960, treats National Socialist philosophy, program and "reality." Describes "the true National Socialism," contrasting myth and reality, and shows how nationalist ideology influenced the National Socialist movement. Includes a concise analysis of the antecedents of the Nazi era, the intellectual and emotional atmosphere of the Weimar Republic and the motives and hopes which led German conservatives and nationalists to support Hitler. Emphasizes the one and only stable element in the flux of Hitler's doctrines – the obsession with anti-Semitism.

428. *BUTLER, Rohan D'Olier. *Roots of National Socialism.* New York: Dutton, 1942.
A Fellow of All Souls College, Oxford, traces National Socialist ideology from the 18th to the 20th centuries. Sees certain dangerous trends in German culture leading to the acceptance of Nazism by a highly gifted and intelligent public. Believes

that the emergence of Hitler went beyond a mistaken economic formula or a military calculation. Where others attributed Hitler's movement to an aberrant phase of German history, Butler discusses contributing factors over a long historical development.

429. CECIL, Robert. *Hitler's Decision to Invade Russia, 1941.* London: Davis-Poynter, 1975; New York: McKay, 1975.
Maintains that the decision to invade the Soviet Union was closely in line with Hitler's ideological beliefs. Traces the evolution in Hitler's mind of the ideas and plans which made the step inevitable. Argues that the *Führer's* goal was to destroy "Jewish-Bolshevism" and to win living space indispensable for German survival. Claims that the invasion was a military move to deny an all-but-conquered Great Britain the hope of future Russian assistance.

430. CECIL, Robert. *The Myth of the Master Race: Alfred Rosenberg and Nazi Ideology.* New York: Dodd, Mead, 1972.
Discusses Hitler's master-race theory. Alfred Rosenberg (1893-1946), son of an Estonian mother and Lithuanian father, was editor of the *Völkischer Beobachter*, newspaper of the Nazi movement, and during the war Reich Minister for the Eastern Occupied Territories. His magnum opus, *The Myth of the Twentieth Century*, presents his view of "the Myth of the Blood, which under the sign of the Swastika released the World Revolution and victoriously put an end to Racial Chaos." Influenced by the ideas of Houston Stewart Chamberlain and Count Arthur de Gobineau, Rosenberg presents his own version of anti-Semitism which was to become official policy in the Third Reich. Cecil describes the character of this leading Nazi ideologue and shows how he worked to present his nationalist and racial ideas. The book's title is a play of words on Rosenberg's self-proclaimed masterpiece, which the publisher called "a fountainhead of fundamental precepts in the field of human history, religion and cultural philosophy, almost overwhelming in magnitude."

431. DE JAEGER, Charles. *The Linz File: Hitler's Plunder of Europe's Art.* New York: Holt, Rinehart & Winston, 1982.
Describes Hitler's plunder of European art and the recovery of thousands of looted works taken from galleries and private col-

lections by the Nazis during World War II. Hitler termed it
"Special Mission Linz," and proposed to build a great art gal-
lery in his hometown, Linz, in Austria. Presents illustrations of
stolen art works as well as an unannotated bibliography and an
appendix listing the still missing art works.

432. DOWNS, Donald Alexander. *Nazis in Skokie.* Notre Dame,
     IN: University of Notre Dame Press, 1985.
     The author, who teaches at the University of Notre Dame,
     shows how the ideology of National Socialism extended beyond
     its demise in Germany. In 1977, a Chicago-based Nazi group
     announced its intention to demonstrate in Skokie, Illinois, the
     home of hundreds of Holocaust survivors. The shocked survi-
     vor community rose in protest. When the issue went to court,
     the American Civil Liberties Union defended the Nazis' right to
     the exercise of free speech. The court ruled in the Nazis' favor.
     Challenges the doctrine of "content neutrality" and argues for
     the minimal abridgment of free speech when that speech is
     intentionally harmful.

433. FEDER, Gottfried. *Der Deutsche Staat auf nationaler und
     sozialer Grundlage* (The National and Social Foundations
     of the German State). Munich: Deutschvölkische
     Verlags-Buchhandlung, 1923.
     One of the earliest expressions of Nazi ideology by Gottfried
     Feder (1883-1941), economics adviser to Hitler in the formative
     days of the Nazi movement. Points to "new ways" in state fi-
     nance and industry. The idea of *Zinsknechtschaft* (interest-
     slavery) was at the core of Feder's teaching. Hitler later became
     convinced that Feder's views were impractical and he rewarded
     the early economics adviser with a humiliating minor position
     in the Nazi hierarchy. The *Führer* deserted the friend who
     dreamed of economic reform.

434. FODOR, M. W. "Austrian Roots of Hitlerism." *Foreign
     Affairs,* XIV (1936), 685-91.
     Concentrates on the Austrian background of Nazi ideology.
     Hitler's sojourning in Vienna, with its anti-Semitism widely
     advocated in cafes, was responsible for moulding much of
     Hitler's philosophy and ideology, especially the deep hatred for
     Jews.

435. FRICK, Wilhelm. *Germany Speaks.* Translated from the
     German. London: Butterworth, 1938.

Wilhelm Frick (1877-1946), Reich Minister of the Interior at the time of his book's publication in London, presents a case for the Nazi cause. The text is heavily weighted with National Socialist philosophy as a basis for the Nazi revolution.

436. GASMAN, Daniel. *The Scientific Origins of National Socialism: Social Darwinism in Ernst Haeckel and the German Monist League.* New York: American Elsevier, 1971.
Analyzes the Social Darwinism of Ernst Haeckel and the German Monist League. The author is concerned about what pseudo-science – or "scientism" – has done in the name of science. Writes about connections between the ideas of Haeckel and National Socialism. Haeckel presented racism, authoritarianism, militarism, imperialism, chauvinism and amoralism, all questionable as bad science and bad philosophy. Nazism accepted them and perverted Darwinism in Germany into a reactionary ideology.

437. GAUCH, Hermann. *Neue Grundlagen der Rassenforschung* (New Foundations of Racial Research). Leipzig: Klein, 1933.
A standard work by Nazi Professor Hermann Gauch was used in German classrooms to train students in all aspects of racism. Reclassifies the animal world into Nordic men and lower animals (other races, including Jews). "Generally speaking, the Nordic race alone can emit sounds of untroubled clearness, whereas among non-Nordics the pronunciation is impure, the individual sounds are more confused and like the noises made by animals, such as barking, snoring, sniffing and squeaking."

438. GILES, Geoffrey J. *Students and National Socialism in Germany.* Princeton, NJ: Princeton University Press, 1985.
Explains the rise and evaluates the strength of the National Socialist Students' Organization (NSDStB) from 1926 to 1945. While university students were subjected to Nazi coordination, their support for the NSDStB was mixed after 1933. The attempt to indoctrinate the entire student population was hindered by ineffective leadership, bureaucratic infighting and student apathy. Opposes the view that German university students offered special loyal support for National Socialism.

439. GLASER, Hermann. *The Cultural Roots of National Socialism.* Translated from the German by Ernest A. Menze. Austin, TX: University of Texas Press, 1978.
Glaser, an official in the education department of the City of Nuremberg, wrote his *Spiesser-Ideologie* in 1968, and this is its translation for the American public. Presents a polemic in which he deplores the decline of German early 19th-century intellectual traditions. Explains how the ideas of German classicism and romanticism were perverted into philistine mediocrity. Claims this change as being central to an understanding of National Socialism. Offers random quotations from Wagner, Rilke, Arndt and Hitler. Expresses great admiration for "German warmth and the German spirit."

440. GLUM, Friedrich. "Ideologische und soziologische Voraussetzung für die Entstehung von Nationalismus und Nationalsozialismus" (Ideological and Sociological Hypotheses for the Genesis of Nationalism and National Socialism). *Die Neue Rundschau*, LXIII (1952), 64-92.
Analyzes the ideas and sociological background which led the German people to accept Hitler and Nazism. Examines nationalism before and after World War I, with attention to the intellectual and cultural aspects of German nationalism with its pride in German *Kultur.* Shows how these facets of German ideology carried over into National Socialism. Devotes much attention to anti-Semitism in Germany.

441. GRUNFELD, Frederic V. *Prophets without Honour: A Background to Freud, Kafka, Einstein and Their World.* New York: Holt, Rinehart & Winston, 1979.
Sketches of 16 German-Jewish intellectuals, all brilliant thinkers who were forced to come to terms with their Jewish heritage in an increasingly hostile environment. Included are vignettes of Einstein, Kafka, Freud, Toller and others — dramatists, poets, novelists and critics. Most figured in the cultural renaissance of the Weimar Republic. All were subjected to unfair treatment in Hitler's Germany, at a time when anti-Semitism was equated with anti-intellectualism. Describes the background of these intellectuals and the circles in which they moved. Allows them to speak for themselves through their writings and letters.

442. *HACKETT, Francis. *What Mein Kampf Means to America.* New York: Reynal, 1941.

Writer Francis Hackett, who had never seen *Mein Kampf*, went
to a tropical island 1400 miles from New York and read it at the
rate of one-hundred pages a day. He was appalled by the book,
"the bible of dementia praecox." His main task was to make
Americans aware of the meaning and implications of Hitler's
blueprint for the future. Discusses the main points of Hitler's
ideology and illustrates them by passages from the book. Describes Hitler's nationalism, racialism, anti-Semitism, contempt
for democracy, political goals at home and abroad and challenge to Great Britain and the United States. Treats the
schizoid aspects of Hitler's character and personality. Considers Hitler's *Mein Kampf* a voice of destruction.

443. *HARTSHORNE, Edward Yarnall, Jr. *The German Universities
     and National Socialism.* Cambridge, MA: Harvard
     University Press, 1937.
Analyzes higher education in the Third Reich during the first
four years of its existence. The author's views differ strongly
from those of Germans with whom he had discussed the subject.
Treats the revolutionary background of university reform, the
reorganization of university administration, student body and
faculty, recasting of the academic curriculum and the new
university atmosphere. Offers excerpts from laws, official
correspondence, private letters and press comments. Describes
how, under the lash of Nazi ideology, the once-proud German
university system descended into an adolescent Spartan military
school complex. Concludes: "Germany is rapidly falling into
a quagmire of intellectual provincialism."

444. HERF, Jeffry. *Revolutionary Modernism: Technology, Culture,
     and Politics in Weimar and the Third Reich.* Cambridge
     (Eng.) and New York: Cambridge University Press, 1984.
Seeks to explain the cultural politics of those philosophical
irrationalists and political antimodernists who paradoxically
also supported technological modernization. Intellectuals in the
Weimar Republic and engineers in the Third Reich associated
technology with spirit and will rather than with materialism and
capitalism. Maintains that ideology was politically decisive
under National Socialism and that technology was regarded as
a reflection of the National Socialist "spirit." Gives attention
to the work of Ernst Jünger, Oswald Spengler, Martin
Heidegger, Carl Schmitt and Werner Sombart.

445. HERZSTEIN, Robert Edwin. *When Nazi Dreams Come True.*
      London: Abacus, 1982.
      Discusses the Nazi mentality from 1933 to 1945, with attention
      to internal struggles among the leaders of the Third Reich and
      their plans for the future of Europe after a German victory.

446. HINZ, Berthold. *Art in the Third Reich.* Translated from the
      German by Robert and Rita Kimber. New York:
      Pantheon, 1980.
      Reveals the well-known triviality of art in the Third Reich, de-
      voted mostly to propaganda on behalf of National Socialism.
      Presents a synthesis of Nazi esthetics and stresses social and
      political aspects of painting and sculpture. The high standards
      of most nations were threatened by Hitler's own personal views
      of art. The *Führer* denounced any modernistic trends as "de-
      generate art."

447. HITLER, Adolf. *Mein Kampf* (My Struggle). Translated from
      the German by Ralph Manheim. Boston: Houghton
      Mifflin, 1943.
      In *My Struggle*, Hitler presents the story of his life and his poli-
      tical program. Regarded inside the Third Reich as the bible of
      National Socialism, the book was also an accurate blueprint of
      what Hitler intended to do in the future. His own title originally
      was *Four and a Half Years of Struggle Against Lies, Stupidity,
      and Cowardice*, but publisher Max Amann shortened it to *Mein
      Kampf*. The book presents Hitler's views on nationalism,
      socialism, Jews, democracy, liberalism, parliamentarianism,
      Catholicism, Marxism and the French. The original edition was
      published in 1924; later versions corrected the innumerable
      grammatical errors. An enormous success in Germany, *Mein
      Kampf* sold 5.2 million copies by 1939 and was translated into
      many languages. Huge sales made Hitler a millionaire.

448. *HULL, David Stewart. *Film in the Third Reich: Art and
      Propaganda in the Third Reich.* New York: Simon &
      Schuster, 1973.
      Originally published by the University of California Press in
      1969, this is an account of Nazi movie-making between 1933
      and the end of World War II. From the beginning of the Nazi
      movement, Dr. Joseph Goebbels, especially, understood well
      the power of film and used it in his control of National Socialist
      art and propaganda. Describes the films that were made, who
      made them, and how it happened that these artists lent their

names to the Nazi movement. Gives his attention to all major actors and directors of the period, especially the work of Leni Riefenstahl. Shows how Goebbels managed the critics (1936) and then absorbed the industry (1937). Devotes a chapter to the anti-Semitic films of 1939-40.

449. JÄCKEL, Eberhard. *Hitler's Weltanschauung: A Blueprint for Power.* Translated from the German by Herbert Arnold. Middletown, CT: Wesleyan University Press, 1972.
The author, at the time of publication a professor at the University of Stuttgart, criticizes other writers on Hitler for neglecting his *Weltanschauung* (world-view). Claims that Hermann Rauschning was an opportunist, Harold Laski did not understand Hitler's commitment to doctrine, nor did Alan Bullock. Finds Hitler's world-view outlined in foreign policy. The *Führer* came gradually to the idea of aggression and opposed Jews because they were against German nationalism and the leader-principle. Presents Hitler's ideology in the *Führer's* own words, with accent on nihilism and racial theory. Emphasizes Hitler's overwhelming desire for political power.

450. JACKMAN, Jarrell C. and Carla M. BORDEN, eds. *The Muses Flee Hitler: Cultural Transfer and Adaptation, 1933-1945.* Washington, DC: Smithsonian Institution Press, 1983.
In 1980 the Smithsonian Institute held two colloquies to honor the centennial of Albert Einstein's birth. This volume consists of nineteen essays from those sessions on the experiences of émigrés from the Third Reich who were noted for their work in many disciplines. The collection deals with émigré migration not only to the United States, but to Great Britain, Canada, China and several countries in Latin America. The text confirms the singular importance of the United States for refugees from the Third Reich.

451. KAMENETSKY, Christa. *Children's Literature in Hitler's Germany.* Columbus, OH: Ohio University Press, 1984.
Describes Hitler's *Gleichschaltung*, the equalization or coordination of every institution in the Third Reich. The author, a former pupil in a Nazi school, relates the "new organicism" in school texts, festivals and holidays. Propaganda Minister Joseph Goebbels and Youth Leader Baldur von Schirach competed with one another to control the minds of children, the future citizens of the "Thousand-Year" Third Reich. Children's

literature in the Nazi milieu stressed absolute obedience to the *Führer*, service to nation and community, and "traditional" values of the German past. Contends that, despite strong efforts by Nazi leaders, the children preferred fairy tales, folklore and cowboy stories.

452. KETTELSON, Uwe-Karsten. *Völkisch-nationale und nationalsozialistische Literatur in Deutschland, 1890-1945* (*Völkisch*-national and National Socialist Literature in Germany, 1890-1945). Stuttgart: Metzler, 1975.
A bibliographical study which analyzes the national and National Socialist literature in Germany from 1890 through the Wilhelminian era, the Weimar Republic and Nazi Germany, presents the literary and cultural figures of the Third Reich. Attempts to place this literature in its social context.

453. *KOHN, Hans. *The Mind of Germany: The Education of a Nation.* New York: Scribner, 1960.
This intellectual history of modern Germany seeks a "tentative reply" to the question: how was it possible for a people with enormous prestige in scholarship, music, literature and philosophy deliberately to attempt national suicide? The answer: responsibility for the disaster must be taken by those Germans who rejected the humanitarian traditions of Western Europe. This alienation from the West was the great tragedy of German history. Nationalism led the Germans on an errant path. Devotes chapters to Goethe, *Turnvater* Jahn, Heinrich Heine and Richard Wagner. Shows how the romanticists placed excessive stress on Germanness, with deplorable later results. Worship of the state led to the excesses of Nazism.

454. KRISPYN, Egbert. *Anti-Nazi Writers in Exile.* Athens, GA: University of Georgia Press, 1978.
This overview of exiled German authors during World War II concludes that the writing of emigrants was ultimately futile and the literature they produced largely a failure due to the very nature of the exile experience. Examines the interdependence of the personal, political and literary qualities that marked the emigration.

455. LANE, Barbara Miller. *Architecture and Politics in Germany, 1918-1945.* Cambridge, MA: Harvard University Press, 1968, 1985.

A specialized study on the relation between architecture and politics in Germany from the end of World War I to the close of World War II. Analyzes Albert Speer (1905-81), Hitler's favorite architect and later Reich Minister for Armaments and War Production. The *Führer* hoped, through his personal relationship with Speer, to realize his youthful architectural ambitions. He commissioned Speer to design buildings for his New Order. Speer was to reconstruct Berlin and other German cities in Hitler's favored monumental, neoclassical style. This type of architecture was to represent the new grandiloquent Greater German Reich. For Hitler, the frustrated architect, his new architecture was to reflect Nazi politics.

456. LANE, Barbara Miller and Leila J. RUPP, translators. *Nazi Ideology before 1933: A Documentation.* Austin, TX: University of Texas Press, 1978.
An anthology of early writings by leading Nazi ideologists, including translations of works by Dietrich Eckart, Alfred Rosenberg, Gottfried Feder, Joseph Goebbels and Heinrich Himmler, as well as party manifestoes and programs. The Munich group (Feder, Eckart and Rosenberg) stressed anti-Semitism, the "Jewish-Bolshevik conspiracy" and the breaking of "interest-slavery" (Feder). Describes and evaluates the significance of each Nazi theorist.

457. *LILGE, Frederic. *The Abuse of Learning: The Failure of the German University.* New York: Macmillan, 1948.
Notes the failure of German higher education during the Nazi regime. "Deeply though I learned to hate during the last fourteen years, as others did who had a living relation to German culture, I have not written to condemn but to understand." Shows how the universities fared under Nazi *Gleichschaltung* (coordination). With Hitler there came dismissals, political appointments and promotions, the burning of books, political censorship and "racial science." Most German professors acquiesced in these developments. "To protest individually, in the absence of united resistance, required more courage than the ordinary man possessed."

458. *MALTITZ, Horst von. *The Evolution of Hitler's Germany: The Ideology, The Personality, The Moment.* New York: McGraw-Hill, 1973.
Presented not as a history of the events but as an examination of the major ideas forming the ideology of National Socialism.

Analyzes and traces in history such components as race theories, *Lebensraum* (living space), anti-Semitism, the Germanic cult, romanticism, nationalism and militarism. Devotes special attention to the German-Jewish relationship and its specific causes. Estimates the extraordinary personality of Hitler, and above all, seeks to show that National Socialism was not merely an aberration in German history but the culmination of a long intellectual development, pushed to extremes by a brutal, abnormal leader.

459. *MANN, Erika. *School for Barbarians: Education Under the Nazis.* New York: Modern Age, 1938.
Erika Mann, daughter of novelist Thomas Mann, denounces the system of education under the Nazis. Reveals how Hitler, in his attempt to break violently with the intellectualism of the Weimar Republic, subjected the entire German educational system to his policy of coordination. He wanted to knock weakness out of children and create an active, dominating, brutal youth. The previous German high educational standards were destroyed and the new German youths were transformed into barbarians. Dispels any wishful thinking about the passing character of Nazism. In the introduction Thomas Mann summarizes Nazi education as a revolt against civilization: "The issue is clear: it is a radical renunciation – ascetic in the worst sense of the word – of the claims of the mind and spirit; and in these words I include the conceptions truth, knowledge, justice – in short, all the highest and purest endeavors of which humanity is capable."

460. MANN, Klaus. "Cowboy Mentor of the *Führer.*" *The Living Age*, CLIV (1940), 217-22.
Karl May was a prolific Sudeten-German author who wrote scores of novels about cowboys and Indians in the United States, although he had never been in America. His books were enormously popular with the German public. Among his dedicated readers was Adolf Hitler, both during his early days and later years. Contends that the *Führer's* blustering ways imitated the cowboy heroes described in May's novels.

461. *MANN, Thomas. *An Exchange of Letters.* Translated by H. T. Lowe-Porter. New York: Knopf, 1937.
When the University of Bonn, responding to demands by Nazi authorities, cancelled Thomas Mann's honorary degree, the famous novelist replied in a scathing denunciation on 13 Decem-

ber 1936. "To what a pass, in less than four years, have they brought Germany. Ruined, sucked dry body and soul by armaments with which they threaten the whole world, holding up the whole world and hindering it in its real task of peace, loved by nobody, regarded with fear and cold aversion by all, it stands on the brink of economic disaster....*God help our darkened and desecrated country and teach it to make its peace with the world and with itself.*"

462. *MANN, Thomas. *Order of the Day.* New York: Knopf, 1942.
German novelist Thomas Mann, called a Goethe in modern formal dress, presents a collection of his political speeches and essays covering the previous two decades. In these chapters, turning from creative work to the business of politics, he discusses National Socialism and the devastation it caused for German culture.

463. MASER, Werner. *Hitler's Mein Kampf.* Translated from the German by Richard Barry. London: Faber & Faber, 1970.
A German specialist on the Nazi regime, Werner Maser presents a study of *Mein Kampf,* the autobiography which outlined Hitler's future course of action. Few readers at the time of its publication understood that the Nazi leader intended to implement every phase of his stated program. These arguments were designed to appeal to every dissatisfied element in German society. His proposals turned out to be remarkably effective in winning mass support for Nazi ideology.

464. *MOSSE, George L. *The Crisis of German Ideology: Intellectual Origins of the Third Reich.* New York: Grosset & Dunlap, 1964.
George L. Mosse, Professor of History at the University of Wisconsin, reports that other scholars have found the ideas underlying National Socialism so nebulous and incomprehensible that they have dismissed them as unimportant. To correct this void in intellectual history, he presents what he believes to be the real story. Sees the ideological base of National Socialism as deeply embedded in German history. Regards the 19th and 20th centuries as the critical era, when anti-liberal and anti-democratic ideology became institutionalized in political parties, veterans' groups and youth movements. Hitler transformed the "German Revolution" into an "anti-Jewish Revolution," and his political program fully assimilated such ideas.

465. *MOSSE, George L., ed. *Nazi Culture: Intellectual, Cultural, and Social Life in the Third Reich.* Translated from the German by Salvator Attanasio and others. New York: Grosset & Dunlap, 1966.

The author of *The Crisis of German Ideology* (1964) presents a collection of materials intended to show what life was like under Hitler and the Nazis. Offer excerpts from diaries, plays, novels, newspaper articles, Hitler's speeches, church officials and university professors. Mosse covers the National Socialist revolution, racism, myths and heroes, science and the Nazi state, education and Christianity. Provides a detailed introduction as well as comments on each selection. New editions were published by Schocken Books in 1981 and 1986.

466. NORTON, Donald H. "Karl Haushofer and the German Academy, 1925-1945." *Central European History*, I (1968), 80-99.

Karl Haushofer (1869-1948), founder of German geopolitics, called for a fusion of geography and politics. Some scholars consider part of his work to be sound science, but other critics deemed it as immature pseudoscience, equipped with a flashy terminology and filled with half-truths. Believing the British Empire to be in decline, Haushofer urged Germany to seek *Lebensraum* (living space) in the east, with the agricultural Ukraine to be appended to the industrial German *Herzland* (heartland). Shows how Haushofer tried to restore German prestige after 1919 by founding the German Academy to promote his views. By 1935, its activities were in decline and Haushofer was displaced as its leader. The Academy then was taken over by Goebbels and the Nazi propaganda machine.

467. PETZOLD, Joachim. "Zur Funktion des Nationalismus, Moeller van den Brucks Beitrag zur faschistischen Ideologie" (On the Function of Nationalism, Moeller van den Bruck's Contribution to Fascist Ideology). *Zeitschrift für Geschichtswissenschaft*, XXI (1973), 1285-1300.

Among German historians there has been a spirited difference of opinion as to whether Arthur Moeller van den Bruck was a Fascist forerunner of Hitler and Nazism or not. Leader of the conservatives during the Weimar era, Moeller presented "the mystique of the national idea" and urged the formation of "a new German self-consciousness." The author stresses Moeller's affinities to the Nazis and shows that his view of nationalism was to utilize it as a weapon to displace Weimar and Versailles.

Moeller's *Das Dritte Reich* (The Third Empire) (1923) provided Nazi Germany with its dramatic name. Petzold concludes that this conservative intellectual was, indeed, a forerunner of Hitler.

468. POIS, Robert, ed. *Race and Race History and Other Essays by Alfred Rosenberg.* New York: Harper & Row, 1970.
Alfred Rosenberg (1893-1946) was the leading proponent of National Socialist ideology, semi-official "philosopher" of the Party, and later head of the Foreign Affairs Department of the Third Reich. Moody, retiring, but glibly persuasive, he edged into Hitler's inner coterie and managed to stay there. In his works he depicted history as a perennial struggle between the glorious Nordic spirit and the corrupting influence of inferior races. He denounced Christianity as a product of the Semitic-Latin spirit and as a dangerous Judaic concept. He reserved his utmost contempt for the Catholic Church, and demanded that the white race be freed from disruptive Etruscan-Syrio-Judaic-Asiatic-Catholic influence. This edition of the Rosenberg works includes an introduction analyzing his ideology, which the editor explains as originating in early 19th-century German Romanticism and influenced by *völkisch* nationalism.

469. *RAUSCHNING, Hermann. *The Revolution of Nihilism: Warning to the West.* Translated from the German by E. W. Dickes. New York: Alliance, 1939.
Alienated from National Socialism, Hermann Rauschning fled to Switzerland, where, safe from Nazi authorities, he published a series of books exposing corruption in the Third Reich. Shows the nihilistic character of National Socialism and warns about its dangers. This book informed the free world that Hitler would stop at nothing to satisfy his lust for power. It points to the Party creed: "We all believe, on this earth, in Adolf Hitler, our Führer, and we acknowledge that National Socialism is the only creed that can bring salvation to our country." Heinrich Himmler placed Rauschning's name on his Special Search List, the Nazi black list of enemies subject to vengeance if caught.

470. *RAUSCHNING, Hermann. *The Voice of Destruction.* New York: Putnam, 1940.
Hermann Rauschning was the former President of the Danzig Senate, who turned on Hitler in 1935 and fled to Switzerland. Originally published under the title *Gespräche mit Hitler* (Conversations with Hitler), this English translation describes

Rauschning's many talks with Hitler in which the *Führer* exhibited his nihilistic ideology. Describes Hitler's rages: "He was an alarming sight, his hair disheveled, his eyes fixed, and his face distorted and purple. I feared that he might collapse or have a stroke." Rauschning writes of Hitler's complaint of the ingratitude of the German people "in the sobbing voice of a down-at-the-heel music-hall performer." Presents Hitler and National Socialism as barbaric throwbacks in German history. The early insider of the Nazi movement turned on it after witnessing Nazi brutality and atrocities.

471. RISTOW, Erich. *Erbsgesundheitsrecht* (Heredity Right Law). Stuttgart and Berlin: Kohlhammer Verlag, 1935.
      A Nazi publication on heredity health law. Proposes compulsory sterilization to promote the strength of the "Aryan race."

472. RITCHIE, James MacPherson. *German Literature under National Socialism.* London: Helm, 1983; Totowa, NJ: Barnes & Noble, 1983.
      A British Germanist discusses pre-Nazi and Nazi literature. Analyzes nationalist-conservative traditions which opposed the "decadence" of the Weimar Republic. Critically examines the literature produced in Nazi Germany both for and against the regime; describes the anti-Fascist works of German exiles; and discusses the literary output during the period since 1945. Devotes much attention to the works of the Mann family. Emphasizes literary production rather than the historical and political circumstances of the era.

473. ROSENBERG, Alfred. *Der Mythos des 20. Jahrhunderts: Eine Wertung der seelisch-geistigen Gestaltenkämpfe unserer Zeit* (The Myth of the Twentieth Century: An Evaluation of the Psychical-Spiritual Formative Struggles of Our Time). Munich: Hoheneichen-Verlag, 1930 *ff.*
      "Masterpiece" by one of Hitler's earliest mentors and semi-official philosopher of National Socialism, Rosenberg's *The Myth of the Twentieth Century* was secondary only to Hitler's *Mein Kampf* as the "bible" of National Socialism. Influenced by the racial theories of Comte de Gobineau and Houston Stewart Chamberlain's *The Foundations of the Nineteenth Century,* which inspired his work, Rosenberg defends the mystique of blood purity. Everything in life, he writes, depends upon racial substance. "The Mythos is the Myth of the Blood, which, under the aegis of the Swastika, released the World Revolution.

It is the awakening of the soul of the Race, which, after a period of long slumber, victoriously put an end to Racial Chaos." Excoriates Jews and denounces Christianity as a dangerous product of the Semitic-Latin spirit and a disintegrative Jewish concept. Rosenberg's book systematized the official philosophy of National Socialism.

474. ROSENBERG, Alfred. *Letzte Aufzeichnung* (Final Inventory). Göttingen: Plesse Verlag, 1958.
The final papers of Hitler's early mentor who eventually became the official philosopher of National Socialism. Presents Rosenberg's views on nationalism, Communism and the Jews. Rosenberg was hanged at Nuremberg on 16 October 1946.

475. ROXAN, David and Ken WANSTALL. *The Rape of Art: The Story of Hitler's Plunder of the Great Masterpieces of Europe.* New York: Coward, McCann, 1965.
The story of Hitler's plunder of the great masterpieces of European art based on a report in the U.S. Army Archives listing Nazi thefts of art treasures. The authors describe Allied efforts to recover stolen art works and restore them to their rightful owners. Call Hitler "the greatest looter of all time," and reveal his intention to establish a huge museum in his home town of Linz. They present long quotations from the documents and details of personal intrigues among the Nazis who vied with one another in stealing valuable objects of art.

476. RYAN, Judith. *The Uncompleted Past: German Novels and the Third Reich.* Detroit, MI: Wayne State University Press, 1983.
Intends to show how postwar German novelists confronted the problems of the Nazi past. Analyzes such books as Günter Grass' *The Tin Drum* (1963) and its place in the sociological interpretation of Nazism. Emphasizes the role of moral consciousness in the work of German authors writing about the Nazi regime.

477. SALOMON, Ernst von. *Der Fragebogen* (The Questionnaire). Hamburg: Rowohlt Verlag, 1951.
After the defeat of Germany in 1945, occupation authorities issued several detailed questionnaires (*Fragebogen*) as a basis for denazification. The questionnaires were served on all Germans suspected of having directed, assisted or collaborated with National Socialists from 1933 to 1945. Salomon, a former right-

wing activist, seeks to disassociate himself from the taint of
Nazism and offers a spirited defense of the German people
against individual or collective guilt for the crimes of Nazism.
Throughout, he uses a tone of amused cynicism and mockery.
The book was enormously successful in Germany, where it sold
one-half million copies within three years.

478. SMITH, Woodruf D. *The Ideological Origins of Nazi
      Imperialism.* New York: Oxford University Press, 1986.
      Maintains that Nazism drew upon the imperialist ideologies
      before and during the Weimar era, including the demand for
      Lebensraum, more land to accommodate Germany's growth,
      and *Weltpolitik,* a "world-policy" directed toward the achieve-
      ment of Germany's economic success.

479. STACKELBERG, Roderick. *Idealism Debased: From Völkisch
      Ideology to National Socialism.* Kent, OH: Kent State
      University Press, 1981.
      In interpreting the intellectual basis for the acceptance of Hitler
      in Germany, the author concentrates on such German *völkisch*
      writers as the novelist and playwright Friedrich Lienhart and
      the racial ideologist Houston Stewart Chamberlain. All these
      "self-styled idealists" projected their own egocentrism on Jews.
      These were the "intellectuals" who helped poison the German
      mind with spurious theories of racial purity and racial superi-
      ority, for which there is not the least scientific evidence.

480. *STERN, Fritz. *The Politics of Cultural Despair: A Study of the
      Rise of Germanic Ideology.* Berkeley, CA: University of
      California Press, 1961; Garden City, NY: Doubleday,
      1965.
      Fritz Stern, Professor of History at Columbia University, ana-
      lyzes the work of Julius Langbehn, Paul Lagarde and Arthur
      Moeller van den Bruck, who were responsible for laying the
      intellectual groundwork for National Socialism and the Third
      Reich. He attempts to find the contributory factors to National
      Socialist ideology. The men presented in this book were the real
      progenitors of National Socialism. Directs attention to shoddy
      and pernicious intellectualism, whose effects were catastrophic.

481. STERN, J. P. *Hitler: The Führer and the People.* Berkeley, CA:
      University of California Press, 1978.
      Believes that Hitler's hold over the German people can be ex-
      plained best in terms of the language the *Führer* used and the

emotions that language aroused. Emphasizes not so much the man as the words he used. Hitler, allegedly, catered to the religious expectations, anxieties and longings of a troubled people. German society was reshaped by the Nazi language and interpretation of cultural values. Maintains that the ideology of National Socialism was already current throughout Europe before World War I, and that its implementation in Germany reflected a wider European audience.

482. TAYLOR, Robert R. *The Word in Stone: The Role of Architecture in the National Socialist Ideology.* Berkeley, CA: University of California Press, 1974.
Contends that Hitler was not, as previously supposed, the dictator in architecture that he was in politics. Although fascinated by art and working hand-in-hand with Albert Speer, the *Führer* was not really able to turn architecture into the direction he favored. Doubts the effectiveness of Nazi propaganda in changing words into stones. Believes that a surprising variety of architectural forms continued to exist during the Third Reich era.

483. UWE, Dietrich Adam. *Hochschule und Nationalsozialismus: Die Universität Tübingen im Dritten Reich* (Higher Education and National Socialism: Tübingen University in the Third Reich). Tübingen: Mohr, 1977.
This specialized study of the University of Tübingen during the National Socialist era argues that despite the "Aryan character" of the faculty, the university managed to survive because of the faculty's will to resist interference and control by the Reich government and the Nazi Party. Insists that the faculty opposed in principle the *Führer*-principle.

484. *VIERECK, Peter. *Metapolitics: The Roots of the Nazi Mind.* New York: Knopf, 1941; New York: Putnam, 1961.
A revised and enlarged version of Peter Viereck's *Metapolitics: From the Romantics to Hitler*, originally published by Knopf in 1941. Viereck, poet and historian, winner of the Pulitzer Prize for Poetry, sees certain elements of Nazi philosophy in German Romantic poetry. From such sources he traces Nazi irrationalism and hysteria and a special belief in a German mission to control the history of the world. Digs deeply with his analysis of Romanticism. Describes two souls in action from 1648 to 1848; discusses Father Jahn, "the first Storm Trooper," and analyzes the evil metapolitics of composer Richard Wagner.

Devotes one chapter to the confrontation between Nazi religion and Christianity.

485. VOGT, Hannah. *The Burden of Guilt: A Short History of Germany, 1914-1945*. Translated from the German by Herbert Strauss. New York: Oxford University Press, 1964.

This brief history of Germany from 1914 to 1945, intended for the younger generation, sold more than 250,000 copies in Germany within a year of publication. Written with the assumption that young Germans were not getting a sufficient account of the Nazi years, the author demolishes the kind of myths that have distorted historical instruction in the past: the stab-in-the-back legend of World War I; the story of the "legality" of Hitler's assumption of power; the theory that Hitler was a sincere lover of peace; that World War II came against his will; and that Germany could have won the war. Stresses the burden of guilt.

486. WEINGARTNER, James J. "The SS Race and Settlement Office: Towards an Orden of Blood and Soil." *Historian*, XXXIV (1971), 62-77.

Emphasizing the concept of Blood and Soil, the SS Race and Settlement Office, administered by agricultural expert Richard Walther Darré, was supposed to implement Hitler's program of racial purification and agricultural revolution. A prolific author on such subjects as race, Marxism and agriculture, Darré was Hitler's watchdog on racial matters from 1931 on.

487. WEINRICH, Max. *Hitler's Professors*. New York: Yivo, 1946.

A narrative text and explanatory documents reveal how the Third Reich's intellectual community supported Hitler's anti-Jewish program. The author comes to the same conclusion as other scholars working in the field, that is, that the German universities, long a stronghold of academic freedom, succumbed to the dictatorship ingloriously. The book should be used together with such studies as Edward Yarnall Hartshorne, *The German Universities and National Socialism* (1937) and Frederic Lilge, *The Abuse of Learning: The Failure of the German University* (1948).

488. WERNER, Karl Ferdinand. *Das N.S.-Geschichtsbild und die deutsche Geschichtswissenschaft* (The National Socialist

Historical Picture and German Historical Science).
Stuttgart: Kohlhammer Verlag, 1967.
A German professor discusses the attitude of German historians
during the Nazi era, and maintains that most of them were not
committed Nazis but were ready to accept Nazi ideology because it did not differ very much from their own conservative-
authoritarian and racist views. Although some German
historians as scholars questioned Nazi views, they made certain
to protect themselves by carefully phrased references to the
ideas promulgated by Hitler.

489. WULF, Josef. *Die bildene Künste im Dritten Reich* (The Plastic
Arts in the Third Reich). Gütersloh: Mohn, 1963.
Analyzes the plastic arts in Nazi Germany with attention to
their use for propaganda, and the decline of the arts to meet the
standards set by Hitler. Most modern art forms were judged to
be "degenerate" in the opinion of "artist" Hitler. Discusses the
policy of *Gleichschaltung* (coordination) and the work of Dr.
Joseph Goebbels and his propaganda ministry.

490. WULF, Josef. *Presse und Funk im Dritten Reich* (Press and
Radio in the Third Reich). Gütersloh: Mohn, 1964.
Presents the story of the press and radio in National Socialist
Germany, showing how both were used in the critical task of
propagandizing Nazi ideology and Hitler's leadership.

491. WUNDERLICH, Frieda. "Education in Nazi Germany." *Social Research*, IV (1937), 342-69.
Shows the catastrophic decline of education in the Third Reich
during the years when it was revised to meet the standards of
dictatorship. Hitler's hostility to teachers, professors and intellectuals in general influenced the Nazi hierarchy to adopt a
similar attitude.

492. *ZIEMER, Gregor. *Education for Death: The Making of the
Nazi.* New York: Oxford University Press, 1941; London:
Constable, 1942.
Examines the Nazi educational system in the midst of World
War II, showing how Hitler's "reforms" were designed to create
a new youth without weakness or tenderness. "I want to see
once more in its eyes the gleam of pride and independence of the
beast of prey." The idea was to prepare German youth for war.
Offers evidence to support this thesis. The German educational
system had been a model for the world: organization of study

from kindergarten to university, the status of teachers and the nature of the curriculum were admired everywhere. Hitler's opposition to intellectual training ("Knowledge is ruin to my young men") turned German education upside down. It was truly an "education for death."

493. ZORTMAN, Bruce. *Hitler's Theater: Ideological Drama in Nazi Germany*. El Paso, TX: Firestein Books, 1984.
This study of ideological drama in Nazi Germany shows how stage presentations were used to promote the propaganda of Dr. Goebbels.

CHAPTER 8

RELIGION IN THE THIRD REICH

*Catholicism, Protestantism, "Positive Christianity,"
Confessional Church*

Hitler was born a Roman Catholic but turned against Christianity in his later years. He rejected it as an alien force, foreign to the pure racial Aryanism of the Germans. "Antiquity," he said, "was better than modern times because it did not know Christianity and syphilis." He saw Christianity as siding with everything weak, as purely Oriental and undesirable. He called Christian ideas of forgiveness of sin, resurrection and salvation as nonsense. He denounced the idea of mercy as dangerous. Christian love was silly. The Christian idea of equality of all human beings meant to him that the inferior, the ill, the crippled, the criminal and the weak were protected.

Once in power, Hitler became involved in a war with the Catholic and Protestant Churches, both of which he would mold into his system of coordination. Realizing the strength of both religions in Germany, he decided to move slowly, biding his time until he was ready to strike. In 1935 he decreed the supremacy of the Nazi state over Protestantism by closing its schools and seizing its property. Some Protestant pastors accepted his domination, others, notably Martin Niemoeller and Dietrich Bonhoeffer, refused to bow to his will. At first he concluded a Concordat with the Catholic Church, but soon turned on it by arresting monks and nuns and accusing them of smuggling gold out of Germany. He censored the Catholic press, forbade Catholic religious processions and banned pastoral letters. On 21 March 1937, Pope Pius XI issued an encyclical, or papal letter, on Germany titled *Mit brennender Sorge* (With Deep Anxiety), which accused Hitler of breaking his pact with the Church and which charged that he had exposed Catholics to "violence as illegal as it was inhuman."

Hitler set up his own version of what he called "Positive Christianity," a German National Church with an Aryan clergy and an Aryan élite. His new religion would throw out the Old Testament, regard Christ not as Jewish but as a Nordic martyr, substitute the swastika for the cross, and emphasize German land, German blood, German soul and German art. Recalcitrant Protestant theologians rejected this Nazi version of religion and established the Confessional Church, a counter-movement opposed to Hitler's pagan cult of blood, race and soil.

Theologians opposed to Hitler could not very well publish during the life of the Hitler regime. But in the postwar era a number of books appeared detailing the struggle of Protestants and Catholics against the state during the twelve years of the Hitler regime. Studies also appeared accusing Pope Pius XII and Franklin D. Roosevelt of not having done enough to rescue the Jews in the Third Reich from a terrible fate. Those churchmen who gave their lives in the struggle against Hitler, especially Pastor Dietrich Bonhoeffer, were honored.

BIBLIOGRAPHY

494. BONHOEFFER, Dietrich. *Gesammelte Schriften* (Collected Works). Munich: Kaiser, 1958.
    The first volume of the collected works of Pastor Dietrich Bonhoeffer (1906-45), evangelical theologian executed because of his opposition to Hitler. A leader of the Confessional Church, which maintained that Christianity was incompatible with National Socialism and its racial doctrine, Bonhoeffer maintained in his writing that the Church was only a church "when she exists outside herself." The Church had an unconditional obligation toward the victims of every social system, even if they did not belong to the church community. His support for "a religionless Christianity" had much influence among Protestants.

495. CONWAY, John S. *The Nazi Persecution of the Churches, 1933-1945.* New York: Basic Books, 1968.
    Shows the methods Hitler used to dominate and control religion in Germany. Calls the treatment of religions "a sad tale of betrayal, timidity, and unbelief." At first the Churches hailed Hitler as "the redeemer of German history," and their leaders

showed irresolution and weakness. Catalogs the various means Nazis used in harassing religions and describes how totalitarianism ruled all aspects of German life. Claims that the Third Reich confiscated Church property and charged ministers with sexual perversion and currency smuggling.

496. DUCLOS, E. P. *La Vatican et le seconde guerre mondiale* (The Vatican and the Second World War). Paris: Pedone, 1955. Discusses the Vatican's silence during the genocidal policies of Hitler, with his concentration and extermination camps in World War II.

497. FALCONE, C. *The Silence of Pius XII.* London: Faber & Faber, 1970.
The documentation by the Holy See in 1966 defending its position on National Socialism did not halt the continuing controversy about the role of Pius XII in the matter of Hitler's persecution of the Jews. This book was typical of the confrontation.

498. FRIEDLÄNDER, Saul. *Pius XII and the Third Reich: A Documentation.* Translated from the French and German by Charles Fullman. New York: Knopf, 1966.
Presents a selection of documents (without access to Vatican archives) to show that Pope Pius XII seemed to have a predilection which apparently did not diminish by the nature of the Nazi regime and which he did not disavow until 1944. Writes that Pius XII feared the Bolshevization of Europe more than anything else. At the end of 1943, according to the author, the Pope and the highest Church dignitaries were still wishing for victorious Nazi resistance in the East. Friedländer's parents were killed at Auschwitz, and the author was hidden in a Catholic monastery until the end of the war.

499. GESCHICHTSVEREIN DER DIÖZESE ROTTENBURG-STUTTGART. *Kirche im Nationalsozialismus* (The Church in National Socialism). Sigmaringen: Thorbecke, 1984.
A collection of papers read at a 1983 conference on the fiftieth anniversary of the Nazi assumption of political power. Academics and surviving participants in the diocese offer eyewitness recollections of the Catholic Church's life in this corner of the former Third Reich. Articles on Nazi persecution of Catholics in the locality, Catholic organizations and the Catholic press

attempt to reconstruct the Catholic milieu under Hitler and the atmosphere of a religious community faced with great dangers.

500.   GURIAN, Waldemar. *Hitler and the Christians.* New York: Sheed & Ward, 1936.
Explains that Adolf Hitler was born into a Catholic family, and at the age of eight his highly religious mother sent him to a monastery school in the hope that he would eventually become a monk. He was expelled when caught smoking on monastery grounds. During his political career he developed a contempt for Christianity and especially for its teaching of forgiveness and turning the other cheek. As Chancellor of Germany in 1933, he inaugurated campaigns to coordinate Catholics and Protestants into his Third Reich, a goal which involved suppression of both denominations. Hitler favored "Positive Christianity," the religious philosophy projected by his ideologist Alfred Rosenberg. Its goals were to purify the German Nordic "race," harmonize belief in Christ with "the laws of blood and soil," restore old Nordic pagan values and substitute the spirit of the hero for that of the Crucifixion. Christianity would then emerge as a new religion and become one with the old Norse paganisms. This German Faith movement came into existence in 1934, with little of Christianity remaining in it.

501.   HARRIGAN, William H. "Nazi Germany and the Holy See, 1933-1936: The Historical Background of *Mit brennender Sorge*." *The Catholic Historical Review*, XLVII (1961), 164-73.
Presents historical information on the papal encyclical *Mit brennender Sorge* (With Deep Anxiety). The alternate title of the encyclical was *On the Condition of the Church in Germany*. Issued on 14 March 1937, by Pope Pius XI, the text accused the Nazi administration of violating the 1933 Concordat between the Third Reich and the Holy See, which had guaranteed "freedom of the profession and the public exercise of the Catholic Religion." Concentrates on the three years preceding the papal encyclical.

502.   HEHL, Ulrich von. *Priester unter Hitlers Terror* (Priests under the Hitler Terror). Mainz: Matthias-Grünewald-Verlag, 1984.
A biographical and statistical account of Catholic priests under the Hitlerite terror, a study sponsored by the German Bishops'

Conference. Obtained much of the material from the Diocesan
Archives.

503. HELMREICH, Ernst C. "The Arrest and Freeing of the
      Protestant Bishops of Württemberg and Bavaria,
      September-October, 1934." *Central European History*, II
      (1969), 159-69.
      To consolidate his power, Hitler subjected every institution in
      the Third Reich to his will. He was especially intent to bring all
      German Churches into line, including Catholics and
      Protestants. The *Gestapo* arrested pastors, priests, nuns and
      monks on charges of currency violations or sexual misbehavior.
      Discusses the arrest of Protestant bishops in two German states
      in September-October 1934 and their subsequent release.

504. *HELMREICH, Ernst C. *The German Churches Under Hitler:
      Background, Struggle and Epilogue.* Detroit: Wayne State
      University Press, 1979.
      Analyzes the background and struggle of the German Churches
      in the Third Reich. Describes the opposition or accom-
      modation which took place, the reasons for the strength or
      weakness of resistance, conflicts among ecclesiastics and the
      ultimate legacy of the struggle. Mainly aims to reveal the clash
      between national leaders and national institutions. Shows how
      German policy and national events affected state policy toward
      religion. Records the responses of Catholic, Lutheran, Re-
      formed and Free Churches to Nazi rule.

505. HERMELINE, Heinrich. *Kirche im Kampf* (The Church in
      Struggle). Tübingen-Stuttgart: Rainer Wunderlich, 1950.
      Examines the struggle of the Catholic and Protestant Churches
      against the Hitler regime and its efforts to bring them into line
      with Nazi ideology.

506. HIRT, Simon, ed. *Mit brennender Sorge: Das päpstliche
      Rundschreiben gegen den Nationalsozialismus und seine
      Folgen in Deutschland* (With Deep Anxiety: The Papal Cir-
      cular Letter against National Socialism and Its Conse-
      quences in Germany). Freiburg-im-Breisgau: Herder,
      1946.
      Study devoted to the papal encyclical, *Mit brennender Sorge*
      (With Deep Anxiety) (opening words of the encyclical), an
      alternate title for the papal letter to the clergy, *On the Condition
      of the Church in Germany*, issued by Pope Pius XI on 14 March

1937. The Pope accused the Nazi government of violating the 1933 Concordat between the Third Reich and the Holy See. Text and comments.

507.   HOCKERTS, Hans Günther. *Die Sittlichkeitsprozesse gegen katholische Ordensangehörige und Priester, 1936-1937* (The Morals Trials against Members of Catholic Orders and Priests, 1936-1937). Mainz: Matthias-Grünewald-Verlag, 1971.
A treatise on the approximately 230 lawsuits between 1936 and 1937 by the Nazi regime against Catholic priests and lay brothers on accusations of homosexuality. Claims that the charges were substantially correct, especially against lay brothers. Dr. Joseph Goebbels, Minister for Public Enlightenment and Propaganda, gave the proceedings more than usual publicity. The propaganda campaign backfired and did not lead, as Goebbels hoped, to an inner loyalty crisis within the German Churches. Discusses the strengths and limitations of Catholic resistance to Nazism.

508.   KÜNNETH, Walter. *Die evangelisch-lutherische Theologie und die Widerstandsrechte* (Evangelical-Lutheran Theology and the Rights of Resistance). Munich: Hermann Rinn, 1956.
Presents the thesis of the conflict between evangelical Lutheran theology and Nazi ideology, with emphasis upon the justification for resistance to the effort to coordinate the Churches into the Nazi system.

509.   LEWY, Guenter. *The Catholic Church and Nazi Germany*. New York: McGraw-Hill, 1964.
In his preface the author concedes the controversial nature of the subject matter. Lewy left his native Germany at the age of fifteen and became an academician specializing in political science at several American universities. Examining German diocesan documents and diplomatic papers, he concludes that the German Catholic Church sympathized with some Nazi policies and programs. Sees the papacy as remaining silent, charges the episcopate with supporting Hitler's expansionist policies and of failing to encourage resistance against Hitler. In the face of the greatest moral depravities, the moral teachings of the Catholic Church, dedicated to love and charity, could be heard in no other form than "vague generalities."

510. LEWY, Guenter. "Pius XII, the Jews, and the German Catholic Church." *Commentary*, XXXVII (1964), 23-5.

 After 1945, Pope Pius XII was subjected to intense criticism because of his alleged silence in the face of Nazi mass murder: "We cannot offer them [the Jews] effective help other than our prayers." Asserts that Pius XII did not look upon the plight of the Jews with expected sense of moral outrage or real urgency. The issue provoked a long controversy, of which this essay is one expression.

511. NEUHÄUSER, Johann. *Kreuz und Hakenkreuz* (Cross and Swastika). Munich: Verlag Katholische Kirche Bayerns, 1946.

 Published under the imprint of the Catholic Church of Bavaria, this study is concerned with the struggle of National Socialism against the Catholic Church and the ecclesiastical resistance against Hitler. The title, *Cross and Swastika*, is designed to show the distance between two ways of life.

512. *PIUS XI. *Mit brennender Sorge: Das päpstliche Rundschreiben gegen den Nationalsozialismus und seine Folgen in Deutschland* (With Deep Anxiety: The Papal Circular Letter against National Socialism and Its Consequences in Germany). Washington, DC: National Catholic Welfare Conference, 1937.

 This is the official text of the 1937 papal encyclical "With Deep Anxiety," in which Pope Piux XI expressed worry about the future of the Catholic Church in the Third Reich. Read from all Catholic pulpits in Germany, this was the first direct involvement of the papacy in the Nazi-Catholic controversy. Accuses the Third Reich of violating the terms of the 1933 Concordat with the Church, which had guaranteed freedom of exercise for the Catholic religion in Nazi Germany. Denounces the persecution of Catholics "as illegal as it is inhuman." "With personal emotion we feel and suffer profoundly with those who have paid such a great price for their attachment to Christ and to the Church."

513. PRIEPKE, Manfred. *Die evangelische Jugend im Dritten Reich, 1933-1936* (Evangelical Youth in the Third Reich, 1933-1936). Hanover: Norddeutsche Verlagsanstalt, 1960.

 A treatise on the reactions of German Protestant youth to the coordination efforts of the Nazi regime during the first three years of its existence. Hitler's goal was to turn the minds of

German youth from their churches to the new religion – "Positive Christianity," which did not recognize the Christian principle of turning the other cheek.

514. SCHMEINMANN, M. *Der Vatikan im Zweiten Weltkrieg* (The Vatican in World War II). Berlin: Dietz, 1954.
Discusses the Vatican's silence during World War II, in the early stage of a bitter controversy on the subject.

515. SCHOLDER, Klaus. "Die evangelische Kirche in der Sicht der nationalsozialistischen Führung bis zum Kriegsausbruch" (The Evangelical Church in the View of the National Socialist Leadership until the Outbreak of War). *Vierteljahrshefte für Zeitgeschichte*, XVI (1968), 15-35.
Analyzes the attitude of the Nazi leadership to the Evangelical Church in Germany up to the outbreak of World War II. Hitler's goal was to control the Protestant religion through the new version of "Positive Christianity," the religious philosophy proposed by Alfred Rosenberg. Hitler would purify the German "race," restore old Nordic values, and substitute the spirit of the hero for that of the Crucifixion.

516. SCHOLDER, Klaus. *Die Kirchen und das dritte Reich* (The Churches and the Third Reich). Frankfurt am Main: Propyläen Verlag, 1977.
A Professor of Modern Church History at the Evangelical Theological Faculty of the University of Tübingen seeks to make sense of the complicated story of the relations of the Churches to the Third Reich. On the one side is the contention that the German Churches opposed Hitler successfully; on the other there is a charge that they were tools of the Nazi regime. Studies the Catholic and Protestant records together. Attributes the ecclesiastical silence on the matter of persecution of Jews more to cowardice than to the preoccupation of churchmen with their own desperate struggle for survival during a reign of terror.

517. *SHUSTER, George Nauman. *Like a Mighty Army: Hitler Versus Established Religion.* New York: Appleton-Century, 1935.
A prominent Catholic writer and one of the earliest experts on National Socialism describes the rise of Hitlerism, particularly in its religious aspects. States that Germany was undergoing the birth of a new religion, the slogan of which could well be: "God

is the German race, and Hitler is his prophet." Describes the early war on the Jews, the Protestant struggle and Hitler versus Rome. Designates the development as "the religious tragedy of Germany." Admits his deep dislike of Hitlerism and the direction it was taking.

518. TROSSMANN, Karl. *Hitler und Rom* (Hitler and Rome). Nürnberg: Sebaldus Verlag, 1931.
During the decade from 1923 to 1933 of Hitler's drive for political power, there was increasing anxiety in the Catholic Church about the nature of National Socialist ideology. Hitler had been born a Catholic, but as an adult he turned more and more against the religion of his youth. Describes Hitler's relations with the papacy as the Nazi movement gathered political strength. The dominantly nihilistic philosophy was in direct opposition to the teachings of the Catholic Church.

519. VOLK, Ludwig. *Das Reichskonkordat vom 20. Juli 1933* (The Reich Concordat of 20 July 1933). Mainz: Matthias-Grünewald-Verlag, 1972.
Describes the Concordat Hitler signed in July 1933 with the Vatican. The *Führer* was eager to lend prestige to his new Nazi regime and therefore offered concessions to the Holy See that no Weimar government had seen fit to give. Using documents from State and Church archives, considers the motives of both sides and how they reacted upon one another. Explains that the Vatican never understood the consequences of signing a treaty with Hitler. Church authorities were interested only in preserving some safeguards for their schools and social organizations. They later learned to their dismay that a treaty with Hitler was meaningless.

520. WRIGHT, J. R. C. *"Above Parties": The Political Attitudes of the German Protestant Church Leadership, 1918-1933*. London: Oxford University Press, 1974.
Examines the political attitudes of German Protestants based on statements of the committees and assemblies of the Protestant Churches from the end of World War I to the advent of Hitler to power. Shows how Protestant conservatism weakened the Weimar government and played into the hands of Hitler and his Nazi movement. Denounces political quietism in critical times and insists that German churchmen should have recognized the character of Hitler and the nature of the Nazi movement.

CHAPTER 9

PSYCHOLOGICAL MOTIVATIONS

Psychohistory, Psychobiography, Propaganda

Any effort to explain the grotesque complexities and incongruities of the Nazi phenomenon needs more than the tools of the historian. An interdisciplinary approach is indicated, including especially the behavioral sciences. Not only historians and political scientists but also social psychologists, psychiatrists and psychoanalysts have contributed their own insights into the nature of National Socialism and the personality and character of its leaders.

Special attention is given to investigating the mind and actions of Hitler as master of a monstrous regime. There are varying opinions as to his mental stability: most writers agree that the man was not insane in the clinical sense but perilously close to the borderline between neurosis and insanity. Stimulated by the work of psychoanalyst Erik Erikson, especially *Young Man Luther* (1958), historians turned to new branches of their profession, psychohistory and psychobiography, to explain the personality of Hitler and the intricacies of Nazism.

As expected, much of the new psychological approach was composed of elaborate guesswork and questionable conclusions. There are exceptions in serious and convincing studies which undoubtedly have merit. Outstanding in the psychohistorical treatment of Hitler's personality are the works of two able scholars: Rudolph Binion with his *Hitler Among the Germans* (1976) and Robert G. L. Waite, *The Psychopathic God: Adolf Hitler* (1977). While there is room for differing opinions, both historians have earned the respect of their colleagues by their venture into new intellectual territory.

This chapter also includes entries on Nazi propaganda and its effects. Estimates may differ on the character of Hitler, but there is general agreement among historians that he was a master of propaganda techniques. Assisted shrewdly by Dr. Joseph Goebbels, his Minister for Public Enlightenment and Propaganda, he successfully used the tools of propaganda to convert a highly civilized people into brainwashed citizens. There was nothing scientific about it — Hitler was moved by intuition, mysticism, astrology and vague, obscure thinking. Somehow it all worked — an apolitical people, proud of their *Kultur* and civilization, were transformed into obedient robots by a shrewd and cunning propagandist.

BIBLIOGRAPHY

521.   ABRAHAMSEN, David. *Men, Mind and Power.* New York, NY: Columbia University Press, 1945.
A psychiatrist specializing in criminal mentality discusses the psychology of the German people (whom he distinguishes from the Nazis), Hitler and his minions and Nazi collaborators in other countries. Offers some general principles to be used in the necessary rehabilitation of the German people.

522.   ACHILLE-DELMAS, François. *Adolf Hitler: Essai de biographie psycho-pathologique* (Adolf Hitler: An Essay on Biographical Psychopathology). Paris: Librairie Marcel Rivière, 1946.
An essay in biographical psychopathology by a French scholar, with emphasis on Hitler's psychology, early years and later life.

523.   ANDERLAHN, Hans. *Gegner erkannt: Kampferlebnisse der SA* (Opponents Recognized: Fighting Experiences of the SA). Munich: Eher Vrlag, 1937.
Nazi propaganda book sponsored by the National Socialist Party, describing the battle experiences of Storm Troopers. Praises the *Sturmabteilung* as a magnificent organization devoted to regeneration of the Fatherland. Credits it with the important task of "restoring the family."

524.   BAIRD, Jay W. *The Mythical World of Nazi War Propaganda, 1939-1945.* Minneapolis, MN: University of Minnesota Press, 1975.
Considers the guiding ideological force behind Nazi propaganda to be the heroic myth that the "best blood" of the German nation, by struggling against satanic forces, was con-

structing a Greater German Reich that would last for a thousand years. Hitler would leave this myth as his heritage to the world, or he would die fighting for it. The myth was accompanied by several leitmotifs – anti-Semitism, the Bolshevik menace and obsession with Frederick the Great. The Nazi propaganda machine supporting the myth was guided by Goebbels and Hitler.

525. BANSE, Ewald. *Germany Prepares for War*. Translated from the German by Alan Harris. London: Dickson, 1934; New York: Harcourt, Brace, 1934.
Immediately after Hitler took office, Ewald Banse was appointed Professor of Political Science at Braunschweig Technical College.   Author of several books on military and geographical subjects which had attracted the attention of Hitler, Banse published *Raum und Volk im Weltkriege* (Space and People in World War), in effect a handbook on German militarism.   Banse praised national sentiment as "self-respect and healthy egoism" and denounced internationalism as "self-abandonment and a degeneration of the tissues." Published in translation in London in 1934, the book was disavowed by Nazi authorities and confiscated. It was widely distributed in Great Britain and the United States as an effective instrument of Allied propaganda in World War II.

526. *BINION, Rudolph. *Hitler Among the Germans*. New York: Elsevier, 1976.
Psychohistorian Rudolph Binion stresses the irrational foundations of Hitler's thinking.   Sees the background of the *Führer* as vital for an understanding of his control over the German people. Presents the thesis that Hitler's anti-Semitism and concept of *Lebensraum* (living space) resulted from a traumatic reliving of a beloved mother's death from iodoform poisoning in the course of breast-cancer treatment. According to the author, the German people were susceptible to Hitler because of a key psychic sore spot – the trauma of defeat in World War I. Such traumas led to Auschwitz (Hitler projected onto the Jews his guilt in prompting the fatal ministrations to his mother), and to Stalingrad (Hitler unconsciously aligned his oral demands with Germany's defeat in World War I).

527. BOELCKE, Willi A. *Kriegspropaganda, 1939-1941* (War Propaganda, 1939-1941).   Stuttgart: Deutsche Verlagsanstalt, 1966.

Analyzes Nazi war propaganda from the outbreak of World War II to Hitler's assault on the Soviet Union in 1941. Presents the secret conferences in the Ministry of Propaganda on methods to be used to maintain public moral support for the war effort.

528. BRAMSTEAD, Ernest K.   *Goebbels and National Socialist Propaganda, 1923-1945.* East Lansing, MI: Michigan State University Press, 1965.
      Explores National Socialist propaganda campaigns before and after Hitler's assumption of political power and the role of Dr. Joseph Goebbels as Minister for Public Enlightenment and Propaganda. Presents the story of *Gleichschaltung*, by which every conceivable institution of the Nazi state was coordinated for the benefit of the Hitler regime.

529. BRAUNMÜHL, Anton.   "War Hitler krank?" (Was Hitler Sick?) *Stimmen der Zeit*, LXXIX (1954), 94-102.
      Discusses Hitler's mental problems with attention to varied diagnoses by physicians.

530. BROMBERG, Norbert.   "Hitler's Character and Its Development: Further Observations." *American Imago*, XXVIII (1971), 289-303.
      Analyzes Hitler's character and concludes that he was a "borderline personality," a type of behavioral pattern that might well be included among mental illnesses. This concept of "borderline personality" as applied to Hitler is accepted by most scholars – that he was not insane, but certainly close to the boundary of insanity.

531. BURDEN, Hamilton T.   *The Nuremberg Party Rallies, 1923-1939.* New York: Praeger, 1967.
      An account of how Hitler used his annual "Party Day" ceremony at Nuremberg to impress the masses. The first and smallest rally was held at Munich at the end of January 1923, when 20,000 spectators and party members gathered to celebrate the Nazi cause. The rallies gathered momentum during the next ten years. The 1933 gathering was called the Congress of Victory to celebrate Hitler's assumption of power. The planning called for a miracle in logistics. The carefully prepared rally held from 5 - 12 September 1938 involved more than a million people in a gigantic celebration. Hundreds of reporters came from all over the world to record the proceedings in a

blaze of publicity. The Nuremberg Rallies became an important part of the Nazi propaganda machine. They highlighted key elements of National Socialism: militarism, nationalism, romanticism and anti-Semitism.

532. CHELIUS, Fritz Heinz. *Aus Hitlers Jugendland und Jugendzeit* (Concerning Hitler's Land of Youth and Adolescence). Leipzig: Verlag der Deutschen Grossbuchhandlung, 1933. Discusses Hitler's early environment and childhood designed to show how the character of the "greatest German" was formed.

533. COCKS, Geoffrey. *Psychotherapy in the Third Reich.* New York: Oxford University Press, 1985. A study of how psychotherapy fared under the Nazis gives special attention to the Goering Institute under the leadership of Hermann Goering's cousin. For the Nazis, psychoanalysis was "a Jewish science," and Sigmund Freud was denounced as a fraud.

534. CRABITÈS, P. "A Master Stroke of Psychology." *The Catholic World*, CXLVIII (1938), 190-97. Treats psychological relations between Hitler and Mussolini in 1938.

535. DICKS, Henry Victor. *Licensed Mass Murder: A Socio-psychological Study of Some SS Killers.* New York: Basic Books, 1972. A British psychiatrist conducts interviews with eight convicted Nazi war criminals serving life sentences for murder. Concludes that while these killers shared characteristics with other authoritarians, all had dominant mother figures in their childhood, with absent or weak fathers. They were influenced by Nazi ideology which they used as an excuse for their murderous behavior.

536. DIETRICH, Otto. *Mit Hitler in der Macht: Persönliche Erlebnisse mit meinem Führer* (With Hitler to Power: Personal Experiences with My *Führer*). Munich: Eher Verlag, 1934. Otto Dietrich (1897-1952) was Reich Press Chief of the Nazi Party from 1933 to 1945 and Hitler's chief publicity agent. As publicist, Dietrich organized the great propaganda campaigns during the elections of 1932. Discusses his role in the rise of the Nazis. He was at Hitler's side in many trips by plane and car.

Through family connections he introduced Hitler to captains of industry who contributed funds to the Nazi movement. Emphasizes "the *Führer's* peaceful struggle for the soul of the German people." The book sold 250,000 copies within a few months after publication.

537. EKSTEINS, Modris. *The Limits of Reason: The German Democratic Press and the Collapse of the Weimar Democracy*. London: Oxford University Press, 1975.
A study of German newspapers during the latter years of the Weimar Republic shows how these papers, although exposing the fallacies of Nazi propaganda and ideology, unwittingly nevertheless helped ease the way of Hitler to power. Describes how German-Jewish publishing houses such as Ullstein were involved with liberal or republican parties and how liberalism and its publishing support were eroded by economic depression and political radicalization.

538. ERIKSON, Erik. "Hitler's Imagery and German Youth." *Psychiatry*, III (1942), 475-93.
Examines the psychiatric point of view of National Socialist ideology and its special appeal to German youth.

539. FORMAN, James D. *Nazism*. New York: Franklin Watts, 1978.
A contribution to juvenile literature for grades six to eight on Hitler and Nazism. Essentially a political biography of Hitler, the book draws on psychoanalytical interpretations to explain the personality of Hitler. Attention is given to his skill as a politician.

540. GANGULEE, Nagendranath. *The Mind and Face of Nazi Germany*. London: Murray, 1942.
Presents excerpts from remarks of Nazi leaders and from the Nazi press illustrating the nature of the Hitler regime.

541. *GATZKE, Hans W. "Hitler and Psychohistory." *The American Historical Review*, LXXVIII (1973), 394-401.
Discusses Walter C. Langer's book on *The Mind of Hitler* (1972). (See No. 557). Analyzes the strong and weak points of psychohistory as a new phenomenon in historical research.

542. GOEBBELS, Joseph. *Michael: Ein deutscher Schicksal in Tagebuchblättern* (Michael: A German Fate in Diary Pages). Munich: Eher Verlag, 1929.
One of many publications by Goebbels before the Nazi assumption of political power and his role as Minister for Public Enlightenment and Propaganda. This early "autobiographical novel" offers excerpts from his diary. Examples: "All a man needs is a mother." "I have no more money. Money is dirt, but dirt is not money." "The mission of women is to be beautiful and to bring children into the world." There is evidence of the propaganda he was later to espouse: a young man must not seek salvation through his intellect; his salvation lay in physical labor.

543. GOEBBELS, Joseph. *My Part in Germany's Fight.* Translated from the German by Kurt Fiedler. London: Hurst & Blackett, 1935.
Details Goebbels' role in the rise of National Socialism to power. Describes himself as a patriot working for the good of his country.

544. GOEBBELS, Joseph, *et al. Adolf Hitler: Pictures from the Life of the Fuehrer, 1931-1935.* Translated from the German by Carl Underhill Quinn. New York: Peebles Press International, 1978.
An English translation of a Nazi propaganda book published in Germany in 1936, the text supervised by Propaganda Minister Goebbels. More than 150 photographs present Hitler in public and private life as an object of adoration. Portrays Hitler's genius as statesman, orator, soldier, road-builder and architect. Pays little attention to Jews, probably because the book was published originally just before the Berlin Olympic Games and Hitler wanted to tone down his anti-Semitism at the time. The publication reveals the nature of Nazi propaganda.

545. HAFFNER, Sebastian. *Germany: Jekyll and Hyde.* Translated from the German by Wilfrid David. New York: Dutton, 1941.
A young German *émigré* analyzes the habits of mind which he believes dominated Germany from Bismarck to Hitler. Suggests that his countrymen have demonstrated their lack of political sense necessary for the peaceable control of a large power state. Concentrates on the Nazi mentality and Nazi aims. Describes Hitler's approach as psychological but completely lack-

ing in understanding of economic issues. This was one of the
earliest studies of the German psychological landscape during
the Hitler regime.

546. HAGEMANN, Walther. *Publizistik im Dritten Reich: Ein
      Beitrag zur Methodik der Massenführung* (Journalism in the
      Third Reich: A Contribution to the Methodology of
      Leadership of the Masses).   Hamburg: Hansischer
      Gildenverlag, 1948.
Analyzes publicity and propaganda in the Third Reich and their
roles in solidifying the dictatorship. Believes the work of Dr.
Joseph Goebbels was critical in maintenance of National
Socialist power.

547. *HALE, Oron J.   *The Captive Press in the Third Reich.*
      Princeton, NJ: Princeton University Press, 1964.
Shows how Hitler and his underlings controlled the German
press and made it a pliant instrument for National Socialism.
During the Weimar Republic the German press enjoyed complete freedom, but under the Nazi regime it was converted into
a tightly regimented, espionage-ridden, slavishly dependent
instrument of governmental thought-control. Produces copious
documentary proof of Hitler's cynical seizure of world-famous
dailies and persecution of any dissenters. By the end of World
War II, the German press was in a shambles, subject to control
by Dr. Goebbels' Propaganda Ministry.

548. *HERZSTEIN, Robert Edwin.   *Adolf Hitler and the German
      Trauma, 1913-1945: An Interpretation of the Nazi Phenom-
      enon.* New York: Putnam, 1974.
Discusses the formation of Hitler's ideas.   Using a
psychohistorical approach, seeks to explain the *Führer's* rise to
power, attributed partially to a reaction to certain psychological
and cultural factors. Synthesizes ideas contributing to the Nazi
phenomenon.

549. HERZSTEIN, Robert Edwin. *The War That Hitler Won: The
      Most Infamous Propaganda Campaign in History.* New
      York: Putnam, 1978.
Describes the propaganda war waged under the direction of Dr.
Joseph Goebbels as the war that Hitler won. Believes it was
successful because the German people, deluged by propaganda,
fought to the end despite overwhelming odds. Shows how the
victory was accomplished: discusses the chief individuals who

ran the operation, their ministries and bureaus and the propaganda devices they employed. Concentrates on the enormous manipulation of public opinion.

550. HOFFMANN, Heinrich. *Hitler befreit das Sudetenland* (Hitler Liberates the Sudetenland). Berlin: Zeitgeschichte-Verlag, 1938.
On 12 September 1938 Hitler, already master of Austria, announced that he demanded the right of self-determination for the Sudeten Germans of Czechoslovakia, and if the Sudeten Germans could not defend themselves, "they will receive help from us." His pressure led to the Munich Pact, which critics asserted "sold Czechoslovakia down the river." This book by Hitler's private photographer tells the story in pictures and text of how Hitler "freed Sudeten Germany."

551. HOFFMANN, Heinrich. *Hitler in Polen* (Hitler in Poland). Berlin: Zeitgeschichte-Verlag, 1939.
A picture book by Heinrich Hoffmann, Hitler's personal photographer, about the German invasion of Poland on 1 September 1939, depicts the *Führer* as a master of *Blitzkrieg*, or lightning war.

552. KECSKEMETI, Paul and Nathan LEITES. "Some Psychological Hypotheses on Nazi Germany." *The Journal of Social Psychology*, XXVI (1947), 141-83, and XXVII (1948), 91-117.
The extraordinary appeal of National Socialism to the German masses inspired numerous attempts by sociologists, psychologists, psychiatrists and psychoanalysts to investigate the causes for the phenomenon. Summarizes and criticizes various hypotheses presented by social psychologists and others to analyze the psychological motivations of the German public.

553. KERSHAW, Ian. *Popular Opinion and Political Dissent in the Third Reich: Bavaria, 1933-1945*. Oxford: Clarendon Press, 1983.
Analyzes Bavarian attitudes toward the Third Reich. Concentrates on grumbling, opposition and collaboration. Divides the Bavarians into social and religious groups, in order to show how Germans managed to lead almost normal lives under a rigid totalitarianism leading to total war and the Holocaust. Religious issues provoked most opposition to the regime. By the mid-war years, most Bavarians were inclined to look upon

Hitler's promises as fraudulent. Nazi propaganda was beginning to wear thin.

554.   KLAEHN, Friedrich Joachim. *Sturm 138: Ernstes und Heiteres aus dem SA-Leben* (Sturm 138: The Serious Side and the Comical in SA-Life). Leipzig: Schaufuss, 1934.
A Nazi publication designed to show the serious side and much amusing about Storm 138, a *Sturmabteilung* (SA) formation of Storm Troopers.

555.   KLAUSS, Hermann. *Feierstunden der deutschen Schule* (Celebration Hours in German Schools). Stuttgart: Franck'sche Verlagshandlung, 1941.
A Nazi propaganda book designed to give directions for festivities in the schools. Attention is given to celebrations during the school year, and especially those under the flag: "The Flag is our Faith."

556.   KRIS, Ernest and Hans SPEIER. *German Radio Propaganda.* London: Oxford University Press, 1944.
Surveys radio propaganda in the Third Reich as managed by Dr. Joseph Goebbels, Minister for Public Enlightenment and Propaganda. As every other institution in Nazi Germany, radio was rigidly controlled while Goebbels aimed to convince the German people that their Leader was the greatest German of all time and was invariably right in his decisions.

557.   *LANGER, Walter C. *The Mind of Adolf Hitler.* New York: Basic Books, 1972.
In 1943, "Wild Bill" Donovan, head of the Office of Strategic Services, requested Dr. Walter C. Langer to submit a secret psychological report concerning the mind of Adolf Hitler, to learn about his possible political moves in the future. The result was a study for a governmental intelligence agency to supply psychoanalytic insight to warfare. For a quarter of a century the report was classified as secret. The work is a psychohistorical reconstruction which treats Hitler's personality and behavior. The author based his work on documents and other writings available at the time and personal interviews arranged by the OSS with informants who had known Hitler before the war. Gives attention to Hitler's troubled background, sexual pathologies, death fears, Messiah complexes, vegetarianism and other characteristics.

558. *LOEWENBERG, Peter. "The Psychohistorical Origins of the
     Nazi Youth Cohort." *The American Historical Review*,
     LXXVI (1971), 1457-1502.
     Discusses what happened to members of the post-World-War-I
     generation of young people in their decisive period of character
     development. Pays attention to their psychological and
     psychosexual development and political socialization that led to
     similar fixations and distortions in adult character. Emphasizes
     the masses of youngsters who endowed their charismatic leader
     with special superhuman qualities. Uses psychoanalytical tech-
     niques. Describes the propaganda designed to win the young to
     National Socialism.

559. *LOEWENBERG, Peter.   "The Unsuccessful Adolescence of
     Heinrich Himmler." *The American Historical Review*,
     LXXVI (1971), 612-41.
     A study of Heinrich Himmler (1900-45), leading Nazi politician
     and practitioner of Nazi terror. Describes Himmler's rearing in
     a devout Catholic home and education in the Landshut, Bavaria
     Gymnasium. Probes the psychological motivations during
     adolescence of a man who later emerged as one of the worst
     mass murderers of all time.

560. LOHE, Werner.   *Roosevelt-Amerika* (Roosevelt-America).
     Munich: Eher Verlag, 1939.
     Nazi propaganda book published by the semi-official publishing
     firm. Heavy in sarcasm and ridicule, criticizes the American
     President and the United States in general for failing to see the
     menace of Bolshevism and for being British-oriented.

561. *MANDELL, Richard D. *The Nazi Olympics*.   New York:
     Macmillan, 1971.
     In 1936 the Olympic Games were held in Berlin. Although the
     Nazi press had denounced the forthcoming games as a "Festival
     of Jews," such criticism ceased suddenly when Hitler made it
     clear that the Olympics would provide an important showcase
     for his regime. The Nazi government spent $25 million in lavish
     preparations, including nine arenas and a magnificent stadium
     in Berlin. Describes in detail the events of the games. Hitler's
     enthusiasm was considerably dampened when Jesse Owens, an
     American black athlete, won four gold medals. The *Führer* was
     present on the day when Owens won his third gold medal but
     pointedly left the stadium before the prizes were awarded to the
     winners. The embarrassment came from Hitler's belief that

blacks "who came from the jungle" were primitive but their physiques were stronger than those of "civilized whites."

562. McRANDLE, James H. *The Track of the Wolf: Essays on National Socialism and Its Leader, Adolf Hitler*. Evanston, IL: Northwestern University Press, 1965.
The title refers to Hitler's addiction to symbolism, Teutonic myths, folklore and astrology. In five essays on the philosophical background the *Führer* inherited and revolutionized, uses a psychoanalytical approach to shed light on Hitler's motivations, stressing the major importance of Hitler's personality in the history of National Socialism. Devotes much attention to explaining the circumstances of Hitler's suicide.

563. MERKL, Peter H. *The Making of a Stormtrooper*. Princeton, NJ: Princeton University Press, 1980.
Shortly after Hitler acceded to political power, Columbia University Sociologist Theodore Abel collected 581 autobiographical sketches of early Nazis, material which was deposited at Stanford University. Merkl uses these sketches to analyze the crucial role played by SA Brown Shirts in the transition from a fringe to a mass movement. Opposes the Marxist-oriented claim about the middle-class origins of Nazism. Sees socio-economic factors as being only one element among a multiplicity of causes. Also emphasizes such psychological motivations as xenophobia, youth anxieties and acceptance of violence.

564. MIALE, Florence R. and Michael SELZER. *The Nuremberg Mind: The Psychology of the Nazi Leaders*. New York: Quadrangle/The New York Times Book Co., 1975.
This study is meant as a contribution to psychohistory. The authors present and interpret the Rorschach records by psychologist Gustave M. Gilbert of sixteen accused war criminals tried at Nuremberg in late 1945 and 1946. They conclude that the Nazis had diseased minds.

565. NS-PRESSEANWEISUNGEN DER VORKRIEGSZEIT 1933-1939 (National Socialist Press Releases in the Prewar Era, 1933-1939). New York: Sauer, 1984-86, 3 vols.
These prewar National Socialist press instructions record the official announcements of Dr. Joseph Goebbels' Ministry for Public Enlightenment and Propaganda. All German journalists were ordered to base their stories on instructions issued by Dr.

Goebbels, then destroy the press announcements, but several reporters salvaged their notes. Provide an insight into Nazi information politics and Goebbels' manipulation of the German media. Render the original instructions as well as the resulting news articles.

566. PAULL, Hermann. *Deutsche Rassenhygiene* (German Racial Hygiene). Görlitz: Verlag für Sippenforschung und Wappenkunde, 1934.
A Nazi publication dedicated to race hygiene, family, marriage, morality and property.

567. RAMLOW, Rudolf. *Hier! Opfer und Sieg der Hitler-Jugend* (Here! Sacrifice and Victory of the Hitler Youth). Stuttgart: Union Deutsche Verlagsgesellschaft, 1933.
A Nazi publication designed to praise "sacrifices and triumphs" of the Hitler Youth. Urges German youngsters to plant the concept of National Socialism into their peers. "The youngster who out of an innate *Volk* sensibility loves his homeland and his Fatherland feels an unconscious bond with those who are of the same tribe."

568. ROGGE, Heinrich. *Hitlers Friedenpolitik* (Hitler's Policies for Peace). Berlin: Schlieffen, 1935.
Published during the critical year of German rearmament, this book by a pro-Nazi writer presents Hitler as an energetic champion of peace.

569. RÖHRS, H. D. *Hitler.* Neckargemünd: Vowinckel, 1965.
A treatise suggesting Hitler as an example of the destruction of a personality. The psychologically oriented text seeks to explain the mystique of Hitler's personality and character.

570. SCHOTT, Georg. *Das Volksbuch vom Hitler* (The People's Book on Hitler). Munich: Eher Verlag, 1933.
The National Socialist publisher Eher Verlag presents Hitler as a champion of the German people.

571. *SCHUMAN, Frederick Lewis. *Nazi Dictatorship: A Study in Social Pathology and the Politics of Fascism.* New York: Knopf, 1935.
Surveys Hitler's rise and the growth of Nazism since the close of World War I. Collected materials for this study in 1933 during an eight-month stay in Germany, aiming to recapture

something of the Third Reich atmosphere. Schuman was one of the first scholars to attempt a psychological interpretation of Hitler and Nazi leaders. Seeks to explain the spirit and working methods of Nazism as well as the pathology of the dictatorship. Synthesizes various points of view on National Socialism. Expresses horror at the excesses of Hitlerism and blames the entire German people.

572. SHOWALTER, Dennis E. *Little Man, What Now? Der Stürmer in the Weimar Republic.* Hamden, CT: Archon Books, 1982.
       Der Stürmer, owned and published by Julius Streicher (1885-1946), Nazi Party militant in Franconia, was a pornographic sheet, an example of journalism at its worst. Its columns were filled with reports of sexual scandals and almost hysterical praise for Hitler and Nazism. Illustrations invariably included subjects such as Christian girls being raped by Jewish men. Examines the content, style, financing and political views of the paper before 1933. Claims that the success of the sheet lay in its ability to translate abstract anti-Semitism and vague, lower middle-class anxieties into concrete terms with which the Nazis could identify. Describes Streicher's repeated accusations of Jewish ritual murders, but concedes that "other articles contained at least a grain of truth."

573. STARK, Johannes. *Nationalsozialismus und Wissenschaft* (National Socialism and Science). Munich: Eher Verlag, 1934.
       A Nazi publication on the relations between National Socialism and science. Maintains that respect for facts and aptitude for exact observation resided exclusively in the Nordic race. Denounces the Jewish spirit in science as being wholly different in its orientation and focused upon its own ego, conception and self-interest.

574. STEINERT, Marlis G. *Hitler's War and the Germans: Public Mood and Attitude during the Second World War.* Translated from the German by Thomas E. J. De Witt. Athens, OH: Ohio University Press, 1977.
       A chronologically organized study of German public opinion about World War II, with more than 1,600 footnotes, based mostly on surviving documents of the SD (Reich Security Service) of the SS (Elite Guard). Asserts that propaganda and public opinion influence and limit one another in the totalitarian society. Conclusions: the Third Reich was only

rarely supported by a unanimous public vote, opinions were not uniform, Germans did not favor aggression, nor were they enthusiastic about war, and they knew little of the regime's mass murders. Investigates the effects of Nazi propaganda and "the actual opinions of large segments of the population."

575. STIERLIN, Helm. *Adolf Hitler: A Family Perspective.* Translated from the German. New York: The Psychohistory Press, 1976.
Published in cooperation with the Institute for Psychohistory, this book by Helm Stierlin, chief of the Division of Psychoanalysis at the University of Heidelberg, stresses the unconscious influence Hitler's mother exercised on her son's future and consequently the history of Western civilization. The admittedly speculative text should be read in conjunction with the psychohistorical studies by Rudolph Binion, *Hitler Among the Germans* (1976) and Robert G. L. Waite, *The Psychopathic God: Adolf Hitler* (1977).

576. TELL, Rolf, pseud., ed. *Nazi Guide to Nazism.* New York: American Council on Public Affairs, 1942.
American edition of a British propaganda title, *Sound and Führer*, which presents quotations from Hitler's speeches and Nazi pronouncements from a number of sources. This wartime publication was designed to convict the Germans out of their own mouths. These excerpts are designed to reveal the inanities and contradictions of the Nazi mind.

577. *THOMPSON, Dorothy. *Listen Hans.* Boston: Houghton, Mifflin, 1942.
During World War II, American journalist Dorothy Thompson delivered her short-wave addresses to a pro-Nazi friend named Hans in Germany, and informed him what the world thought of the Nazi regime. Analyzes the German mind and reveals what she believes the German people really wanted. Speaks the language of the liberal world at a time when liberalism was being pushed farther and farther into the background.

578. *WAITE, Robert George Leeson. "Adolf Hitler's Guilt Feelings: A Problem in History and Psychology." *Journal of Interdisciplinary History,* I (1971), 229-49.
A preliminary study using a psychohistorical approach to ascertain Hitler's character and personality. Emphasizes guilt feelings as contributing to Hitler's mental problems. The ideas

of this analysis appeared in Waite's *The Psychopathic God: Adolf Hitler* (1977).

579. *WAITE, Robert George Leeson. *The Psychopathic God: Adolf Hitler*. New York: Basic Books, 1977.
     This study of Hitler from the perspective of psychohistory describes the *Führer* as a person, reviews the origin and nature of his ideas, and analyzes his youth, personality, development and sex.   Also examines elements in German history which have made it plausible, although not inevitable, for such a person to become Chancellor.   Sees Hitler as a borderline personality, who, although mentally ill, could function very effectively in many respects.   Like other psychohistorians, Waite was confronted by the fact that little is really known about Hitler's youth.   Discusses such subjects as the supposedly missing testicle of the *Führer*, and the impact of his mother's death from cancer while in the care of a Jewish physician.   Comments on the centrality of anti-Semitism in Hitler's ideology and policies.

580. *ZEMAN, Z. A. B. *Nazi Propaganda*. Published in association with the Wiener Library. London: Oxford University Press, 1964, 1973.
     Examines the Nazi propaganda machine, which was responsible for much of Hitler's success on the domestic scene. In the Nazi drive for power and throughout the life of the Third Reich, Dr. Joseph Goebbels, Minister for Public Enlightenment and Propaganda, directed an intensive propaganda campaign. Many of Hitler's goals were implemented by the remarkable talents of the Propaganda Minister. Insatiable for power, Goebbels took control of every means to mold the minds of the German people – press, radio, books, plays, art, music and tourism. So well organized and effective was his work that a popular witticism relegated the German government to a subdivision of the Propaganda Ministry.

CHAPTER 10

FOREIGN POLICY

Denunciation of Versailles, the Axis, Lebensraum,
Two-Front War, Aggression

Hitler's foreign policy was based on two premises, one concerned with the peace treaty after World War I, and the other with the acquisition of territory. In his autobiography *Mein Kampf* and throughout the Nazi drive for political power, Hitler denounced the Treaty of Versailles as an iniquitous document, as a Carthaginian peace designed to keep the German people in a permanent state of subjugation. He would correct what he considered to be the shameful wrong of Versailles. Moreover, he was dissatisfied with Germany's position in Central Europe because the country was hemmed in on all sides and prevented from attaining its "natural growth."

Most scholars concerned with Nazi foreign policy see Hitler's goals as simple aggression. In no way could he have achieved what he wanted without the Allies abdicating their position in Europe and relinquishing the gains they had made after the bloody four years of war from 1914 to 1918. Hitler had only contempt for the Weimar Republic and its attempt to bring about a change through a program of conciliation. Germany, he insisted, had not been defeated in the Great War – on the contrary, "she had been stabbed-in-the-back by Jews and Social Democrats," the alleged traitors on the domestic scene.

Hitler began his giant rearmament program within one year after his accession to power. At first secretly then openly, he violated the disarmament provisions of the Treaty of Versailles. He saw to it that huge expenditures were made for building up the armed forces. He was certain that this was the only language the Allies understood. He made it clear that if they refused to give Germany her legitimate rights, they must accept the fact that he would fight for justice.

At the same time, Hitler strengthened his policy of rearmament by a program of economic reorientation aimed at self-sufficiency (*Autarkie*) in the event of war. While pursuing these goals, he also attempted to confuse the Allies in a psychological campaign designed to convince Allied statesmen that he was a man of peace. His aim was to lull his enemies into lethargy.

BIBLIOGRAPHY

581.   BOURGEOIS, Daniel.   *Le Troisième Reich et la Suisse, 1933-1941* (The Third Reich and the Swiss, 1933-1941). Neuchâtel: Editions de la Baconnière, 1974.
Examines the relations between the Third Reich and Switzerland during the time of peace and the first wartime years, until the invasion of the Soviet Union turned Hitler's mind away from Switzerland. As a European state with part German population, Switzerland had cause for nervousness. The Nazi regarded Swiss Germans as *Volksdeutsche*, "ethnic Germans," and they were eventually to be included in a Greater German Reich as a matter of ideology. The Swiss were determined to maintain their state; they did not respond to Nazi propaganda, despite the large funds used for that purpose. Shows that small countries have few options in defending their territory against neighboring great powers.

582.   BROWN NETWORK. New York: Knight Publications, 1936.
The second book after *The Brown Book of the Hitler Terror*, both published by the World Committee for the Victims of German Fascism, documents the activities of Nazi agents in foreign countries. Demonstrates that for three years the Third Reich had been at war with virtually the entire world. Details the story of the kidnapping of Berthold Jacobs by Nazi agents in Switzerland. Describes the global ramifications of National Socialism as a new kind of Pan-Germanism. The anonymous authors predict that unless Hitler succeeded in finding more competent agents than he had found thus far, the new Germany would end up as the loneliest state in history.

583.   CARR, William. *Arms, Autarky and Aggression*. New York: Norton, 1973.

This study in German foreign policy from 1933 to 1939 examines Hitler's foreign policy in the light of Nazi economic policy and rearmament. Hitler deduced the need for rearmament from his ideological premises, aware that his army needed an industrial and economic base of considerable strength. Discusses the diplomatic developments between the wars, much of them based on Gerhard L. Weinberg's *The Foreign Policy of Hitler's Germany* (1970).

584.   COMPTON, James V. *The Swastika and the Eagle: Hitler, the United States, and the Origins of World War II.* Boston: Houghton Mifflin, 1967.
Presents what the author believes to be an entirely new point of view on the genesis of the war. Describes how the United States appeared to Hitler and his advisors before Pearl Harbor, when Germany's fateful decisions were reached. Also details Hitler's myopic view of the United States before the war. "Perhaps never before in history have the vital affairs of a great nation been reached with such blindness and deliberate disregard as they were in Hitler's Germany." Shows how blunder was piled on blunder, misunderstanding on misunderstanding, until the United States, a country devoted to neutrality, was literally forced into arms and became the decisive factor in the destruction of the Third Reich.

585. *DEAKIN, Frederick William. *The Brutal Friendship: Mussolini, Hitler and the Fall of Italian Fascism.* New York: Harper & Row, 1962.
An account of the personal relations, at first warm and then strained, between Hitler and the Italian Fascist dictator, by the Warden of St. Anthony's College, Oxford. Describes Mussolini's power in Italy and the *Duce*'s ruin under the impact of a war that could not be won. Reveals that Hitler's attitude to the *Duce* was one of brutal self-assurance. Based on a critical examination of documentary sources and secondary works, this detailed study is intended for the author's peers and not for the general public.

586.   DENNE, Ludwig. *Das Danzig-Problem in der deutschen Aussenpolitik, 1934-39* (The Problem of Danzig in German Foreign Policy, 1934-39). Bonn: Röhrscheid Verlag, 1959.
Examines every conceivable phase of the Danzig problem in the context of German foreign policy from 1934 to 1939. Concludes that Hitler did not start World War II over the issue of

Danzig or over the so-called suppressed Germans in Poland, but over living space in the East, and that was the phantom he chased "and through which he brought the entire world against him." In other words, Hitler considered Danzig and Poland as being merely preliminary steps in his drive for *Lebensraum* (living space). Describes Hitler's foreign policy as the work of a "psychopath," who applied the methods of domestic politics to foreign policy, namely bluff and power.

587. *DIRKSEN, Herbert von. *Moscow, Tokyo, London: Twenty Years of German Foreign Policy*. Norman, OK: University of Oklahoma Press, 1952.
A career diplomat in the German Foreign Service, Herbert von Dirksen contributes an account of German foreign policy between the two World Wars. Relates the story of his diplomatic life, with attention to German-Polish relations, Berchtesgaden, Godesberg, the Munich Pact, and in general the "tragic development" of German foreign policy. Under the Nazis Dirksen served as a kind of aristocratic supercargo, useful to a dictator fascinated by titles. His work for Hitler was an exercise in humiliation and frustration. He never became reconciled to the "insincerity, superficiality and the inefficiency" of the German Foreign Office under Hitler. He despised Ribbentrop with all the contempt of an aristocrat for a parvenu, "an unwholesome, half-comical figure."

588. DRECHSLER, Karl, Hans DRESS and Gerhard HASS. "Europläne des deutschen Imperialismus im zweiten Weltkrieg" (European Designs of German Imperialism in the Second World War). *Zeitschrift für Geschichtswissenschaft*, XIX (1971), 916-31.
The authors analyze *Mitteleuropa*, as seen by Nazi economic experts. It was to extend from Gibraltar to Siberia and from Cyprus to the North Pole. The Nazi goal was to hide this planned expansion behind what would be designated as "European economy." Seek to show the continuity between German war aims in World War I and World War II.

589. *EUBANK, Keith. *Munich*. Norman: University of Oklahoma Press, 1963.
A study of the background and development of the 29 September 1938 pact among Germany, the United Kingdom, France and Italy, by which the signatories conceded to Hitler virtually everything he demanded in Czechoslovakia. The agreement,

immediately stamped as appeasement by its critics, was regarded by most observers as a step toward World War II.

590. FABRY, Philipp W. *Der Hitler-Stalin Pakt, 1939-1941* (The Hitler-Stalin Pact, 1939-1941). Darmstadt: Fundus Verlag, 1962.
The Russo-German Nonaggression Pact, signed 23 August 1939, was a ten-year agreement between Hitler and Stalin, whereby the two countries would in no case resort to war against each other. Shows how Hitler and Stalin were practicing their own versions of *Realpolitik* — Hitler seeking to avoid a war on two fronts and Stalin buying time for Russian rearmament.

591. *FOX, John P. *Germany and the Far Eastern Crisis, 1931-1938: A Study in Diplomacy and Ideology.* New York: Oxford University Press, 1982.
Examines German policy toward the developing crisis in East Asia from the occupation of Manchuria by Japan to the German decision to abandon its interest in China and side with Japan in the Sino-Japanese War. Demonstrates how the ideological goals of National Socialism took precedence over economic interests and traditional diplomacy. Asserts that it was Nazi ideology which finally triumphed over German diplomacy in the formulation and execution of Germany's Far Eastern policy. The German attitude moved like a pendulum, sometimes to the Chinese, sometimes to the Japanese side, but eventually opted for Japan.

592. FRIEDLÄNDER, Saul. *Prelude to Downfall: Hitler and the United States, 1939-1941.* Translated from the French by Aline B. and Alexander Werth. New York: Knopf, 1967.
The author of *Pius XII and the Third Reich: A Documentation* (1966) presents a record of the diplomatic struggle for advantage as Hitler's Third Reich and the United States moved toward war. Uses manuscript sources, collections of political, diplomatic and military journals, correspondence, memoranda and instructions in government archives. Explains that in the two war years before Pearl Harbor, German policy reflected not only internal obstacles to action in the United States, but also prolonged British and Russian resistance, insurgency inside Vichy France and the curious duplicity of the Japanese. All played their part in Hitler's tortuous maneuverings.

593. FUNK, Walther. *Grundsätze der deutschen Aussenpolitik und das Problem der internationalen Verschuldung* (Foundations of German Foreign Policy and the Problem of International Guilt). Berlin: Junker & Dünnhaupt, 1938.
Walther Funk (1890-1960), Nazi Minister of Economic Affairs from 1933 to 1945, presents the basic elements of German foreign policy under Hitler. Funk was an important figure in the early financial structure of the Third Reich, but after 1938 had little weight in the upper echelons of the Party. He was found guilty at Nuremberg of war crimes and sentenced to life imprisonment, but was released in 1957 for reasons of health.

594. *GATZKE, Hans W. *Germany and the United States: "A Special Relationship?"* Cambridge, MA: Harvard University Press, 1980.
An account for the general reader of what the United States and Germany have meant to each other over the past two centuries. Places the shifting ambivalent relations of the two nations in historical perspective. Explains that the 19th century saw mutual admiration as well as condescension between the two countries. Gatzke's account of the origins of World War II stands in contrast to A. J. P. Taylor's revisionism. Offers extensive comment on the Nazi era.

595. HILDEBRAND, Klaus. *The Foreign Policy of the Third Reich.* Translated from the German by Anthony Fothergill. Berkeley, CA: University of California Press, 1973.
Analyzes two fundamental questions: what was the relationship between foreign and domestic policies inside the Third Reich, and to what degree did that foreign policy represent either a continuation of or a break with the past? Denies any sense of continuity in Hitler's work, which was activated by a new program for racial world domination. Hitler would win territory in the East, and avoid the mistake of William II in alienating Great Britain by an aggressive naval and colonial policy. Once secure in his continental base, he would then make his bid for world power.

596. HILDEBRAND, Klaus, ed. *Deutsche Frage und europäisches Gleichgewicht* (The German Question and the European Balance of Power). Cologne: Böhlau Verlag, 1985.
Collection of essays in honor of historian Andreas Hillgruber's 60th birthday includes contributions by several American historians on phases of National Socialism, including Donald

Cameron Watt, "The Debate over Hitler's Foreign Policy: Problems of Reality or *Faux Problèmes*;" Gordon A. Craig, "Roosevelt and Hitler: The Problem of Perception;" and Norman Rich, "Resistance and Collaboration: Dilemmas and Paradoxes." György Ránki writes on "Hitler's Verhandlungen mit osteuropäischen Staatsmännern, 1939-1944."

597. HILTON, Stanley E. *Hitler's Secret War in South America, 1939-1945: German Military Espionage and Allied Counterespionage in Brazil.* Baton Rouge, LA: Louisiana State University Press, 1981.
Discusses *Abwehr* espionage operations in South America, especially Brazil, to harry Allied shipping in the South Atlantic and beyond. The goal was to attack troopships and freighters carrying supplies to Great Britain and elsewhere. Offers many instances of the amateurishness of the Nazi agents and explains how Allied counterintelligence smashed *Abwehr* espionage operations.

598. HIRSZOWICZ, Lukasz. *The Third Reich and the Arab East.* London: Routledge & Kegan Paul, 1966.
An account of Hitler's foreign policy as it concerned the nations of the Middle East.

599. JACOBSEN, Hans Adolf. *Nationalsozialistische Aussenpolitik, 1933-1938* (National Socialist Foreign Policy, 1933-1938). Frankfurt am Main: Metzner Verlag, 1968.
Analyzes how German foreign policy was made, as well as the nature of the influences working on the policymakers. Describes the structure of German politics, the decision-making process and the problem of ideology. Contends that Nazi foreign policy, the unique product of Nazi ideology and the Nazi system of government, was not a continuity but a complete break with the past. Hitler did not want territorial expansion for its own sake but instead aimed to construct an empire on racial principles. This point of view was popular among post-Hitler era German historians.

600. KIMMICH, Christoph M. *The Free City: Danzig and German Foreign Policy.* New Haven, CT: Yale University Press, 1968.
Explains that Danzig, the Baltic seaport on the left bank of the Vistula, became a Free City after World War I. For Hitler, the return of Danzig became a matter of prime importance: his de-

mand to control the city became a cause for the invasion of Poland in 1939.

601. KORDT, Erich. *Nicht aus den Akten* (Not from the Documents). Stuttgart: Union Deutsche Verlagsgesellschaft, 1950.
      Not from the Documents is a personalized account of the Wilhelmstrasse from 1928 to 1945. An important official in the German Foreign Office, Kordt took part in high-level conferences and state visits, and was able to observe what really went on behind the façade of Nazism. Offers a devastating description of the character and ability of Joachim von Ribbentrop, Hitler's Minister of Foreign Affairs, whom he accuses of making an unholy mess of Germany's foreign policy: "Ribbentrop's reports to Hitler were filled with obscenities and absurdities and besides were written in miserable German." Reveals how the hopes of the small group of conspirators, whose aim was to rescue the peace, were exploded by Hitler's uncanny luck. Claims that he and a small group of "good Germans" were bitterly opposed to the machinations of Hitler and his Nazi cohorts.

602. KRAUSNICK, Helmut. "Legende um Hitlers Aussenpolitik" (Legends Surrounding Hitler's Foreign Policy). *Vierteljahrshefte für Zeitgeschichte*, II (1954), 217-39.
      A detailed study of the "legends" of Hitler's foreign policy emphasizes the concept of *Lebensraum* (living space).

603. KUUSISTO, Keppo. *Alfred Rosenberg in der nationalsozialistischen Aussenpolitik, 1933-39* (Alfred Rosenberg in National Socialist Foreign Policy, 1933-39). Helsinki: Suomen Historiallinen Seura, 1984.
      A Finnish journalist turned historian presents a study of the Nazi Party's *Aussenpolitisches Amt* (APA), under the direction of Alfred Rosenberg, who was known as the official National Socialist philosopher. For a time Rosenberg was in line for the post of Hitler's Foreign Minister. Describes Rosenberg as a poor administrator and an amateur in the struggle against Goebbels and Ribbentrop. The APA was noted for its confusion and improvisation. Its primary emphasis was directed toward the East, where Rosenberg hoped for the overthrow of Bolshevism and the splitting of the Soviet Union into its "ethnic" components. Other agencies concerned with foreign policy, notably the Foreign Ministry and Ribbentrop's

Dienststelle (Service Bureau) had much more influence than the APA under Rosenberg's inefficient direction.

604. *LOW, Alfred D. *The Anschluss Movement, 1918-1938: Background and Aftermath.* New York & London: Garland, 1984.
An annotated bibliography of German and Austrian nationalism. The book is designed to assist scholars and students of the *Anschluss* movement, the union of Germany and Austria, in their investigations of some of the aspects of the movement, and to identify directly or indirectly current gaps in our knowledge of *Anschluss.* Sections are devoted to the roots of the *Anschluss* movement from 1848 to 1918, with attention to the Austro-Germans, Imperial Germany and Pan-Germanism; the *Anschluss* movement from 1918 to 1938; Hitler's control of Austria from 1938 to 1945 (*"Ein Volk – Ein Reich"*); and Allied occupation and the rebirth of the Austrian state and nation from 1945 to the present.

605. LUŽA, Radomír. *Austro-German Relations in the Anschluss Era.* Princeton, NJ: Princeton University Press, 1975.
Examines the problems of Austro-German relations as well as the nature and policies of the Third Reich. Sees Austria's annexation as one of Hitler's vacillations, which reflected the chaos and constant infighting of the central administration in Berlin. Hitler may have destroyed his native Austria, but he allowed channels of regionalism as well as Austrian traditionalism. Austria really found its national identity as well as full access to modernity through occupation and defeat.

606. McMURRY, Dean Scott. *Deutschland und die Sowjet Union, 1933-1936* (Germany and the Soviet Union, 1933-1936). Cologne: Böhlau Verlag, 1979.
A history of the first three years of Hitler-Stalin relations, with accent on ideology, power politics and industrial relations. Contends that Hitler's basic ideological commitment was the destruction of "Jews-Bolsheviks." Using this ideological framework, Hitler intended to use power politics to conquer Soviet territory and enslave the Russian people. At first the Foreign Office opposed this goal, but soon faltered and went along with the *Führer.* Hitler's diplomats agreed with the aim to establish Germany as the dominant power in Europe.

607.   McSHERRY, James E. *Stalin, Hitler, and Europe: The Imbalance of Power, 1939-1941.* Cleveland and New York: World, 1970, vol. 2.
       Emphasizes Soviet foreign policy, but devotes much attention to Hitler. After June 1940 the story essentially concerns the relations between the two top leaders and the suspicions and fears each two had of the other. Hitler tried to lull the Russian dictator into a false sense of security. Stalin stiffened as Axis reverses began, when the Greeks drove the Italians into Albania. Hitler reportedly reached his decision to attack the Soviet Union in late 1940.

608.   MESKILL, Johanna Menzel. *Hitler and Japan: The Hollow Alliance.* New York: Atherton Press, 1966.
       Analyzes the alliance between Nazi Germany and Japan, with emphasis upon Hitler's relationship with one of two wartime allies. Describes the union as "a hollow alliance," with little respect on either side. Believes that these allies failed to coordinate their efforts because of mutual distrust and incompatible geopolitical goals. The Axis alliance was a failure as a political instrument. The Tripartite Pact of 1940 was supposed to be between friendly allies but it never achieved its ultimate purpose.

609.   MICHALKA, Wolfgang. *Ribbentrop und die deutsche Weltpolitik, 1933-1940* (Ribbentrop and German Global Politics, 1933-1940). Munich: Fink Verlag, 1980.
       Examines the role of Joachim von Ribbentrop (1893-1946), Hitler's unofficial adviser in foreign affairs from 1933 to 1938 and thereafter Foreign Minister. Argues that the Third Reich's foreign and domestic policies were not the result of monolithic planning and decision-making, but of constant infighting. Ribbentrop remained an amateur in foreign affairs, a diplomat who would have done anything to ingratiate himself with the *Führer*. Describes Ribbentrop as an opportunist and manipulator.

610.   MURRAY, Williamson. *The Change in the European Balance of Power 1938-1939: The Path to Ruin.* Princeton, NJ: Princeton University Press, 1984.
       A study of the years of Hitler's triumph, which the author regards as anything but inevitable. Accepts the earlier view that the Western Allies would have been in a better position to counteract Hitlerism in 1938 than in 1939, and that appease-

ment promoted what its advocates feared most — German aggression leading to protracted war.

611. ORLOW, Dietrich. *The Nazis in the Balkans: A Case Study of Totalitarian Policies.* Pittsburgh: University of Pittsburgh Press, 1968.
Deals with one organization, the *Südosteuropa Gesellschaft*, the Southeast Europe Society, as an example of the extension of Nazi foreign policy in the Balkans. Offers details about the intricacies and contradictions of bureaucratic life under the Nazi regime. Describes the disordered and chaotic nature of officialdom in the Nazi state. The intrusion in the Balkans was supposed to be "unofficial," but it was beset by conflicting attitudes in the bureaucracy.

612. PAULEY, Richard F. *Hitler and the Forgotten Nazis.* Chapel Hill, NC: University of North Carolina Press, 1981.
An account of Austrian National Socialism from its germination by anti-Semite Georg von Schönerer in the 1880s to the *Anschluss* in 1938. Treats the social composition of the Austrian Nazis, leadership problems, slow growth in the 1920s, impact of the Great Depression and the extent of the Nazi terror. Believes that Austrian Nazis were not merely the tools of Hitler but had an impact of their own.

613. PRESSEISEN, Ernst L. *Germany and Japan: A Study in Totalitarian Diplomacy.* The Hague: Nijhoff, 1958.
Analyzes the relations between the Third Reich and Japan from 1933 to 1941. Presents Hitler's foreign policy as an exercise in totalitarian diplomacy.

614. QUESCH, Johann. *Jugoslawien und das Dritte Reich* (Yugoslavia and the Third Reich). Stuttgart: Seewald Verlag, 1968.
Analyzes Hitler's foreign policy as it concerned Yugoslavia.

615. ROBERTSON, Esmonde M. *Hitler's Prewar Policy and Military Plans, 1933-1939.* London: Longmans, Green, 1963.
Discusses foreign policy from Hitler's accession to power until the outbreak of World War II, with attention to the rearmament program and plans for strategy in a possible war.

616. SCHUBERT, Günther.   *Anfänge   nationalsozialistischer
         Aussenpolitik* (Beginnings of National Socialist Foreign
         Policy). Cologne: Verlag Wissenschaft & Politik, 1963.
      Investigates the beginnings of National Socialist foreign policy
      after Hitler's assumption of the chancellorship.

617. SCOTT, William Evans.   *Alliance Against Hitler: The Origins
         of the Franco-Soviet Pact.* Durham, NC: Duke University
         Press, 1962.
      An account of the negotiations beginning in 1931 for a
      commercial agreement and nonaggression pact between the
      French Republic and Soviet Russia signed in Paris in May 1935.
      Asserts that Hitler's advent to power spurred Franco-Soviet
      rapprochement. The Nazi introduction of conscription gave the
      final impulse for the pact.

618. SMELSER, Ronald.   *The Sudeten Problem, 1933-1936.*
         Middletown, CT: Wesleyan University Press, 1975.
      Along the mountainous borders of western Bohemia lived some
      3.5 million German-speaking Sudetens, who comprised a useful
      lever for Hitler's plan to annihilate the entire Czech state. In-
      sisting on self-determination, Hitler professed to protect
      "kindred blood." Considers Nazi *Volkstumspolitik* (politics of
      national characteristics) and the formulation of Hitler's foreign
      policy.

619. *TREFOUSSE, Hans Louis. *Germany and American Neutrality,
         1939-1941.* New York: Bookman Associates, 1951.
      Analyzes the developing policies of the Third Reich toward the
      United States during the years immediately preceding the out-
      break of war between the two countries. Shows the complete
      inefficiency of the underlings who surrounded Hitler, especially
      the inept party followers assigned to the Foreign Office.
      Trefousse, a former captain in military intelligence, documents
      Hitler's mentality in diplomatic action. Describes the *Führer's*
      pattern: first the assurance to foreign governments that Hitler
      was an apostle of peace; then an attempt to isolate them from
      allies; and finally, after his enemies were reduced to impotence,
      he would strike. The policy worked in Europe, but it failed for
      the United States. President Roosevelt refused to be confused
      by Hitler's diplomacy.

620. WEBER, Reinhold W. *Die Entstehungsgeschichte des Hitler-Stalin Paktes, 1939* (History of the Origins of the Hitler-Stalin Pact, 1939). Frankfurt am Main: Lang, 1980.
Attempts to explain the failure of the 1939 Anglo-French-Soviet alliance and the origins of the Nazi-Soviet Pact. Relies on cabinet papers, published sources and Foreign Office correspondence.

621. *WEINBERG, Gerhard L. *The Foreign Policy of Hitler's Germany: Diplomatic Revolution in Europe, 1933-1936.* Chicago: University of Chicago Press, 1970.

622. *WEINBERG, Gerhard L. *The Foreign Policy of Hitler's Germany Starting World War II, 1937-1939.* Chicago: University of Chicago Press, 1980.
Presents a detailed analysis of the ideas, politics, events and negotiations that shaped the *Führer*'s foreign policy. The two volumes treat not only the German leadership but also the important diplomats of other countries. Demonstrates that Hitler's goals and policies remained consistent, with the ultimate aim of depopulating Eastern Europe to make *Lebensraum* (living space) for the Third Reich. Emphasizes the initiative of Germany as Europe's most advanced and mighty industrial and military power. Seeks to show the origins of World War II, "how the world came to be involved in a massive conflagration for the second time in a quarter of a century."

623. *WISKEMAN, Elizabeth. *The Rome-Berlin Axis: A Study of the Relations between Hitler and Mussolini.* London: Collins, 1966.
After withdrawing Italy from the League of Nations, dictator Mussolini formed the Rome-Berlin Axis on 25 October 1936, and made it formal on 22 May 1939, as the so-called Pact of Steel. Traces the origins of the pact which bound each party to cooperation in the event of war.

CHAPTER 11

THE RESISTANCE MOVEMENT

Opposition, Resistance, Conspiracy

Winston Churchill said it best: "[*Members of the Resistance*] were the greatest and most noble political group of our time." It was an accurate judgment. Many civilized Germans were appalled by the ideology of Hitler and his cohorts and by what was being done to disgrace the German name before all the world. Among them were men of conscience who refused to remain silent even though they knew they were placing their lives in jeopardy in a vicious dictatorship. They came from diverse professions and walks of life: all were motivated by love of country and by the conviction that something had to be done to remove the stains of Nazism from German history.

During the early years of the Nazi regime and during the war years, little was known about the underground resentment against Hitler and Nazism. In the postwar era one book appeared after another giving detailed evidence and indisputable proof that resistance to the dictator had begun long before the late war years when the Third Reich slid into decline. There were three stages – opposition, resistance and conspiracy. Nazi repression was so severe that even a gentle pastor such as Dietrich Bonhoeffer could only come to the conclusion that Hitler had to be removed by assassination. One of the great tragedies of the era was the execution of this remarkable man only days before liberation by the triumphant Allies.

After World War II, scholarly and popular studies appeared of Resistance leaders such as Colonel Claus von Stauffenberg, key figure in the 20 July 1944 plot on Hitler's life; Carl Goerdeler, former Lord Mayor of Leipzig; legalist Helmuth James Count von Moltke, bearer of a distinguished military name; Hans and Sophie Scholl, brother-and-sister members of the student White Rose group; Martin Niemoeller, former U-boat captain turned pastor and pacifist; and others. These were the extraordinary representatives of that Other Germany which refused subservience to a totalitarian regime.

As a matter of convenience, books by members of the Resistance movement are entered here instead of in Chapter 3 dealing with biography, memoirs and reminiscences.

BIBLIOGRAPHY

624. BAUMONT, Maurice. *Le grande conspiration contre Hitler* (The Great Conspiracy against Hitler). Paris: Del Duca, 1963.
Details the events of the unsuccessful *Putsch* of 20 July 1944 led by Count Claus von Stauffenberg at Rastenburg, Hitler's field headquarters in East Prussia. Records the succession of events which nearly cost the *Führer* his life.

625. BAYNE, E. A. "Resistance in the German Foreign Office." *Human Events*, III (1946), 1-8.
Demonstrates that opposition, resistance and conspiracy against Hitler and Nazism existed even in the German Foreign Office before and during World War II. There was much criticism inside the Foreign Office of Joachim von Ribbentrop and his lack of qualification for the post of Foreign Minister.

626. BERBEN, P. *L'attentat contre Hitler, 20 juillet 1944* (The Attempt against Hitler's Life, 20 July 1944). Paris: R. Laffont, 1962.
Describes the techniques and morality of the conspirators against Hitler in the attempt on his life on 20 July 1944.

627. BUCHHEIT, Gert. *Soldatentum und Rebellion: Die Tragödie der deutschen Wehrmacht* (Soldiery and Rebellion: The Tragedy of the German *Wehrmacht*). Rastatt/Baden: Grote, 1961.
Relates the story of the military and rebellion in the "tragedy of the German *Wehrmacht*." Senior and junior officers who had little use for Hitler and the Nazis were caught in the web of an enforced oath of allegiance. Most of such officers suffered in silence, but a few entered into the conspiracy to assassinate Hitler.

628. CAHEN, Max. *Men Against Hitler.* Adapted with an intro-
     duction by Wythe Williams. Indianapolis, IN: Bobbs-
     Merrill, 1939.
     Discusses the opposition to Hitler just before the outbreak of
     World War II.

629. CARSTEN, Francis L. "Stauffenberg's Bomb." *Encounter,*
     XXIII (1964), 64-67.
     Describes the bomb and the attempt on Hitler's life on 20 July
     1944, for which Stauffenberg was executed.

630. *DEUTSCH, Harold C. *The Conspiracy Against Hitler in the
     Twilight War.* Minneapolis, MN: University of Minnesota
     Press, 1968.
     Focuses on the period from September 1939 to May 1940, at a
     time when the conspiracy inside Germany seemed ready to
     strike, and at a time when an important contact existed between
     the German opposition and Great Britain through Pius XII as
     intermediary. Describes the fading opposition among the
     German military, negotiations with London through the
     Vatican and how the Resistance inside Germany tried to warn
     first the Scandinavian countries and then Holland and Great
     Britain. Maintains that the Resistance movement began long
     before the tide of war turned against Nazi Germany. Pays
     tribute to the "other Germans" who tried unsuccessfully to rid
     their country of Hitler and to redeem the German name.

631. DULLES, Allen Welsh. *Germany's Underground.* New York:
     Macmillan, 1947.
     An account by a prominent member of the U.S. Office of
     Strategic Services of his efforts to maintain relations with the
     German Resistance movement during World War II. Brother
     of John Foster Dulles, postwar American Secretary of State,
     Allen Dulles renders an account of his contacts with the
     German Underground with attention to his own role. Describes
     the part played by German generals, politicians and others from
     university and church circles. Conveys the impression that the
     conspiracies were inconsequential and brought to naught by
     accidents which could not be foreseen.

632. DUMBACH, Annette E. and Jud NEWBORN. *Shattering the
     German Night: The Story of the White Rose.* Boston: Lit-
     tle, Brown, 1986.

Recounts the story of the medical students in Munich who organized the White Rose, and the brother and sister who defied Hitler by distributing illegal pamphlets denouncing the atrocities of the Nazi Third Reich. Calls the White Rose a German youth resistance organization whose existence was a startling anomaly in the history of World War II and which made headlines throughout the world when it was discovered, despite Nazi attempts to suppress it. Reconstructs the history of the White Rose from interviews with surviving relatives, court records, diaries and letters. Pays tribute to courageous innocents struggling against repulsive evil.

633. GALANTE, Pierre and Eugene SILIANOFF. *Operation Valkyrie: The German Generals' Plot Against Hitler.* Translated from the French by Mark Howson and Cary Ryan. New York: Harper & Row, 1981.
Originally published in France in 1981 as *Hitler est-il mort?*, this book by two journalists recapitulates the events of the German generals' plot to assassinate Hitler in 1944. The story is based on interviews, diaries and records of survivors, especially Adolf Heusinger. Gives attention to Hitler's military capacity. Suggests that the war was lost because of many mistakes in strategy.

634. GALLIN, Mary Alice. *German Resistance to Hitler.* Washington, DC: Catholic University of America Press, 1962.
Examines the ethical and religious factors of the German opposition to Hitler, especially the Catholic Resistance movement.

635. *German Resistance to Hitler.* Edited by Walter Schmitthenner and Hans Buchheim. Translated from the German by Peter and Betty Ross. Berkeley, CA: University of California Press, 1970.
A collection of essays on Resistance written by German specialists. Hermann Graml writes about Resistance thinking on foreign policy; Hans Mommsen on social views and constitutional plans of the Resistance; Hans-Joachim Reichart on Resistance in the labor movement; and Ernst Wolf on political and moral motives behind the movement. All the essays reveal that opposition to Nazism was real and even widespread — if altogether ineffective.

636. GOLLWITZER, Helmut, *et al.*, eds. *Du hast Mich Heimgesucht bei Nacht: Abschiedsbriefe und Aufzeichnungen des*

Widerstandes, 1933-1945 (You Have Haunted Me in the Night: Farewell Letters and Notes of the Resistance, 1933-1945). Munich: C. Kaiser, 1955 .
Notes and records, including especially the final words of members of the Resistance who were persecuted and/or killed by the Nazis from 1933 to 1945. Includes letters, diaries, poetry, and statements of men and women who were victims of the Nazi terror – generals, aristocrats, students, workers and farmers.

637. HAESTRUP, Jørgen. *Secret Alliance: A Study of the Danish Resistance Movement, 1940-1945.* New York, NY: New York University Press, 1985, 3 vols.
Based on hitherto secret documents, unpublished letters and interviews in the immediate postwar years with surviving members of the Danish Resistance. Covers such aspects of the movement as the early development of opposition in Denmark; the country's special position (Denmark was never formally at war with the Third Reich but at the same time took part in the Allied struggle); and a description of ties with the outside world, especially Great Britain. Rates Danish resistance to Nazi occupation as a remarkable episode in the history of World War II.

638. HAFFNER, Sebastian. "Beinahe: Die Geschichte des 20. Juli." *Neue Auslese,* II (1947), 1-12.
An account of the events of 20 July 1944, the attempt on Hitler's life at his Rastenburg field headquarters, a plot which was "almost" successful.

639. HOFFMANN, Peter. *Hitler's Personal Security.* Cambridge, MA: Massachusetts Institute of Technology Press, 1979.
Details the security measures used to protect Hitler. Recounts some fifty attempts to assassinate the *Führer* between 1921 and 1945. Gives attention to SS security arrangements, transportation, residences, public appearances and wartime headquarters. Hitler professed unconcern for his own safety, but shows that he insisted on more and more security.

640. *HOFFMANN, Peter. *The History of the German Resistance, 1933-1945.* Translated from the German by Richard Barry. Cambridge, MA: Massachusetts Institute of Technology Press, 1977.
Investigates the movements, groups and individuals who sought in varying ways, including assassination, to overthrow Hitler.

Its German title, *Widerstand, Staatsstreich, Attentat* (Resistance, *Coup d'État*, Assassination Attempt), describes the contents of this giant study, which includes maps, diagrams and some 200 pages of footnotes.

641.   JANSEN, Jon B., pseud. and Stefan WEIL, pseud. *Silent War: The Underground Movement in Germany.* Translated from the German by Anna Caples. Philadelphia: Lippincott, 1943.

One of the earliest books on the Underground movement in Nazi Germany, what it was, what it accomplished, and what could be expected of it. The authors maintain that a strong anti-Nazi sentiment had sprung up in almost every stratum of German society. Most of the material came from the authors' own experiences in what was later called the Resistance movement in Germany.

642.   KOSTHORST, Erich. *Die deutsche Opposition gegen Hitler zwischen Polen und Frankreichfeldzug* (German Opposition against Hitler between the Polish and French Campaigns). Bonn: Bundeszentrale für Heimatsdienst, 1954.

A report of the opposition against Hitler and Nazism, concentrating on the short period between the invasion of Poland in late 1939 and the campaign against France in 1940.

643.   KRAMARZ, Joachim. *Stauffenberg: The Architect of the Famous July 20th Conspiracy to Assassinate Hitler.* Translated from the German by R. H. Barry. New York: Macmillan, 1967.

Recounts the 20 July 1944 conspiracy to assassinate Hitler, based on correspondence and interviews with Stauffenberg's friends and associates. Presents not only the life, character and social background of Count Claus von Stauffenberg, but also tells the story of the conspiracy which nearly took the life of the dictator. Shows how this officer moved from the passive resistance of his social class to the conclusion that only the elimination of Hitler could save the Fatherland from its descent into vulgarity. The son of an old noble family sacrificed his life in the unsuccessful attempt on Hitler's life.

644.   LAMPE, David. *The Danish Resistance.* New York: Ballantine, 1960.

Describes the opposition of the Danish people to Nazism. Danish resistance was outstanding among peoples whose countries were occupied by the Nazis. Hitler ordered reprisals to be carried out in secret for the killing of German soldiers in Denmark "in the proportion of five to one." The Danes reacted with contempt. Under dangerous conditions they helped most Danish Jews to escape to Sweden.

645. *LASKA, Vera, ed. *Women in the Resistance and in the Holocaust: The Voices of Eyewitnesses.* Westport, CT: Greenwood, 1983.

Laska, a Resistance activist of Czech background and now a university teacher in Massachusetts, relates her own experiences as well as those of other eyewitnesses who survived the horrors of the concentration and extermination camps. Includes vignettes of courageous and suffering women. Describes how women prisoners were degraded at Auschwitz – no privacy, little food and the continual threat of death.

646. *LEBER, Annedore. *Conscience in Revolt.* Translated from the German by Rosemary O'Neill. London: Vallentine, Mitchell, 1957.

Records sixty-four accounts of the lives of Resistance martyrs in the Third Reich from 1933 to 1945, each entry emphasizing the heroism, sometimes spectacular, sometimes quiet, often commonplace, of ordinary decent Germans who could not reconcile their consciences with the barbarities and inhumanities of the Nazi state. These are almost all tragic stories of ordinary men and women facing an impossible dilemma. Annedore Leber was the widow of Julius Leber, former Social Democratic Party deputy, leading figure of the German Resistance who was condemned to death by the People's Court for high treason, and one of the martyrs of the 20 July 1944 plot against Hitler's life. The author was assisted by Willy Brandt, later *Bundeskanzler* of the German Federal Republic, and historian Karl Dietrich Bracher.

647. *MANVELL, Roger and Heinrich FRAENKEL. *The July Plot: The Attempt in 1944 on Hitler's Life and the Men Behind it.* London: The Bodley Head, 1964.

A concise retelling of one of the most extraordinary stories of the Hitler era – the officers' plot to kill Hitler on 20 July 1944, at Rastenburg, the *Führer's* East Prussian headquarters. At 12:37 P.M., a one-armed colonel, Count Claus von Stauffenberg, went into the conference barracks, saluted, apologized for his lateness and then placed a bulging briefcase under the heavy table at which Hitler sat listening to the news from the Russian front. Five minutes later the bomb exploded, smashing the hut to pieces. Hitler emerged shaken but alive. The authors discuss the roles of General Ludwig Beck, former Chief of the German General Staff, and Carl Goerdeler, one-time Mayor of Leipzig – the military and civilian leaders of the plot.

648. MASTNY, Vojtech. *The Czechs under Nazi Rule: The Failure of National Resistance, 1939-1942.* New York: Columbia University Press, 1971.
A study concentrating on the efforts of the Czechs to resist the Nazis from the opening of World War to 1942.

649. MICHEL, Henri. *The Shadow War.* Translated from the French by Richard Barry. New York: Harper & Row, 1972.
Surveys the development of the Resistance movement throughout Europe, traces its origins and shows its position in relation to the Allies on the one hand and to the occupying forces on the other. Gives attention to the component parts of the Resistance, and shows how it drew its members from all political and social groups of the continent. Reveals how the Resistance was equipped, organized and recruited, and describes the various tactics used in different countries. Devotes special attention to the *Maquis* in France and Partisans elsewhere. The author was for twenty years secretary-general of the French Historical Committee for the Second World War.

650. *MOLTKE, Graf Helmuth James. *Letzte Briefe aus dem Gefängnis Tegel* (Last Letters from Tegel Prison). Berlin: Henssel, 1951.
Collection of the last letters sent from Tegel Prison by Count Helmuth James Moltke (1907-45), legal adviser to the Counter-Intelligence Department of the German High Command (OKW) and a leading figure in the German Resistance movement. These letters, which made a profound impression in the Bonn Republic, clarified that von Moltke was being executed not for any specific actions but for his Christian beliefs. He wrote to his family in hourly expectation of death, and hoped that his wife and children would be protected in the troublesome times ahead through the power of faith. He claimed not to be worried about his last sunset: "I am in the best of spirits. Only I beg our Heavenly Father that he will keep me in them, for so

to die is easier for the flesh. How good has God been to me."
In his last moments he objected to violence as a manifestation
of the beast in man. In his final letter to his wife he wrote that
he did not aim at martyrdom but regarded it as "an estimable
advantage to die for something which (a) we really have done,
and (b) is worthwhile."

651. OPPEN, Beate Ruhm von. "Student Rebellion and the Nazis:
    'The White Rose' in Its Setting." *St. John's Review*, XXXV
    (1984), 2-21.
    Beate von Oppen is a tutor at St. John's College, Annapolis,
    where the curriculum emphasizes the Hundred Great Books.
    Devotes this article, based on her experiences as a student in
    Nazi Germany, to the political background which led to the
    formation of the White Rose, a student group at the University
    of Munich which secretly printed and distributed leaflets criti-
    cizing Hitler and the Third Reich. Describes students Hans
    Scholl, Willi Graf, Christoph Probst, Alexander Schmorell,
    Sophie Scholl (age 21) and their teacher, Professor Kurt Huber.
    These students caused great concern for the watchdogs of the
    regime. The White Rose showed extraordinary courage and
    strength to defy the power of the manipulators.

652. PRITTIE, Terence. *Germans Against Hitler*. Boston: Little,
    Brown, 1964.
    A British newspaperman tells the story of the German Resist-
    ance – the development of conspiracies inside the army, and the
    resistance of Roman Catholic and Protestant Churches, the
    Kreisau Circle, university students and underground Commu-
    nist cells.

653. REMER, Otto-Ernst. *20. Juli 1944*. Hamburg: Siep, 1951.
    An inside story of the 20 July 1944 attempt on Hitler's life at
    Rastenburg, as observed by Otto-Ernst Remer (1912-), who
    played a leading role in arresting the conspirators at the
    Bendlerstrasse in Berlin. Commanding a crack military unit
    stationed near Berlin, Remer was ordered to move into the city
    and seal off the ministries in the Wilhelmstrasse. He became the
    nemesis of the conspirators at the War Ministry when he took
    into custody Count Claus von Stauffenberg and other plotters.
    In this work he supported General Friedrich Fromm, who also
    turned on the conspirators. For his role in suppressing the plot,
    Major Remer was promoted to major-general. During the
    Bonn Republic, Remer supported various neo-Nazi organi-

zations. Defends his part in the 20 July incident as a German officer merely carrying out his orders.

654. RITTER, Gerhard. *The German Resistance: Carl Goerdeler's Struggle Against Tyranny.* Translated from the German by R. T. Clark. New York: Praeger, 1959.
Relates the story of Carl Goerdeler (1884-1945), jurist, Lord Mayor of Leipzig and civilian leader of the Resistance movement against Hitler. A man of puritanical character, Goerdeler moved rapidly from opposition to resistance to conspiracy against Hitler, and became a tireless propagandist against National Socialism. He argued that "to continue the war with no chance of victory was an obvious crime." Arrested and sentenced to death by the People's Court, he was hanged on 2 February 1945 in the Prinz Albrechtstrasse prison.

655. ROMOSER, George K. "The Politics of Uncertainty: The German Resistance Movement." *Social Research*, XXXI (1964), 73-9.
Analyzes political aspects of the German opposition, resistance and conspiracy movements.

656. ROTHFELS, Hans. "Die Roten Kämpfer. Zur Geschichte einer linken Widerstandsgruppe." *Vierteljahrshefte für Zeitgeschichte*, VII (1959), 438-60.
Hans Rothfels, specialist on the origins, character and work of the German Resistance movement, discusses the activities of the Communists in the domestic struggle against Hitler and Nazism. In the early days of National Socialism, Hitler's Storm Troopers won the battle of the streets against Red Fighters. Communist units continued their opposition to Nazism throughout the years from 1933 to 1945.

657. ROTHFELS, Hans. *The German Opposition to Hitler: An Assessment.* Translated from the German by Lawrence Wilson. London: Wolff, 1961.
A German historian recounts the extent of the German Resistance, its composition, aim and efforts. Shows how a body of dedicated men from all walks of life resolved not merely to put an end to Nazi tyranny, but to build in its place a new European order based on free and equal cooperation among nations. They failed due not to a lack of resolution but to the peculiar difficulties confronting a resistance movement to any totalitarian regime. Emphasizes the basic character of the

opposition, German "submissiveness," attitude to Jews, plans and actions, and relations between the opposition and the Allies.

658. SCHMITTHENNER, Walter and Hans BUCHHEIM, eds. *Der deutsche Widerstand gegen Hitler* (The German Resistance against Hitler). Cologne and Berlin: Kiepenheuer & Witsch, 1966.
Four historical-critical studies about the German Resistance by historians Hermann Graml, Hans Mommsen, Hans Joachim Reichhardt and Ernst Wolf. The scholars pay tribute to those Germans who as a matter of conscience placed their lives in jeopardy by opposing the dictator.

659. SCHOLL, Inge. *Students Against Tyranny: The Resistance of the White Rose, Munich, 1942-1943*. Translated from the German by Arthur R. Schultz. Middletown, CT: Wesleyan University Press, 1970, 1983.
Written originally in German in 1947, this book was published there in 1969 by the sister of Munich students Hans and Sophie Scholl, who were executed for distributing leaflets against the Nazi regime. This is the story of the White Rose, an organization formed in 1942 at Munich to oppose Hitler and the Nazi government. The students proposed to knock down "the iron wall of fear and terror." It is a tragic tale of idealistic students caught in a reign of terror and sacrificing their lives for their belief in decency and justice. The 1973 edition has an additional introduction by theologian Dorothee Soelle, who includes a diatribe against NATO, the Pentagon, the arms race and Ronald Reagan.

660. SCHRAMM, Wilhelm, Ritter von. *Conspiracy Among Generals*. Translated from the German by R. T. Clark. New York: Scribner, 1956.
The story of military conspiracy against Hitler as told by a reporter attached to the headquarters of General Erwin Rommel. Recounts the details of the generals' plot of 20 July 1944 on Hitler's life at the *Führer's* headquarters in Rastenburg on the Eastern Front. Although not himself involved, the author was sympathetic to the conspiracy. Emphasizes "the Prussian virtues" and "gentlemanly behavior" of the officers involved.

661. VANROON, G. *German Resistance to Hitler*. New York: Van Nostrand-Reinhold, 1971.

Analyzes the German opposition to Hitler and Nazism with attention to the role of Count Helmuth von Moltke (1907-45), bearer of a distinguished name in German military history and leader of the German Resistance movement. Describes the activities of the Kreisau Circle, the small group of officers and professional civilians formed in 1933 and led by von Moltke. The circle agreed that it was necessary to revive Christianity as a *sine qua non* for ridding the nation of Nazism.

662. WARMBRUN, Werner. *The Dutch under German Occupation.* Stanford, CA: Stanford University Press, 1963.
An account of how the Dutch people reacted during the Nazi occupation from 1940 to 1945 throughout World War II after the conquest of their country by Hitler. Describes the resistance of Dutch citizens to Nazi control.

663. *WOLFF, Ilse R., ed. *Persecution and Resistance under the Nazis.* London: Wiener Library, 1960.
No. 1 in the catalog series of the unique Wiener Library in London, this early guide and bibliographical reference presents extensive material on the persecution of opponents, especially Jews, in Nazi Germany and also files on the Resistance movement.

664. ZELLER, Eberhard. *The Flame of Freedom: The German Struggle Against Hitler.* Translated from the German by R. P. Heller and D. R. Masters. Miami, FL: University of Miami Press, 1969.
An account of the background, motivations and failure of the men of the Resistance in their struggle against Nazism. Describes the nobility and courage of Stauffenberg, Goerdeler, Beck, Bonhoeffer and others who sacrificed their lives in the attempt to rid the world of Hitler. Most attention is given to the 20 July 1944 plot on Hitler's life.

665. ZENTNER, K. *La Résistance allemande, 1933-1945* (The German Resistance, 1933-1945). Paris: Stock, 1968.
A study of the German Resistance movement against Hitler, with detailed descriptions of plots and conspiracies to end the Nazi state.

666. ZIMMERMANN, Erich and Hans Adolf JACOBSEN, eds. *Germans Against Hitler.* Translated from the German by Allen and Lieselotte Yahraes. Bonn: Berto Verlag, 1960.

A collection of documentary material published by the Press and Information Office of the Federal Republic of West Germany at Bonn. Contains contributions by some of the conspirators who survived, as well as material by those who lost their lives (Goerdeler, Beck, Moltke, Stauffenberg, *et al.*).

CHAPTER 12

ANTI-SEMITISM AND THE HOLOCAUST

Nuremberg Laws, Final Solution, Concentration and Extermination Camps, Genocide, the Holocaust

When Allied troops liberated the concentration and extermination camps at the end of World War II, what they saw shocked and nauseated them. There were piles of corpses and emaciated survivors who seemed to be walking skeletons. In the camps the unbelieving troops found stockpiles of shoes, clothing, human hair, gold teeth and wedding rings. Buchenwald, Dachau, Treblinka, Chelmno – there has been little to compare with it in the history of civilization in its totality, its technical efficiency, its utter dehumanization of people by biological annihilation.

The tradition of anti-Semitism went deeply into German history. In 1096 there were pogroms in many German cities and some 5,000 Jews who refused to be baptized as Christians were put to death. In the mid-14th century the Black Death was attributed in German states as well as the rest of Europe to an alleged Jewish conspiracy. In the late 19th century, German conservative parties had an anti-Semitic clause in their political platforms. In the hands of Hitler, anti-Semitism was transformed into a campaign to "purify the Indo-European-Aryan-Nordic race of a polluted Jewish element."

Hitler laid the legal basis in 1935 with his Nuremberg race laws, the Reich Citizenship Act and Act to Protect German Blood and Honor. Reich citizenship was reserved only for those of German or kindred blood; there were to be no mixed marriages. These race laws legitimized the terror let loose against Jews since 1933. After the outbreak of World War II, the "soft" campaign against Jews merged into a drive to achieve the complete extermination of an entire people.

The whole macabre story was revealed after the war in book after book which recorded the facts — gas chambers, the futile efforts at resistance, politics inside the camps, sadistic male and female guards, refinements meant to keep the truth from victims until the last moment, choice for the ovens, horrible medical experiments, lampshades made of human skins and carting away the ashes. And on the walls the slogans: "Work Makes Free," "Clean is Good," "Lice Can Kill."

Incriminating evidence was presented before the International Military Tribunal at Nuremberg — moving pictures, photographs, depositions and testimony which revealed that more than five million Jews had been slaughtered in Hitler's death camps. In the postwar era, neo-Nazis claimed that the charge of wholesale massacre was exaggerated and the Holocaust never took place. A succession of books proved the utter falsity of this claim, as both scholars and survivors presented irrefutable facts about Nazi genocide.

The literature on Nazi anti-Semitism reveals the extent of Hitler's monomania on Jews. Hitler blamed them as traitors "who had stabbed Germany in the back" and caused the loss of World War I. He charged the Jews with being communists and capitalists: they were seeking to rule the whole world and had to be eliminated. "The wretched Jew," he said, "is the enemy of the human race and the cause of all our suffering." The self-confessed greatest German of all time would rid Europe of its "parasites" — his euphemism for wholesale slaughter.

The Holocaust has attracted more attention among scholars, journalists, laymen and especially victims than most any other subject concerned with National Socialism. Andreas Hillgruber's book (see No. 706) set off a new debate. Critics accused Hillgruber of seeking through a "new revisionism" to endow West Germany with "a NATO philosophy with a German national coloring." They attacked him for his "apologetic tendencies." Taking Hillgruber's side, historian Ernst Nolte (*Three Faces of Fascism*) (1966) held that with the exception of gassing procedures, Nazi war crimes had ample historical precedents, especially in the Russian Revolution, and that Hitler had really committed "an Asiatic Deed." "Was not the Gulag Archipelago more original than Auschwitz?" Critics assailed Nolte's arguments as "a perfidious apology." Author Joachim Fest defended the new revisionism by asserting that while the Nazis killed on the basis of race, the Bolsheviks killed on the basis of class.

BIBLIOGRAPHY

667. *ABRAHAMSON, Irving, ed. *Against Silence: The Voice of Elie Wiesel.* New York: Holocaust Library, 1985, 3 vols.
A collection of the writings of concentration camp survivor Elie Wiesel, much of it concerned directly with the Holocaust. The subjects include essays on Jewish identity, open letters, book reviews, television scripts and statements by the President's Commission on the Holocaust. Wiesel designates the Holocaust as the most meaningful phenomenon of our time — an event of total darkness. "Since I live, I must be faithful to memory. Though I want to celebrate the sun, to sing of love, I must be the emissary of the dead, even though the role is painful." Wiesel seeks to introduce a moral element in a purely political atmosphere.

668. ABZUG, Robert H. *Inside the Vicious Heart.* New York: Oxford University Press, 1985.
This study, devoted to Americans and the liberation of Nazi concentration camps, attempts to assess the impact of concentration and extermination camps upon the liberators, writers and the general public. When Allied soldiers entered Buchenwald, Belsen, Dachau and other camps, they came face to face with the human ruins of the Nazi system of slave labor and genocide. They were sickened by the piles of dead, mass graves, crematories and skeleton-like survivors. The witnesses include Generals Eisenhower, Patton and Bradley, editor Joseph Pulitzer, novelist Meyer Levin, photographer Margaret Bourke-White, and most of all, the common American GI's who opened the gates, buried the dead and tried to save those still alive. Writes that irrefutable evidence uncovered by Allied soldiers marked a turning point in the moral imagination of the American public.

669. ACKERMAN, Nathan W. and Marie JAHODA. *Anti-Semitism and Emotional Disorder.* New York: Harper, 1950.
A psychoanalytical interpretation of anti-Semitism with emphasis upon emotional disorders connected with it. The authors seek to explain the treatment of Jews in the Third Reich and the real meaning of Nazi anti-Semitism.

670. ADLER, H. G. "Ideas Toward a Sociology of the Concentration Camp." *The American Journal of Sociology*, LXIII (1958), 513-22.

In the postwar years many attempts were made to understand the nature of the concentration camp system set up by Hitler to hold those he regarded as outside the periphery of the master race. Considers the sociological implications of the system. Shows that even under the most adverse conditions human beings seek the security to be found in combination with fellow sufferers.

671. ADLER, H. G. *Theresienstadt, 1941-1945.* Tübingen: Mohr, 1955.

Uses historical, sociological and psychological approaches in describing the concentration camp at Theresienstadt (Terezín), situated in northern Bohemia about 35 miles from Prague. Originally, the camp had the reputation of an especially humane detention center. Jews from Prague who were held there believed that they were safe in "a model Ghetto." This legend of a humane camp died when Reinhard Heydrich designated Theresienstadt a transit station on the way to extermination camps. The camp was liberated and leveled in 1945.

672. ARAD, Yitzhak. *Ghetto in Flames: The Struggle and Destruction of the Jews in Vilna in the Holocaust.* New York: Ktav, 1980.

The city of Vilna, "the Jerusalem of Lithuania," for many centuries played a central role not only in the cultural life of Jews but also in that of world Jewry. This city was the first to be destroyed when the Nazis began their "Final Solution of the Jewish question." Records the life, struggles and systematic destruction of the Vilna Jewish community during three years of German occupation. Asserts that the fate of the Jews of Vilna was shared by most Jewish communities in Nazi-occupied Europe.

673. *ARENDT, Hannah. *Eichmann in Jerusalem: A Report on the Banality of Evil.* New York: Viking, 1963.

Adolf Eichmann (1906-62) was an SS officer and "Jewish Specialist" of the Reich Main Security Office during World War II, and the individual charged with implementation of the "Final Solution" calling for the total extermination of European Jewry. On 11 May 1960 Israeli agents found him in Argentina and smuggled him to Israel. His trial in Jerusalem, 11 to 14

April 1961, aroused worldwide attention. Found guilty, he was hanged on 31 May 1962. Introduces the phrase "banality of evil," which caused much discussion among scholars specializing in the history of the Third Reich.

674. ARENDT, Hannah. "Social Science Techniques and the Study of Concentration Camps." *Jewish Social Studies*, XII (1950), 49-64.
Aims to shed some light on the varied techniques used to explain the existence and practices of Hitler's system of concentration and extermination camps.

675. ARNDT, Ino and Wolfgang SCHEFFER. "Organisierter Massenmord an Juden in nationalsozialistischen Vernichtungslagern," (Organized Massacre of Jews in National Socialist Extermination Camps). *Vierteljahrshefte für Zeitgeschichte*, XXIV (1976), 105-35.
In an essay on the organization of mass murder of Jews in National Socialist extermination camps the authors present a commentary designed to show the falsity of apologetic literature on the subject.

676. ARONSFELD, Caesar C. *Text of the Holocaust*. Marblehead, MA: Micah Publications, 1985.
A study devoted to Nazi extermination propaganda from 1919 to 1945.

677. BALL-KADUN, Kurt Jakob. *Das Leben der Juden in Deutschland im Jahre 1933* (The Life of Jews in Germany in the Year 1933). Frankfurt am Main: Europäische Verlagsanstalt, 1963.
An account of the everyday life of Jews in Nazi Germany during 1933. Describes the fears and insecurity of Jews in Frankfurt am Main. The anti-Semitic campaign was under way, but in 1933 real signs of the Holocaust that was to come were absent.

678. BAUM, Rainer C. *The Holocaust and the German Elite: Genocide and National Suicide in Germany, 1871-1945*. Totowa, NJ: Rowman & Littlefield, 1981.
Using a sociological approach, maintains that most Germans did not share the anti-Semitism of Hitler and his close followers. The population was so confused that it remained passive in response to the murderous policies reflecting the *Führer's* hatred of Jews. The "Final Solution" was unique and set apart from

all other genocides in history. Opposes the concept that the Holocaust was a product of a long history of anti-Semitism or even the result of the charismatic appeal of Hitler. Believes that it was a mere "sideshow" for the Nazi élite, which was interested mostly in Hitler's policy of living space.

679. BERGMANN, Martin S. and Milton E. JUCOVY, eds. *Generations of the Holocaust*. New York: Basic Books, 1982.
Several psychoanalysts contribute chapters regarding the effects of the Holocaust on the children of survivors as well as the off-spring of Nazi parents. The authors show the interactions between trauma and individual psychopathology.

680. BRAHAM, Randolph L. *The Eichmann Case: A Source Book*. New York: World Confederation of Hungarian Jews, 1969.
Adolf Eichmann (1906-62), chief of Subsection IV-B-4 of the Reich Main Security Office as an expert on Jewish affairs, was accused of being responsible for the death of millions of Jews. Arrested at the end of World War II, he escaped unrecognized from an internment camp in the American zone in 1946 and disappeared. On 11 May 1960 the Israeli secret service found him in Argentina and smuggled him to Israel. He was tried on charges of crimes against the Jewish people, crimes against humanity and war crimes. Found guilty, he was hanged on 31 May 1962. Presents a bibliography of books and articles in many languages on the Eichmann case, including attention to world reaction to his trial and the controversy engendered by Hannah Arendt on "the banality of evil."

681. BROSZAT, Martin. "Hitler und die Genesis der Endlösung" (Hitler and the Genesis of the Final Solution). *Vierteljahrshefte für Zeitgeschichte*, XXV (1977), 739-75.
Analyzes the "Final Solution." Broszat, who represents the functionalists (Hitler was a weak dictator because he was ham-pered by bureaucratic chaos) claims that the *Führer* did not or-der the Holocaust, but the killing program evolved gradually from a series of separate operations in 1941 and 1942 and from the impossibility of further evacuation or resettlement of Jews in Europe. Those holding the opposite view claim that, al-though there was not a single killing order, a wide variety of orders added up to the Holocaust, and that Hitler, as Head of State, had expressly advocated systematic killing as a means of resolving "the Jewish question."

682. BROSZAT, Martin, ed. *Kommandant in Auschwitz: Autobiographische Aufzeichnungen von Rudolf Höss* (Commandant in Auschwitz: Autobiographical Notes of Rudolf Höss). Stuttgart: Deutsche Verlagsanstalt, 1958.
Autobiographical notes by Rudolf Franz Höss (or Hoess) (1900-47), commandant of the extermination camp at Auschwitz, who was said to be responsible for the execution of more than 2.5 million inmates. Added to Höss's compulsion to follow orders was the fact that the commandant had been brought up to believe that anti-Semitism was a form of pest control. To him the business of exterminatig Jews was strictly an impersonal, mechanical system with the precision of modern industry. The notes are remarkable for Höss's testimony. He had been told by Himmler in the summer of 1941 that Hitler had ordered the "Final Solution of the Jewish problem."

683. BRUSS, Regina. *Die Bremer Juden unter dem Nationalsozialismus* (The Jews of Bremen under National Socialism). Bremen: Das Archive, No. 341, n.d.
Using the copious records of the Bremen Senate and Chamber of Commerce, which survived the war, presents a regional study on Jews between 1933 and 1945. Shows how Jews were excluded from public service, professions and economic life. Accompanies the quantitative data by the evidence of individual professionals and businessmen. Reveals how the scale of violence to human life and property went beyond the burning of synagogues. Hitler's early SA Storm Troopers and after 1934 the SS guards, terrorized Bremen's Jewish population.

684. COHEN, Elie A. *Human Behavior in the Concentration Camp.* Translated by M. H. Braaksma. New York: Norton, 1955.
Attempts to evaluate the varied types of reactions by prisoners caught in the concentration and extermination camps. Distinguishes between those who accepted their fate and those who fought back against their oppressors. Emphasizes prisoners' psychological motivations in facing persecution.

685. COHN, Norman. *Warrant for Genocide: The Myth of the Jewish World-Conspiracy and the Protocols of the Elders of Zion.* London: Eyre & Spottiswoode, 1967; New York: Harper & Row, 1967.
Exposes and effectively demolishes the myth of the *Protocols of the Elders of Zion*, a forged publication used by Hitler in his campaign against the Jews. Most of it was copied from a

French pamphlet of 1864, a polemic against Napoleon III. In Czarist Russia the secret political police used the *Protocols* to justify the government's persecution of the Jews. In the Third Reich, Alfred Rosenberg edited a German version. In *Mein Kampf* Hitler declared that the entire being of Jews rested in a "continuing lie, as shown in unparalleled form in the *Protocols of the Elders of Zion*, so interminably hated by the Jews." The forged publication was officially recommended by Nazi authorities for use in schools.

686. *DAWIDOWICZ, Lucy S. *The Holocaust and the Historians.*
     Cambridge, MA: Harvard University Press, 1981, 1983.
     The author of *The War Against the Jews, 1933-1945* (1975) presents the view that most historians have not given the Holocaust the attention it deserves in European history. Believes the subject merited more attention, because "never before in human history had a state and a political movement dedicated itself to the destruction of a whole people." Criticizes writers who asserted that Hitler neither desired nor knew of the "Final Solution." Asserts that the Jews were left to their fate in Europe, and that they were disregarded in the United States and even considered with disdain in Great Britain.

687. *DAWIDOWICZ, Lucy S.   *The War Against the Jews, 1933-1945.* New York: Holt, Rinehart & Winston, 1975; Bantam, 1976.
     Professor of History Dawidowicz at Yeshiva University presents a chronicle of Hitler's Jewish policy. Maintains that anti-Semitism was the linchpin of all the *Führer's* plans, and that for Hitler World War II was directed primarily against the Jews. Asserts that Hitler did not kill Jews because he was waging war; he waged war in order to kill Jews. Defends the response of the Jewish community in Germany and Poland and demonstrates in detail the great strength of Jewish solidarity and of the Jewish determination to survive under heartbreaking circumstances. Describes the self-serving actions of political and socioeconomic groups inside the ghettos. Discusses the victims from imprisonment, ghettoization and starvation, to mass murder.

688. DICKINSON, John K. *German and Jew: The Life and Death of Sigmund Stein.* Chicago: Quadrangle Books, 1967.
     Relates the story of Sigmund Stein, a "little man who happened to be Jewish," and his life inside the Third Reich. A lawyer in the town of Hochberg, Stein was also a German who had deep

roots in rural Germany. When fellow Jews urged him to leave the country, he refused, pointing out that he could best serve his people by acting as a buffer between the Jewish community and the Nazis. He tried from 1933 to 1944, but was methodically stripped of his rights as a citizen and his dignity as a human being. The torment of his Jewish heritage and his proud German upbringing was finally resolved when Stein disappeared into the abyss of Hitler's concentration camps.

689. *DONAT, Alexander. *The Holocaust Kingdom: A Memoir.* New York: Holt, Rinehart & Winston, 1965.
On page after page of this book the reader is assaulted by the odor of corpses, the smell of human bestiality, the overpowering stench of Nazi detritus. Far more frightening than Dante's imagined Inferno, this 20th-century hell was the product of man-made cruelty, refined to perfection by every act of modern technology and designed to destroy human beings physically and spiritually. This is the story of a Jewish family – man, wife and son – who, by a combination of ingenuity and plain luck, managed to survive the Nazi terror. Donat, a printer at the time in New York, writes: "Of course, I suffer from sleeplessness and bitter nightmares, but I cannot forget the experience of the Hitler years, let alone forgive."

690. DRUKS, Herbert. *The Failure to Rescue.* New York: Speller, 1977.
An account charging the United States with shutting its doors to persecuted Jews and collaborating with Great Britain to keep Israel closed to Jews from 1939 to 1945. Accuses the Allies of refusing to bomb the rails leading to the concentration camps and denounces what he calls the "fakery" of President Roosevelt's last-minute rescue efforts through the War Refugee Board. Criticizes the "perfidious myth created by Ben Hecht" that Zionists failed to help the Jews of Europe. Blames some American Jewish leaders for being more worried about anti-Semitism in the United States than about the systematic destruction of European Jewry.

691. ELISSAR, Eliahu Ben-. *La diplomatie du IIIe Reich et les Juifs (1933-1939)* (The Diplomacy of the Third Reich and the Jews [1933-1939]). Paris: Juilliard, 1969.
The Israeli author believes that Hitler's racial policies were sensitive to pressure from abroad. In discussing the diplomacy of the Third Reich as it concerned Jews from 1933 to 1939, re-

lates how pressure on Jews eased during the 1936 Olympics and was resumed in 1938 with anti-Semitic outrages. The Jews were victims of appeasement, a process dating from April 1933 with the reluctance of the British and Americans to boycott German goods. Archival material documents the origin and failure of schemes to save Jewish lives, as well as plans to shift Jews to Palestine, Angola, Madagascar or Shanghai. All failed due to lack of funds and of vigor by Hitler's enemies.

692. *FEINGOLD, Henry L. *The Politics of Rescue: The Roosevelt Administration and the Holocaust, 1938-1945.* New Brunswick, NJ: Rutgers University Press, 1970.
A political scientist discusses the failure of the Roosevelt administration to rescue European Jewry in the Holocaust. Provides evidence to show that Washington officials, although aware of what was occurring in Europe, adopted a policy of evasion and indifference in glaring contrast to the reputation of the United States as a haven for the oppressed. The government barred Jews at a critical time in their history and failed to rescue them during the slaughter in extermination camps. Also faults American Jewish agencies for their insufficient desire for intervention.

693. FLEMING, Gerald. *Hitler and the Final Solution.* Berkeley, CA: University of California Press, 1984.
Another entry in the current scholarly controversy over Hitler's failure to issue any written order for the "Final Solution." According to one theory, the "Final Solution" was not masterminded by Hitler at all, but rather it arose out of ill-coordinated anti-Semitic initiative throughout Europe as the Germans won control of the Continent. Argues that the *Führer* exercised close personal control over the whole undercover operation from start to finish. Offers many examples of how Hitler's operatives throughout Europe repeated his killing orders transmitted orally: "It is the Führer's wish...." Documentary material is presented to counteract the studies minimizing Hitler's role in the "Final Solution."

694. *FRIEDLANDER, Henry and Sybil MILTON, eds. *The Holocaust: Ideology, Bureaucracy, and Genocide: The San José Papers.* Millwood, NY: Kraus-Thomson, 1981.
Papers presented at the Holocaust Conference in San José in 1977 and 1978 sponsored by the National Conference of Christians and Jews include essays by Raul Hilberg and Henry

Feingold in this multidisciplinary collection. Attention is given to the professions in Nazi Germany and the United States and the Holocaust, as well as theological reflections on it.

695. FRIEDMAN, Philip G. *Their Brothers' Keepers.* New York: Crown, 1957.
Concentrates on those countries, notably Denmark, which made efforts to save Jews from the *Gestapo* and Hitler's concentration and extermination camps.

696. GENIZI, Haim. *American Apathy.* Ramat-Gan: Bar-Ilan University Press, 1983.
A highly critical study of the failure of President Roosevelt's administration to do more in the rescue of Jews trapped in the "Final Solution."

697. GENSCHEL, Helmut. *Die Verdrängung der Juden aus der Wirtschaft im Dritten Reich* (The Displacement of Jews in the Economy in the Third Reich). Göttingen: Musterschmidt Wissenschaftlicher Verlag, 1966.
Examines the elimination of German Jews from economic life in the Third Reich. Claims that the strong representation of Jews in German banking, finance, trade and industry generated lower middle-class anti-Semitism and, in turn, transformed racist anti-Semitism into a mass movement. Also asserts that the elimination of Jewry could come only under the impact of a racist total war.

698. *GILBERT, Martin. *The Holocaust: A History of the Jews of Europe during the Second World War.* New York: Holt, Rinehart & Winston, 1986.
Martin Gilbert, the official biographer of Winston Churchill, contributes a 959-page history of the Holocaust, a story of suffering, cruelty, degradation, torture, starvation and mass murder, certainly one of the low points in the history of civilization. The text, based on documentary research and the testimony of survivors, describes a prolonged, cold-blooded, almost inconceivable malignity, of horrible assaults on human dignity. Among those sacrificed were three sisters of Sigmund Freud, two murdered in Treblinka and one in Auschwitz, and Anne Frank's sister Margot, who died of shock in Belsen after falling out of her bunk and hitting the floor. In the Lithuanian village of Jedwabnes on a July day in 1941 the 1,600 Jews who lived there "were driven into the market place by the SS, tortured for

several hours, then driven into a barn and burned alive."
Gilbert writes: "There were many Jedwabneses."

699. GILBERT, Martin. *The Macmillan Atlas of the Holocaust.*
      New York: Macmillan, 1982.
      An atlas concerned with every phase of the
      Holocaust — background, random killings, enforced expulsions,
      setting up of ghettoes, roundups and deportations, creation of
      extermination camps, slave labor system, death marches, exe-
      cutions, liberation and similar subjects. There are more than
      300 maps and many photographs. Rejects the view that the
      Jews submitted like sheep to their destruction.

700. GOLDHAGEN, Erich. "Weltanschauung und Endlösung:
      Zum Antisemitismus der national-sozialistischen
      Führungsschicht" (Conception of the World and Final
      Solution: On Anti-Semitism in the National Socialist
      Leadership Command). *Vierteljahrshefte für
      Zeitgeschichte*, XXIV (1976), 379-405.
      This study of the relationship between National Socialist ideol-
      ogy and the "Final Solution" traces the Nazi racist belief in a
      joint Jewish-Bolshevist conspiracy. The bitter hatred of Jews
      reflected in Hitler's personal antipathy became the central idea
      of Nazi philosophy. This overwhelming acceptance of the
      biological structure of nations eventually led to its logical
      end — an attempt to wipe European Jewry from the face of the
      earth.

701. GORDRON, Sarah. *Hitler, Germans and the "Jewish
      Question."* Princeton, NJ: Princeton University Press,
      1984.
      Examines the background of the Nazi persecution and murder
      of European Jews as well as German reaction to the slaughter.
      Finds anti-Semitism in 19th-century Germany no more virulent
      than elsewhere in Europe. Believes that hatred of Jews was
      minimal in bringing Hitler to power. The "Final Solution" was
      a political development based on Hitler's ethnic theory about
      the struggle between superior Aryans and inferior Jews. Inves-
      tigation of *Gestapo* files demonstrates pockets of opposition to
      the persecution of Jews: this sentiment existed among the mili-
      tary, bureaucracy, press and even the Nazi Party itself.

702. GOSTNER, Erwin. *1000 Tage in KZ* (1000 Days in Concentration Camp). Innsbruck: Wagner'sche Universitäts-Buchdruckerei, 1945.
An account of conditions in one of Hitler's concentration camps, in which the author spent a thousand days. Describes the atrocities and barbarities of Hitler's system to cleanse the Aryan "race" of impurities.

703. GUTMAN, Israel. *The Jews of Warsaw, 1939-1943: Ghetto, Underground, Revolt.* Translated from the Hebrew by Ina Freedman. Bloomington, IN: Indiana University Press, 1982.
Examines the character and conduct of the Jewish community of Warsaw during the era of Nazi persecution. Describes intellectual and psychological means adopted by Jews to cope with their tragic problems. Stresses the significance of the resistance under inhuman conditons.

704. HAUSNER, Gideon. *Justice in Jerusalem.* New York: Harper & Row, 1966.
The former Attorney General of Israel and the prosecutor at the trial of Adolf Eichmann recounts not only the proceedings but the total German involvement in the extermination of Jews. Analyzes the testimony of survivors and describes what happened to his fellow-Jews. Denounces Eichmann and criticizes Pope Pius XII as being guilty of silence.

705. *HILBERG, Raul. *The Destruction of the European Jews.* Chicago: Quadrangle, 1961; New York: Holmes & Meier, 1985.
A revised edition of Hilberg's massive study originally published in 1961. The author, formerly a member of the Documentation Project in the Federal Records Center at Alexandria, Virginia, devoted years to gathering the facts in this study of the Holocaust, said to be the greatest human destruction process in history. Challenges those neo-Nazis who contend that the destruction of European Jews never took place. In examining Jewish institutions Hilberg does so primarily through the eyes of the Germans as tools used in the system of genocide. Sees the process as a matter of extremes. "That is why it can serve as a test of social and political theories." Asserts that it is not enough to know that the Jews were destroyed, but how the deed was done.

706.   HILLGRUBER,   Andreas.   *Zweierlei   Untergang: Die Zerschlagung des Deutschen Reiches und das Ende des europäischen Judentums* (Two Kinds of Destruction: The Shattering of the German Reich and the End of European Jewry). Berlin: Siedler-Verlag, 1986.

Andreas Hillgruber, historian at Cologne University, suggests a link between the collapse of Hitler's Eastern Front and the Holocaust. Describes the "catastrophe" during the winter of 1944-45 as the Soviet Army pushed forward to Berlin, as a result of which millions of Germans had to flee their homes, leaving two millions or more dead. Accusses the Soviets of mass rape and "barbarian" behavior in contacts with the German public. By associating the collapse of Germany's Eastern Front with the Holocaust, Hillgruber implies a moral comparison of the two events. Argues that Austria, more than Germany, fostered the kind of anti-Semitism that produced the death camps.

707.   KOCHAN, Lionel.   *Pogrom: 10 November 1938*.   London: Deutsch, 1957.

On 7 November 1938 Ernst vom Rath, Third Secretary of the German Embassy in Paris, was assassinated by Hirschel Grynszpan, a Polish Jew. In retaliation, Reinhard Heydrich, chief of the SD, the Security Service, ordered the destruction of all Jewish places of worship in Germany and Austria. The night of 9-10 November 1938, known as *Kristallnacht*, or Night of the Broken Glass, saw terror attacks on Jewish synagogues and stores. That night and the next day bands of Nazis systematically pillaged thousands of Jewish-owned shops. Labels the event a latter-day pogrom.

708.   *KOGON, Eugen.   *The Theory and Practice of Hell: The German Concentration Camps and the System Behind Them*. Translated from the German by Heinz Norden.   New York: Farrar, Straus, 1950; New York: Berkley Windover Books, 1975.

Originally published in Germany as *Der SS Staat*, Eugen Kogon's text describes "the closest thing to hell in human history." Presents the story of the role of Hitler's SS in the horror of the concentration camps. Shows not only every possible form of cruelty, but also the dishonesty among the Nazi overlords. It is a chilling record of human depravity, a catalog of barbarism unprecedented in the history of mankind.

709. KURTH, Gertrud M. "The Jew and Adolf Hitler."
    Psychoanalytic Quarterly, XVI (1947), 11-32.
    Explores the psychological aspects of Hitler's attitude toward
    the Jews, an attempt to explore the complexities of what may
    have been an unbalanced mind.

710. LANGHOFF, Wolfgang. *Rubber Truncheon*. Translated from
    the German by Leo Linke. New York: Dutton, 1935.
    A young German actor describes his thirteen months in a
    German concentration camp. Tells of inhuman treatment by
    his Nazi warders, but also notes the growing opposition to the
    Third Reich beginning among the victims incarcerated in
    concentration camps. Provides names of guards and victims.
    In the Introduction, novelist Lion Feuchtwanger explains that
    the author has made a successful effort to set down to the last
    detail "nothing but the naked truth."

711. LAQUEUR, Walter Z. *The Terrible Secret: Suppression of the
    Truth about Hitler's 'Final Solution.'* Boston: Little, Brown,
    1981.
    This investigation of the evidence on Hitler's "Final Solution"
    focuses on the eighteen months from June 1941 to the end of
    1942. Gradually, the Nazi urge to annihilate enemies was
    developed into a system of organized murder. Asserts that
    "millions of people cannot be killed without participants in the
    murder and without witnesses." Criticizes Allied politicians,
    neutral countries, the Vatican and the Red Cross, all accused
    of knowing what was going on but keeping silent out of fear.
    Maintains that many people, including Jews, could not accept
    the facts even in the face of proof. "The truth was so frightful
    that nobody wanted to be told and nobody wanted to believe
    it."

712. *LESCHNITZER, Adolf. *The Magic Background of Modern
    Anti-Semitism: An Analysis of the German-Jewish Rela-
    tionship*. New York: International Universities Press, 1956.
    Himself a victim of the tragic events in Germany, Dr.
    Leschnitzer analyzes the German-Jewish relationship. In elic-
    iting the reasons why Jews were made victims of Hitler's
    monomania, he considers economic and social changes, the
    psychological reactions to such changes and the interrela-
    tionship and cross-fertilization of all three. Believes that, while
    for millions of Jews Nazism was a catastrophe, it was no disaster
    for Judaism, despite Hitler's hopes. "It was German civilization

that collapsed, burying, along with many of her own, the adopted children who had loved her so much." It was a new witchcraft mania, but antipathy was always there smoldering under the surface, until after 1933 the murderous arson began.

713. *LEVIN, Nora. *The Holocaust: The Destruction of European Jewry, 1933-1945.* New York: Crowell, 1968.
Analyzes the microcosm and macrocosm of the Hitler terror. Gives an account of how six million Jews were slaughtered during World War II by premeditated official plan. It is a story of how a great nation was forced to descend from the plane of anti-Semitic ideology to the stain of genocide. Explains what happened when the Nazis ruptured the continuum of the Western moral order. Traces the destructive process from the impact of racial myths on German thought to the extermination of the gas chambers. Led by Himmler and Heydrich, the Nazi terror operation transformed economic and legal restrictions against the Jews into inhuman labor camps and ghettos. In turn, these gave way to the death camps. Weaves into the chronicle the political and military events in Europe that clinched Nazi power and sealed the fate of European Jews.

714. *LIFTON, Robert Jay. *Medical Killing and the Psychology of Genocide.* New York: Basic, 1986.
Psychiatrist Robert Jay Lifton interviewed directly nineteen men "who had been significantly involved at high levels with Nazi medicine," and five of whom had worked in concentration camps (three in Auschwitz) either as SS physicians assigned there or in connection with medical experiments. Passes professional judgment on these physicians and presents an analysis of the process by which an individual sworn to the art of healing becomes a professional mass killer. Explains how doctors dedicated to the collective ideology of National Socialism took a few short steps to the idea of removing "diseased" individuals from society's organism — the real essence of genocide. Shows how seemingly decent people became acclimated to the genocidal culture of the extermination camps. There was a simultaneous process of psychic numbing, often by means of alcohol and "doubling" or dividing the self into two functioning wholes, so that "a part acts as an entire self." In this way the author shows how killing could be justified as "healing" and how decent men allowed themselves to become part of the "medical bureaucracy of killing."

715. LIPSTADT, Deborah E. *Beyond Belief: The American Press and the Coming of the Holocaust, 1933-1945.* New York: Free Press, 1985.
Contends that the American press and radio, especially daily newspapers, gave generally uninformed coverage, with some notable exceptions, on the Holocaust. The title refers to the unwillingness of some but not all important dailies to publish results of the "Final Solution" because they were "beyond belief." Does not mean to suggest a conspiracy to suppress news about the Holocaust, but the prestigious newspapers and radio networks were skeptical and scornful of reports made by refugees. The public was thus left in the dark about the horrible excesses of Nazism and Congress was ignorant of their importance. Had the truth been known, there would have been a more enlightened and humane immigration policy and later, after authentication, more aggressive military action against the death camps.

716. *LOW, Alfred D. *Jews in the Eyes of the Germans: From the Enlightenment to Imperial Germany.* Philadelphia: Institute for the Study of Human Issues, 1979.
Analyzes the relations and attitudes of Germans to Jews and Judaism. The book was planned when the author was a student at the University of Vienna, in response to the Nazi claim that all great Germans were anti-Semites. The Austrian takeover by Hitler at that time prevented its publication. Presents evidence to rescue Frederick the Great, Goethe, Nietzsche, Schiller, Metternich, even Fichte, from Nazi perversions. Asserts that some of these great men may have been prejudiced against Jews, but they cannot be regarded as foreshadowing the ideology of National Socialism.

717. LUKAS, Richard C. *Forgotten Holocaust: The Poles Under German Occupation, 1938-1944.* Lexington, KY: The University Press of Kentucky, 1986.
An account of the Nazis' systematic genocide of Poles contains analyses of the relationship of Poland's Jewish and Gentile communities, the development of the Resistance, the exile leadership and the Warsaw uprisings.

718. *MELTZER, Milton. *Never to Forget: The Jews of the Holocaust.* New York: Harper, 1975.
Milton Meltzer, author of many children's books, discusses the roots of Nazi anti-Semitism, the rise of Hitler to political power

and the methodology of the Nazi death machine. Presents eye-witness accounts of the persecution and massacre of Jews and their experiences in ghettos, work camps and finally in the extermination camps. The text is designed for boys and girls from the sixth to the twelfth grades.

719. MOCZARSKI, Kazimierz. *Conversations with an Executioner.* Edited by Mariana Fitzpatrick. Translated from the German. Englewood Cliffs, NJ: Prentice-Hall, 1971.
SS Major-General Juergen Stroop, member of the inner circle of Nazi power, was in charge of the liquidation of the Warsaw ghetto in 1943. After the war he was tried in Poland and sentenced to death. Moczarski shared the same cell with him for nine months. This book reproduces his conversations with a Nazi executioner. Stroop accepted Nazi ideology whole-heartedly and never showed the least signs of repentance for his deeds. Without conscience, he was interested only in Nazism and his own aggrandizement. (See Juergen Stroop, *The Stroop Report* [1980], entry No. 53 for his official report to Himmler on the liquidation of the Warsaw ghetto).

720. *MOMMSEN, Hans. "Der nationalsozialistische Polizeistaat und die Judenverfolgung von 1938" (The National Socialist Police State and Persecution of Jews in 1938). *Vierteljahrshefte für Zeitgeschichte*, X (1962), 68-87.
A German historian, bearer of a famous name in German historiography, analyzes the Nazi campaign against German Jews, with special attention to the *Kristallnacht* (Night of the Broken Glass), 9-10 November 1938 when, following the assassination of Ernst vom Rath, Third Secretary of the German Embassy in Paris, Hitler ordered the destruction of Jewish places of worship in Germany and Austria. Jews were required to pay "for the damage they had provoked" with a fine of one billion marks. Recounts the story of the National Socialist police state and its persecution of Jews in 1938.

721. MORSE, Arthur D. *While Six Million Died.* New York: Random House, 1967.
This account of the Holocaust discusses governmental as well as public "American apathy." Asserts that President Roosevelt and others in the American administration did not do as much as they could have in a humanitarian effort to lessen the plight of Jews in Nazi Germany.

722. NAUMANN, Bernd. *Auschwitz*. Translated from the German
by Jean Steinberg. New York: Praeger, 1966.
A report on the proceedings against Robert Karl Ludwig Mulka
and others before the court at Frankfurt am Main. It is estimated that from 1 to 4 million "special incidents" took place at
Auschwitz — mass and isolated murders as part of Hitler's
"Final Solution of the Jewish problem." On 20 December 1963
twenty-two former SS men were brought before the court for
their role in the "special incidents." The defendants, mostly
middle-class, showed contempt for the court, insulted witnesses
and demanded that the prosecutors apologize. Most of them
insisted that they merely carried out orders for their superiors.
Sentences ranged from three years to life at hard labor; three
defendants were acquitted. Naumann, representing the
Frankfurter Allgemeine Zeitung, was present in the courtroom
at the longest legal case in German records — from 20 December
1963 to 20 August 1965.

723. NYISZLI, Miklos. *Auschwitz*. Greenwich, CT: Fawcett, 1960.
A doctor's eyewitness account of conditions at Auschwitz, the
notorious Nazi extermination camp on a marshy tract between
the Vistula and its tributary, the Sola, 160 miles southwest of
Warsaw. Describes the horrendous circumstances of life at
Auschwitz, where hundreds of thousands of inmates died in its
gas chambers. Devotes special attention to the role of doctors
in the daily life of the camp.

724. POSNER, Gerald L. and John WARE. *Mengele: The Complete
Story*. New York: McGraw-Hill, 1986.
A new biography of Dr. Josef Mengele, notorious extermination
camp director at Auschwitz, who selected those sent to the gas
chambers and who was accused of horrifying medical experiments. Based in large part on Dr. Mengele's diaries and other
family material presented to the authors by Mengele's son Rolf,
a West German lawyer.

725. PRESSER, Jacob. *The Destruction of the German Jews*.
Translated from the Dutch by Arnold Pomerans. New
York: Dutton, 1969.
A Dutch historian presents the story of how Hitler attempted to
destroy the entire Jewish population of Germany in his goal of
winning "a pure-blooded Aryan-Nordic race." The author,
himself a Jew and at the time of writing this book a professor

of history at the University of Amsterdam, had lost his first wife, who was murdered in an extermination camp.

726. REICHMANN, Eva G. *Hostages of Civilization: The Social Sources of National Socialist Anti-Semitism.* London: Gollancz, 1950; Boston: Beacon, 1951.
This study seeks to determine whether a special Jewish community was expelled and destroyed because the Gentiles among whom the Jews lived decided that life with the Jews had become unbearable for them. Analyzes modern German society as a whole, describes each social class and discusses the place of Jews in that setting. Suggests that hatred of Jews in recent German history was not the result of actual group conflict, but was grounded on traditional stereotypes projecting German fears and insecurities.

727. *REITLINGER, Gerald. *The Final Solution: The Attempt to Exterminate the Jews of Europe, 1939-1945.* London: Vallentine, Mitchell, 1953.
This was one of the first books on this subject. Presenting a summary of what came to be known as the "Final Solution," recounts Hitler's campaign to obliterate the Jews of Europe. Reveals that the Nazi police state unwittingly left behind hundreds of tons of documents and many thousands of witnesses. Treats the preparation and beginning of the "Solution," with attention to the pogroms of November 1938, the early deportations, the ghettos, the Auschwitz plan and the gas chambers. Is also concerned with implementation of the policy throughout conquered Europe. Page after page describes corpses piled like firewood and Jews led unsuspecting to the gas chambers. To them – this was the last step from nationalism to bestiality.

728. RINGELBLUM, Emmanuel. *Notes from the Warsaw Ghetto.* Translated from the Yiddish by Jacob Sloan. New York: McGraw-Hill, 1958.
This journal covers the terror against the Jews from 1939, when the Germans took over Warsaw, to the end of 1942, when Jews of the ghetto fought against the Nazis and many of them died in the process. Ringelblum buried these notes. He was eventually caught and with his wife and twelve-year-old son executed. Presents grim fact after fact. The story of the Warsaw ghetto was told in John Hersey's *The Wall* (1950); this book substantiates Hersey's account.

729. ROBINSON, Jacob and Philip G. FRIEDMAN. *Guide to Jewish History under Nazi Impact.* New York: Yivo Institute for Jewish Research, 1960.
A massive guide to Jewish history with special attention to the fate of Jews under National Socialism. The authors' entries treat every aspect of the Holocaust, including references to available documents, plus a list of libraries housing material on the subject. The book is intended as an aid to Holocaust research.

730. *ROSSEL, Seymour. *The Holocaust.* New York: Franklin Watts, 1981.
This introduction to the Holocaust for beginning students discusses the nature and mechanics of prejudice, the rise of Hitler, Nazi anti-Semitism, the creation of ghettos and concentration camps and the place of the Holocaust in history.

731. SCHLEUNES, Karl A. *The Twisted Road to Auschwitz: Nazi Policy Toward German Jews, 1933-1939.* Urbana, IL: University of Illinois Press, 1970.
This account of Nazi policy toward Jews contends that, although anti-Semitism was the keystone of the Nazi movement, the Nazis actually knew little about the Jews and had little ideas about what to do to them until Hitler's monomania encouraged them into action. Shows how the lower middle class, as well as other levels of the Nazi hierarchy, profited from Hitler's anti-Semitic drive. Sees Nazi pressure against Jews as being not the product of a single policy, because Hitler did not resolve internal conflicts and seemed unable to issue decisive orders. Cites confusion and strain in the Nazi machinery of destruction. This book supplements Raul Hilberg's *The Destruction of European Jews* (1961, 1985).

732. SCHOENBINER, Gerhard. *The Yellow Star.* Translated from the German by Susan Sweet. New York: Bantam Books, 1973.
This discussion of Jewish inmates in Nazi concentration and extermination camps asserts that all prisoners had to wear prescribed markings on their clothing, including a serial number and colored triangles affixed to the left breast and the right trouser leg. At Auschwitz the serial number was tattooed on the left forearm. Political prisoners wore a red triangle; criminals, green; shiftless elements, black; homosexuals, pink; and Gypsies, brown. Jews were required to wear a yellow triangle in

addition to the classification triangle. The yellow triangle pointed up, the other down, thus forming the six-pointed Star of David. Any Jew classified as a "racial defiler" had to wear a black border around the yellow triangle.

733. SCHOEPS, Hans-Joachim. *"Bereit für Deutschland." Der Patriotismus deutscher Juden und der Nationalsozialismus* ("Ready for Germany." The Patriotism of German Jews and National Socialism). Berlin: Haude & Spener'sche Verlagsbuchhandlung, 1970.
In the 1930s Hans-Joachim Schoeps, a historian who described himself as "conservative, Prussian and Jew," in that order, published a series of essays about the predicament of Jews under the Nazi regime. In February 1933, shortly after the accession of Hitler to power, Schoeps founded a small organization of about one-hundred Jews to proclaim love for the Fatherland. Rejecting Zionism and itself rejected by the Third Reich, the organization used the slogan "Ready for Germany." Schoeps' first pamphlet was titled, "We Walk a German Road." This German publisher reissued Schoeps' essays.

734. SEGER, Gerhard. *A Nation Terrorized*. New York: Reilly & Lee, 1935.
The author relates his experiences during six months spent in Oranienburg concentration camp, from which he escaped. This was the first report by a fugitive from a camp. A former Socialist Deputy in the *Reichstag*, Seger describes how Hitler was dealing with dissenters he accused of political crimes and offenses. This book was followed by scores more on the same theme.

735. SHARF, Andrew. *The British Press and Jews Under the Nazi Rule*. London: Oxford University Press, 1964.
Examines the British public's attitude toward reports of extreme anti-Semitic persecutions in Nazi Germany. Maintains that the British press tended to evade what was unpleasant and what was disturbing to its conscience. However, praises the coverage of *The Times* and especially the *Manchester Guardian*.

736. SMITH, Marcus J. *The Harrowing of Hell: Dachau*. Albuquerque, NM: University of New Mexico Press, 1972.
This account of conditions at Dachau concentration camp in Bavaria, 12 miles northeast of Munich, one of three camps set up in 1932 to form the nucleus of a concentration camp system

(the two others were Buchenwald in central Germany and Sachsenhausen in the north) offers details concerning life in this notorious camp. Reports that Dachau was the scene of medical experiments performed on its inmates.

737. *STEIN, Leon. *The Racial Thinking of Richard Wagner.* New York: Philosophical Library, 1956.
Demonstrates that there was much more to composer Richard Wagner than his music. He wrote not only music but German prose, in much of which he revealed his status as a bigot. He glorified German profundity, integrity, innocence, veracity and strength. His "Judaism in Music" was actually an attack on Jewish composers Mendelssohn and Meyerbeer. He denounced Jews as being alien to German culture. His nationalism and racialism appealed strongly to Hitler, who fairly worshipped him. This self-assertive, impulsive, quarreling, vitriolic composer was acceptable to Nazi ideology. Describes the golden figure of the Wagnerian cult as a shabby, gilded idol, a master of musical form but an utter failure as a human being.

738. STEINER, Jean-François. *Treblinka.* Translated from the German by Helen Weaver. New York: Simon & Schuster, 1967.
The story of the extermination camp on the Bug River in Poland, which with Chelmno, Belzec and Sobibór, was one of the four main Polish camps used as receiving centers primarily for Jews. Almost exclusively a death camp, Treblinka was the scene of mass killings by Zyklon-B gas. The knowledge of certain death at Treblinka was responsible in part for the Warsaw ghetto uprising in early 1943.

739. STREICHER, Julius. *Kampf dem Weltfeind: Reden aus der Kampfzeit* (Fight Against the World Enemy: Speeches from the Time of Struggle). Nürnberg: Verlag Der Stürmer, 1938.
Julius Streicher (1885-1946), National Socialist politician, pornographer and Jew-hater, presents his "Fight Against the World Enemy," speeches he had delivered against the Jews during "the period of battle." The book was published by his illustrated newspaper *Der Stürmer.*

740. SYRKIN, Marie. "The Literature of the Holocaust." *Midstream*, XII (1966), 3-20.

A summary of the extensive literature to 1966 on the Holocaust, the term used to describe Hitler's attempt to exterminate all European Jews.

741. *TEC, Nechama. *When Light Pierced the Darkness.* New York: Oxford University Press, 1985.
A study of those "righteous Christians" in Poland who protected hunted Jews during the Holocaust and in their own way defied the Nazis. Poland, a country with as many as 3.5 million Jews (about 10% of the population), had a long history of anti-Semitism. Among the Poles were citizens who refused to accept Nazi bestiality and who gave sanctuary to helpless Jews. In her previous book *Dry Tears* (1984), Tec, now a sociologist at the University of Connecticut, told how she managed to survive by "passing" as a Catholic schoolgirl. Gives the results of interviews with other survivors. Where some priests continued to speak harshly against Jews, others gave shelter to scores of Jewish children. Writes that every class of Polish society had decent Christians who as a matter of principle helped Jews in a tragic situation.

742. TENENBAUM, Joseph. "The Einsatzgruppen" (The Task Forces). *Jewish Social Studies*, XVII (1955), 43-64.
Describes the *Einsatzgruppen*, or task forces, special mobile units charged with implementing the liquidation policy in occupied countries. These formations were assigned to the task of carrying out the "Final Solution of the Jewish problem" by extermination. The *Einsatzgruppen* were responsible for the deaths of two million of the estimated six million Jews killed.

743. THALMANN, Rita and Emmanuel FEINERMANN. *Crystal Night, 9-10 November, 1938.* Translated from the French by Gilles Cremonesi. New York: Coward, McCann & Geoghegan, 1974.
Reconstructs the events of the 1938 pogrom in Germany following the assassination of Ernst vom Rath, Third Secretary at the German Embassy in Paris, by Hirschel Grynszpan, a young Polish Jew. The term "Crystal Night" (also called "Night of the Broken Glass") was used because of the smashing of windows of Jewish-owned stores. At the time the Nazis described it as "the Jew action." The authors point out that, when the incident took place, the French National Assembly did not even discuss the matter. They emphasize the premeditated nature of the Crystal Night.

744. TRUNK, Isaiah. *Judenrat* (Jewish Council). New York: Macmillan, 1972.
A study of the *Judenräte*, the special bodies representing Jews *vis-à-vis* the Nazi government. These councils were set up not only in the Third Reich, but throughout German-occupied Europe. Gives special attention to the *Judenrat* functioning during the Warsaw ghetto uprising in the spring of 1943, the final struggle of one-thousand Jews against German troops and police in occupied Warsaw, Poland.

745. WANGH, Martin. "National Socialism and the Genocide of the Jews: A Psycho-analytic Study of a Historical Event." *The International Journal of Psycho-analysis*, XLV (1964), 386-95.
Analyzes psychoanalytical aspects of Hitler's "Final Solution" and the genocide which accompanied it.

746. WIESENTHAL, Simon. *The Murderers Among Us: The Simon Wiesenthal Memoirs.* New York: McGraw-Hill, 1967; New York: Bantam Books, 1968, 1973.
Memoirs of relentless Nazi-hunter Simon Wiesenthal, with special attention to Operation Odessa, the secret escape organization of the SS underground, and the international manhunt for Hitler's escaped henchmen. Wiesenthal, originally from Polish Galicia, was imprisoned for some four years in several concentration camps: he decided to spend the rest of his life tracking down wanted Nazi criminals. He is credited as "the man who found Adolf Eichmann." This book reveals Wiesenthal as a determined agent of retribution.

747. WORMSER-MIGOT, Olga. *Le système concentrationnaire nazi 1933-1945* (The Nazi Concentration Camp System 1933-1945). Paris: Presses universitaires de France, 1968.
A historical survey, more encyclopedic than interpretive, of the system established for the operation of Nazi concentration camps, with special sttention to the origins and subsequent evolution of the system. Sources include records of the International Red Cross, archives throughout Europe and documents of the Nuremberg Trial.

748. WYMAN, Davis S. *The Abandonment of the Jews: America and the Holocaust, 1941-1945.* New York: Pantheon, 1984.
Presents an inquiry into the response of Americans in the early 1940s to evidence that Hitler was exterminating the Jews of

Europe. Claims that the White House, the State Department, Congress and the military all resisted recommendations that they oppose the massacre of Jews. The governments of Great Britain and the United States feared a large influx of Jewish refugees into their countries. American Christian churches retreated into almost total silence. Charges that even the American Jewish community, enmeshed in feuds, was ambivalent in seeking the rescue of European Jews. Implicates passive bystanders and perpetrators.

749. YAHIL, Leni. *The Rescue of Danish Jewry.* Philadelphia: Jewish Publication Society of America, 1969.
Denmark played an important role in the desperate plight of European Jews in the Nazi Holocaust. On a humanitarian basis and also as a means of showing their contempt for Nazism, Danes organized an underground campaign to rescue Jews from arrest and almost certain extermination. Recounts how hunted Jews were saved and sent surreptitiously to Sweden. Regards the rescue of Jews in October 1943 as the true test of a working democracy.

750. ZIMMELS, H. J. *The Echo of the Nazi Holocaust in Rabbinic Literature.* New York: Ktav, 1977.
A reference work on the scholar's approach to the Holocaust, as guided by religious doctrine. The author, an Orthodox rabbi, stresses the faithfulness of European Jews to their religious heritage during a time of pitiless persecution. Examines the rabbinic literature on the Holocaust and relates it to the various stages of Nazi oppression.

CHAPTER 13

NATIONAL SOCIALISM IN WORLD WAR II

German Military Structure, Hitler as Strategist, War Operations, Nuremberg Trial

No attempt is made in this chapter to present entries on the thousands of books on Germany in World War II. Instead, these titles are limited to those concerned especially with the role of National Socialism in the war as indicated in the subtitles above. Included are studies about the rearmament of Germany beginning as early as 1934 and the building of a war machine to win the objectives Hitler had outlined in *Mein Kampf*. Military historians have shown the greatest interest in Hitler's ability as a war strategist and tactician, with attention to early victories and later damaging defeats. Surprising unanimity exists on the subject – the war lord made mistake after mistake in such major encounters as Operation Barbarossa and the Battle of the Bulge. Attention is given to the postwar trials of Nazi leaders at Nuremberg; these entries are included here to avoid too many chapters.

As is to be expected, the question of war responsibility has engaged historians and journalists who have written on the origins of World War II. By far the large majority of experts seeking to provide an unbiased account of what happened, see the origins in a complexity of unresolved political, economic and military confrontations, but agree that primary responsibility for the immediate outbreak of hostilities must be attributed to Hitler and Nazi Germany. The bitter soldier of World War I, once he was propelled to the seat of power in Germany, refused to accept that defeat as final. He unceremoniously rearmed his people and then pushed them into the war to destroy the

Treaty of Versailles and give Germany the living space he decreed for her.

Only a handful of revisionist historians, led by Briton A. J. P. Taylor and several ultranationalist German scholars, have challenged this view and presented what has been called an apologia for Hitler. Taylor, especially, has been greeted by his peers not with respected criticism but with ridicule and disbelief. They denounce his stand as the unfortunate extension into adulthood of the British schoolboy's eccentric compulsion to be different.

BIBLIOGRAPHY

751. ADDINGTON, Larry H. *The Blitzkrieg Era and the German General Staff, 1865-1941.* New Brunswick, NJ: Rutgers University Pess, 1971.
      Traces the role of the German General Staff in the military history of Germany from just before the war between Prussia and Austria in 1866 to 1941 immediately preceding Hitler's attack on the Soviet Union. Shows how the General Staff utilized *Blitzkrieg*, or lightning war, in the first two years of World War II.

752. ANDERS, Wladyslaw. *Hitler's Defeat in Russia.* Chicago: Regnery, 1953.
      When Hitler turned on the Soviet Union on 22 June 1941, he broke his own resolve not to fight a war on two fronts. Analyzes details of the Nazi catastrophe in Russia, with attention to the mistakes made by a self-professed military genius. Anders, Polish general and former commander of the Free Poland Forces, discusses Nazi policy toward the occupied population and war prisoners and details Western aid to the Soviet Union. Tells of Nazi brutality and political stupidity in handling the local population. Concludes that the Russian campaign was a defeat for Hitler because of his own ineptitude and not because of heroic fighting by the Soviets.

753. ANSEL, Walter. *Hitler Confronts England.* Durham, NC: University of North Carolina Press, 1960.
      A study of the confrontation between Hitler and Great Britain during 1940, when the Nazi series of conquests was stopped in the Battle of Britain.

754. ASSMANN, Kurt. *Deutsche Seestrategie in zwei Weltkriegen* (German Naval Strategy in Two World Wars). Heidelberg: K. Vowinckel, 1957.
Describes German strategy on the high seas in both World Wars.

755. ASSMANN, Kurt. "The Battle for Moscow." *Foreign Affairs*, XXVIII (1950), 309-26.
Analyzes Hitler's vain attempt to defeat the Russians before Moscow.

756. BARTZ, Karl. *Swastika in the Air*. London: Kimber, 1956.
This account of the role of the German *Luftwaffe* under the command of General Hermann Goering describes the attacks on Warsaw, Rotterdam, Coventry and elsewhere, and traces the gradual diminution of its power in the air.

757. BAUMGARDT, Winfried. "Zur Ansprache Hitlers vor den Führern der Wehrmacht am 22. August 1939: Eine quellenkritische Untersuchung" (On Hitler's Appeal to the Leadership of the *Wehrmacht* : A Critical Examination of the Source Material). *Vierteljahrshefte für Zeitgeschichte*, XVI (1968), 120-49.
A critical examination of the sources for Hitler's interviews with leaders of the *Wehrmacht* (the German Armed Forces), in late August 1939, only a few days before the invasion of Poland.

758. BEKKER, Cajus. *Hitler's Naval War*. Translated from the German by Frank Ziegler. Garden City, NY: Doubleday, 1974.
An introduction to the German side of the naval war from 1939 to 1943, with discussions of operations in the Atlantic, Mediterranean and the Arctic. Analyzes the differences in strategic thinking within the German naval command. Shows the importance which the German Naval High Command paid to arms supplied to Soviet Russia by the Arctic convoys, and pays tribute to the British merchant seamen who challenged the freezing climate of the convoys to northern Russia. Believes that Hitler's failings as a naval strategist, along with the controversies between the traditional battleship officers and champions of U-boat warfare, irretrievably cost Germany the war.

759. BENTON, Wilbourn Eugene and Georg GRIMM, eds.
      Nuremberg: German Views of the War Trials. Translated
      from the German.   Dallas, TX: Southern Methodist
      University Press, 1955.
      Offers opinions of representative German scholars on the
      precedent-breaking Nuremberg Trial. Includes translations of
      ten articles from German legal journals and the statements
      made at the trial by defense counsel. Considers these views as
      "an exchange of ideas...rather than a debate." Some of the
      contributors claim that the trial was not a properly conducted
      international criminal court of justice, others do not allow their
      technical objections to obscure the belief in its importance and
      merits.   Several essays support the entire concept of the pro-
      ceedings and admit the grave nature of Nazi crimes.   Others
      express doubts about the legality of the trial.

760. BERNADOTTE, Folke. *The Curtain Falls: Last Days of the
      Third Reich.*   Translated from the Swedish by Erich
      Lewenhaupt. New York: Knopf, 1945.
      An account of the final days of the Hitler regime by Count
      Folke   Bernadotte   of   Wisborg   (1895-1948),   soldier,
      humanitarian and diplomat, who was assassinated on 17
      September 1948 while acting for the United Nations as a
      mediator between Israelis and Arabs. As head of the Swedish
      Red Cross in World War II, he was credited with saving some
      20,000 inmates of Nazi concentration camps.   Relates how
      Heinrich Himmler urged him to transmit an offer on 24 April
      1945 that Germany would surrender unconditionally to Great
      Britain and the United States but not to Soviet Russia. Also
      writes how he sought to get all Danes and Norwegians held
      captive in the Third Reich returned to their homes.

761. *BEST, S. Payne. *The Venlo Incident.* London: Hutchinson,
      1950.
      Relates the Venlo incident, a clash between German and British
      intelligence units at the beginning of World War II, a contest
      won by the Germans. Learning that German officers repre-
      senting a conspiracy against Hitler wanted to make contact with
      the British, London sent two agents, Captain S. Payne Best and
      Major R. H.   Stevens, to Venlo, a frontier town in the
      Netherlands. The two were kidnapped by an armed detachment
      from across the frontier and smuggled into Germany. They re-
      mained captives until the end of the war, when they were liber-
      ated by Americans.

762. BOELCKE, Willi A. *Deutschlands Rüstung im Zweiten Weltkrieg: Hitlers Konferenzen mit Albert Speer, 1942-1945* (Germany's Arming in the Second World War: Hitler's Conferences with Albert Speer, 1942-1945). Frankfurt am Main: Akademische Verlagsgesellschaft Athenaion, 1969.
A German study of the rearmament of Hitler's Germany starting in 1934 and steps in arming the country during World War II.

763. BOLTING, Douglas. *From the Ruins of the Reich, 1945-1948.* New York: Crown, 1985.
Although concerned primarily with the situation in postwar Germany, describes the invasion of Hitler's Third Reich by the Allies, the discovery of the death camps, the conquest of Berlin and the final days in the *Führer's* underground bunker. Draws the moral that Nazi Germany achieved a new level of sub-animal behavior.

764. BOSCH, William J. *Judgment on Nuremberg: American Attitudes toward the Major German War-Crimes Trials.* Chapel Hill, NC: University of North Carolina Press, 1970.
Stresses American reactions to the postwar war-crimes trials. Seeks to reveal "fundamental aspects of the American mind." Indicates that most Americans approved the trials, but some historians and experts in international relations disapproved.

765. BROSS, Werner. *Gespräche mit Goering während des Nürnberger Prozesses* (Conversations with Goering during the Nuremberg Trial). Flensburg and Hamburg: Wolff, 1950.
In his cell during his trial before the International Military Tribunal, Hermann Goering was interviewed by German journalist Werner Bross. These talks reveal much about the attitude of the former No. 2 Nazi while on trial for his life. Goering defended himself with skill and aggressiveness, seeing himself as the ranking officer in the prisoners' dock and demanding that all the accused follow his orders. He believed to be merely a victim of "victors' justice" and demanded treatment as an honorable opponent. He was confident of posthumous rehabilitation and later wrote in his last letter to his wife: "In 50 or 60 years there will be statues to Hermann Goering all over Germany. Little statues maybe but one in every German home."

766. CAIDIN, Martin. *The Night Hamburg Died.* New York: Ballantine Books, 1960.
Explains that for the British Bomber Command, Hamburg, one of Germany's major cities, was a target of prime importance. Just 64 miles from the mouth of the Elbe, it was Germany's largest seaport with such industries as shipbuilding, oil refining, metal and rubber goods, optical and electrical equipment and foodstuffs. Massive air raids came from Great Britain from 24 July to 3 August 1943. In more than 3,000 sorties, some 9,000 tons of bombs dropped on the city. German fighter planes and anti-aircraft crews were confused and helpless in the chaos. Thousands died in the raids: in the city center a tremendous firestorm snuffed out oxygen. Asphalt in the streets blazed; people were suffocated in their cellars or burned to death in the streets. Relates that the bombings had a devastating effect on German morale. Germans denounced them as uncivilized; Allied spokesmen described them as an inevitable response to Nazi terrorism and bombing of British cities.

767. CALVORESSI, Peter. *The Facts, the Law and the Consequences.* New York: Macmillan, 1948.
The author, who served with the British prosecution team at Nuremberg, presents a critical analysis of the work of the International Military Tribunal. Concentrates on the military aspects of what happened in the courtroom and offers his own interpretations of the personalities involved.

768. CARELL, Paul. *Hitler Moves East, 1941-1943.* Translated from the German by Ewald Osers. Boston: Little, Brown, 1965.
Reports on the military events of Operation Barbarossa, Hitler's campaign against Soviet Russia, which began in 1941 and ended at Stalingrad. Uses divisional and other unit histories, many published in Germany during the early postwar years. Provides precise descriptions of German strategy and the blunders for which Hitler was responsible, and many maps showing combat action in detail. Stresses the fierceness of the fighting under almost incredible conditions.

769. CARELL, Paul. *The Foxes of the Desert.* Translated from the German by Mervyn Savill. New York: Dutton, 1960.
Relates the story of the Afrika Korps from 1941 to 1942. Writes about the "desert foxes" who followed General Erwin Rommel and chased the British in North Africa without ever catching

them.   All the famous encounters are here — Tobruk, "Hellfire Pass," El Alamein and Tunisia.

770.   COLLIER, Basil.   *The Battle of Britain.*   London: Batsford, 1962; New York: Macmillan, 1962.
Account of the air battle over Great Britain between the German *Luftwaffe* and the Royal Air Force in the summer of 1940.   British victory in the confrontation in the skies was the first great turning point of the war.   Failure to subdue the Royal Air Force cost Hitler the war.   He lost the Battle of Britain first, because of determined British resistance, and second, because he made a critical mistake by shifting his air attack indiscriminately from target to target instead of concentrating on one target at a time, thus scattering his strength.   The *Führer* discovered to his dismay that he could not cope with both the RAF and the unbreakable British spirit, which hardened under massive blows.   Churchill paid tribute to the RAF in a famous line: "Never in the field of human conflict was so much owed by so many to so few."

771.   COLLIER, Basil.   *The Battle of the V-Weapons, 1944-45.*   London: Hodder & Stoughton, 1964.
A British account of the two V-Weapons (*Vergeltungswaffen* 1 *und* 2), the Vengeance or Reprisal weapons Hitler used near the end of the war to wrest victory from defeat.   Altogether the Germans fired 9,251 V-1s ("Buzz Bombs") against England, of which 4,621 were destroyed.   Cites estimates that they caused heavy damage, but both weapons proved to be too little and too late.   In the long run, they were ineffective for the already defeated Hitler, who had failed to order a massive assembly-line production of such flying bombs and rockets.

772.   CONOT, Robert E.   *Justice at Nuremberg.*   New York: Harper & Row, 1983.
Discusses for a general readership the philosophical, political and legal questions that lay behind the Nuremberg Trial.   Gives attention to political pressures determining the charges, the persons to be indicted, and each Allied country's choice of prosecutors and judges.

773.   *COOPER, R. W.   *The Nuremberg Trial.*   New York: Penguin, 1947.
Admits being aware of the many gaps and deficiencies in this hurried summary.   Renders extensive excerpts from the key

documents presented in court, and shows how United Nations' representatives struggled with concrete problems in international cooperation. Describes how they worked "to unite four different legal systems into the service of mankind."

774. CREVELD, Martin van. *Hitler's Strategy, 1940-1941.*
      Cambridge (Eng.): Cambridge University Press, 1973.
      An account of Hitler's strategy as war lord during the second
      year of World War II, when Nazi Germany enjoyed one military
      success after another.

775. *DAVIDSON, Eugene. *The Trial of the Germans: An Account
      of the Twenty-two Defendants before the International Mili-
      tary Tribunal at Nuremberg.* New York: Macmillan, 1966.
      Recapitulates the story of the Nuremberg Trial held in 1945-46.
      The author worked in many European research centers, inter-
      viewed three defendants (Admiral Doenitz, Hjalmar Schacht,
      and Franz von Papen), as well as survivors of concentration
      camps, prisoners of war and Luise Jodl, wife of the executed
      General Alfred Jodl. Considers problems of guilt, mass murder
      and the crime of aggression. Investigates the defendants' life
      stories. Seeks "hidden springs of the National Socialist state"
      in the careers of the men in the dock. Believes that the much
      criticized trial had to take place for political and psychological
      reasons because of shocking crimes on a vast scale.
      "Nuremberg was attempting to say something that was uni-
      versally felt."

776. DEIGHTON, Len. *Blitzkrieg: From the Rise of Hitler to the
      Fall of Dunkirk.* New York: Knopf, 1980.
      A study of the ideas, planning and realization of Hitler's
      Blitzkrieg tactics. Stresses the invasion of the battlefield by the
      Industrial Revolution, the text supported by maps and
      drawings.

777. *De JONG, Louis. *The German Fifth Column in the Second
      World War.* Translated from the Dutch by C. M. Geyl.
      Chicago: University of Chicago Press, 1956.
      De Jong, Director of the Netherlands Institute for War
      Documentation, discusses the Nazi Fifth Column in the
      Netherlands during World War II. Provides facts and figures
      on Hitler's plans for destruction from within. Explains how the
      Nazi propaganda machine labored at the task of manufacturing
      fear in the goal "of destroying the enemy from within, to con-

quer him through himself." Argues that the Fifth Column of popular belief is exaggerated as far as the Netherlands are concerned. Although a few Dutchmen swore allegiance to the swastika, most Dutch citizens were contemptuous of Hitler and his ideology.

778. DER DEUTSCHE IMPERIALISMUS UNTER DEM ZWEITEN WELTKRIEG. BAND II. BEITRÄGE ZUM THEMA: "DIE VORBEREITUNG DES ZWEITEN WELTKRIEGES DURCH DEN DEUTSCHEN IMPERIALISMUS" (German Imperialism under the Secnd World War. Volume II. Contribution to the Theme: The Preparation of the Second World War through German Imperialism). Berlin: Rütten & Loening, 1961.
A compilation of forty-six papers by mostly East German and Soviet Russian historians at a conference in East Berlin in December 1959, using the theme, "the origins of World War II through German Imperialism." Many of the essays attempt to show how American interests instigated the war despite the heroic efforts of European Communist parties and the Kremlin to avoid it. Several contributors defend the Nazi-Soviet pact of 1939.

779. *DEUTSCH, Harold C. *Hitler and His Generals: The Hidden Crisis, January-June 1938.* Minneapolis, MN: University of Minnesota Press, 1974.
Examines and analyzes the military crisis in Germany from January to June 1938. By various stratagems Hitler got rid of two members of the High Command, both of whom opposed his aggressive designs. Field Marshal Werner von Blomberg, Minister of Defense and Supreme Commander of the Armed Forces in the early days of the Nazi regime, was forced to resign his post after he married a woman with a questionable past. Colonel General Werner Freiherr von Fritsch, Commander-in-Chief of the German Army, was driven into retirement after being accused of homosexual offenses. With the fall of these two top generals, Hitler himself took over as Supreme Commander of the Armed Forces. He had succeeded in penetrating the closed society of the generals and could now pursue his plans for creation of a Greater Germany "without the annoying opposition of weak professionals."

780. DOUGLAS-HAMILTON, James. *Motives for a Mission: The Story Behind Hess's Flight to Britain.* New York: Macmillan, St. Martin's Press, 1971.
      This book, written by the son of the Duke of Hamilton, explains how Hess got his idea, how he misjudged Hitler's reaction completely and what later happened to Hess. The 10 May 1941 airplane flight to Scotland of Rudolf Hess, Deputy *Führer* of the Third Reich and supposedly Hitler's right-hand man, was ostensibly to seek British collaboration against the Russians. It was one of the most bizarre episodes of World War II. During the Olympic Games of 1936, Hess had met a British aristocrat who later became the Duke of Hamilton. When Hess left Germany, he hoped to land his plane on the estate of the Duke of Hamilton and through him win access to important circles in Great Britain to solicit their help. He believed himself acting out of loyalty to Hitler rather than from treachery, and he hoped to obtain British agreement to a peace settlement.

781. DÜLFFER, Jost. *Weimar, Hitler und die Marine: Reichpolitik und Flottenbau, 1920-1939* (Weimar, Hitler and the Navy: Reich Politics and Fleet Construction, 1920-1939). Düsseldorf: Droste, 1973.
      Analyzes the significance of naval politics for domestic and foreign policy in the Weimar Republic and the Third Reich. Uses extensive archival research to contradict those who see Hitler as an opportunist and those who believe that the *Führer* never understood sea power. Insists that Hitler had a long-range program of extending Wilhelminian Germany's goal of world power. This meant the construction of a large and powerful navy.

782. DUPUY, T. N. *A Genius for War: The German Army and General Staff, 1807-1945.* Englewood Cliffs, NJ: Prentice-Hall, 1977.
      A military historian traces the evolution of the German Army as a military instrument, which in both World Wars demonstrated a significant superiority over its British and American rivals. Explains the reason: the Prussian state and its successors learned how to institutionalize military excellence.

783. FISHMAN, Jack. *The Seven Men of Spandau.* London: Allen, 1954.
      Relates the story of the imprisonment of seven Nazi leaders at Spandau, a fortress prison in West Berlin at the mouth of the

Spree River, after their conviction by the International Military
Tribunal at Nuremberg. Given numbers from 1 to 7 they were
(1) Baldur von Schirach (20 years); (2) Grand Admiral Karl
Doenitz (10 years); (3) Constantin Freiherr von Neurath (15
years); (4) Grand Admiral Erich Raeder (life); (5) Albert Speer
(20 years); (6) Walther Funk (life); and (7) Rudolf Hess (life).
Four Allied Powers were obligated to keep the prisoners in close
captivity. The upkeep expense was defrayed by the city of
Berlin and the federal government at Bonn. Describes in detail
the daily life of the prisoners under a harsh prison regime.

784. *FLEMING, Peter. *Operation Sea Lion*. New York: Simon &
      Schuster, 1957.
      Discusses Hitler's projected invasion of England in 1940, with
      accent on German preparations and the British countermeas-
      ures. In Directive No. 16 of 16 July 1940 Hitler stated that de-
      spite the hopelessness of Great Britain's present position, "I
      have decided to prepare for, and if necessary to carry out, an
      invasion of England." Examines all the factors which led up to
      the planned invasion, presented alternately from the British and
      German points of view. Reveals Hitler's utter misunderstand-
      ing of the British character. To the end, the *Führer* believed that
      the British would capitulate in panic. Speculates what might
      have happened if the British had lost the Battle of Britain.

785. FREDBORG, Arvid. *Behind the Steel Wall*. New York:
      Viking, 1944.
      A Swedish journalist describes the situation in Berlin from 1941
      to 1943 while stationed there. Relates the reactions of Germans
      in their daily life from the viewpoint of a neutral newspaperman.

786. FRUCHTER, S. *Der Luftkrieg* (War in the Air). Frankfurt am
      Main: Athenäum Verlag, 1965.
      Describes the war in the air during World War II to explain the
      gradual deterioration of the *Luftwaffe* under Hermann
      Goering's leadership.

787. GALLAND, Adolf. *The First and the Last: The Rise and Fall
      of the German Fighter Forces, 1938-1945*. Translated from
      the German by Mervyn Saville. New York: Holt, 1954;
      London: Methuen, 1955.
      Adolf Galland (b. 1911), a German fighter ace and *Luftwaffe*
      organizer, was active in almost every World War II theater of
      operations, including the British Isles during the Battle of Brit-

ain in 1940. *Luftwaffe* statistics credited him with 103 air kills, and he was awarded many decorations. In 1942, he was appointed General of Fighters, a post he held until January 1945. Offers a history of the *Luftwaffe*'s decline. Maintains that the loss of air superiority as well as the defeat of the Third Reich had similar causes — both unnecessary.

788. GARLINSKI, Josef. *Hitler's Last Weapons: The Underground War Against the V-1 and V-2.* New York: Times Books, 1978.
Offers a popular account of the efforts of agents and resistance fighters in occupied Europe who tried to uncover and relay to London the secrets of Nazi weapons V-1 and V-2, the *Vergeltungswaffen* (revenge weapons) with which Hitler hoped to win the war.

789. *GÖRLITZ, Walter. *History of the German General Staff, 1657-1945.* Translated from the German by Brian Battershaw. New York: Praeger, 1953.
Analyzes the German General Staff from its beginnings to the end of World War II, revealing the importance of military leadership in German history. This military organization served as a model for most countries, including the United States. Maintains that had it not been for Hitler's amateurish interference, the General Staff might well have won World War II. Suggests that the General Staff was far too intelligent to have started the war that it knew it could not win. Discusses the continued obedience of the generals to Hitler long after they had become aware of his incompetence as a strategist.

790. HALDER, Franz. *Hitler als Feldherr* (Hitler as Commander-in-Chief). Munich: Münchener Dom Verlag, 1949.
German General Franz Halder (1884-1972), Chief of the Army General Staff from 1938 to 1942, a professional soldier, was dismissed on 24 September 1942 after a disagreement with Hitler on tactics before Stalingrad. Denounces Hitler as a fanatic who understood little of strategy, who was indifferent to the welfare of troops fighting for him, who believed will power more important than military planning, and who brought about Germany's defeat by his failure to place confidence in his professional advisers.

791. HART, W. E. *Hitler's Generals.* London: Cresset Press, 1944.

Studies the relations between the *Führer* and his generals, with attention to those who remained loyal (Keitel and Jodl) and those who did not take seriously their vow of obedience (Halder, Witzleben and Beck). Explains that Hitler had little faith in most of his generals and considered his own strategy and intuitions as being more important than the advice of his military collaborators.

792. HAUPT, W. *La dernière bataille de Hitler* (Hitler's Last Battle). Paris: France-Empire, 1966.
Recounts the Battle of Berlin, "Hitler's last battle." Describes the final assault of Soviet Russian armies on the German capital in April 1945. On 27 April 1945, Russian troops, after engaging scattered bands of fanatical German youngsters and older men, hoisted a victory banner inside the shattered city. The German garrison in Berlin surrendered on 2 May 1945.

793. HIBBERT, Christopher. *The Battle of Arnhem.* New York: Macmillan, 1962.
Operation Market-Garden, the biggest airborne invasion in history, came on 17 September 1944, some one-hundred days after the landings in Normandy. The British assault, which was regarded as a sure success, turned into a tragic nightmare, when 9,000 Red Devils were pressed by the Germans into "a little patch of hell." Drawing material from many sources, including survivors and Allied senior commanders, relates the entire story of the unsuccessful venture. British military historians laid much of the blame on General Eisenhower, who did not fully support General Montgomery's strategy for a single, powerful dart into East Germany, and instead opted for an advance on as broad a front as possible.

794. HILLGRUBER, Andreas. *Hitlers Strategie: Politik und Kriegsführung, 1940-1941* (Hitler's Strategy: Politics and War Leadership, 1940-1941). Frankfurt am Main: Bernard & Graefe Verlag für Wehrwesen, 1965.
Discusses German strategy during the early years of World War II, when Hitler won a series of victories against the Allies in Western Europe. Ties political actions with Hitler's war leadership. The critical mistakes allegedly came after 22 June 1941, with the unexpected invasion of the Soviet Union.

795. HINSLEY, Francis Harry. *Hitler's Strategy: The Naval Evidence*. Cambridge (Eng.): Cambridge University Press, 1951.

Assesses Hitler's share in the conduct of operations, in the execution of plans for the war as a whole. Stresses Hitler's intellectual and strategic limitations. For sources, uses the German conferences on naval affairs, the complete record of which fell into British hands, as well as the ponderous documents of the Nuremberg Trial. Concludes that, although Hitler made mistake after mistake in his moves as war lord and was never completely logical, still he nearly conquered the world.

796. HOSSBACH, Friedrich. *Infanterie im Ostfeldzug* (Infantry in Campaigns in the East). Osterode: Giebel & Dehlschlagel, 1951.

Friedrich Hossbach (1894-1980) was appointed Adjutant to Hitler in 1934 and Chief of the Central Section of the General Staff and *Wehrmacht*, posts he held until January 1938. On 10 November 1937 he wrote the famous memorandum – the Hossbach Protocol – recording the minutes of the conference led by Hitler and outlining the *Führer's* plan of continental expansion. Appointed General of Infantry in 1943, he spent the next two years on the Eastern Front, but was dismissed in January 1945 for withdrawing his troops in disregard of Hitler's orders. Relates the story of German infantry in the Eastern campaign and defends his decision to recall his men in defiance of Hitler's orders.

797. HUMBLE, Richard. *Hitler's Generals*. Garden City, NY: Doubleday, 1974.

A British military historian discusses the rebirth and degeneration of the German military machine from Hitler's accession to political power to the downfall of the Third Reich in 1945. Gives attention to the talents and failings of such strategists as Rommel, Guderian and von Rundstedt, with special treatment of Rommel. Recognizes Rommel's asset as an inspiring leader of men in a swiftly moving attack, but doubts the General's strategic talent. Lauds the ability of Guderian and von Manstein.

798. IRVING, David. *Hitler's War*. New York: Viking, 1977.

A British historian's revisionist study reveals interviews with hundreds of survivors of the Third Reich and incorporates their replies to his questions. Aims to describe the war as Hitler saw it.   Writes about the *Führer* as a pragmatic leader who erred through indecision and mistrust.   Criticizes the standard view of Hitler's malevolence as a myth, and shifts the moral burden of the war to others.   Contends that the real responsibility for the Holocaust rests upon the SS and not upon Hitler.   Argues that Hitler's hatred for Jews manifested itself primarily in fantasies, and that the *Führer* only intended to exile Jews to Madagascar.   Claims that Himmler and Heydrich, not Hitler, threw the extermination machinery into high gear.

799.   IRVING, David.   *The Destruction of Dresden.*   London: Kimber, 1963; New York: Holt, Rinehart & Winston, 1964.
The German city of Dresden was subjected to a devastating airfire attack by the British Bomber Command in early 1945. Called the "German Florence," because of its magnificent rococo art collections and splendid baroque buildings, Dresden was also a major communications and industrial center.   The city was filled with refugees who had fled the advancing Russians, as well as its 630,000 inhabitants.   The worst raid came on the night of 12-13 February 1943, when the city was caught in a firestorm that engulfed people and buildings, with tens of thousands dying in the terrible destruction.   Germans denounced the bombing as an inexcusable act of barbarism; the British pointed to earlier damaging German air attacks on Warsaw, Rotterdam and Coventry.

800.   *JACKSON, Robert H.   *The Nuremberg Case: Together with Other Documents.*   New York: Knopf, 1947.
The chief American prosecutor at the Nuremberg Trial, Justice Robert R. Jackson (1892-1954), offers selections from his own opening and closing statements, excerpts from the examination of several of the defendants and other pertinent records.   Aiming to uncover the anatomy of dictatorship, shows how a small group of determined Nazis used "legal means" to seize power and then led the country to near destruction.

801.   KAHN, David.   *Hitler's Spies: German Military Intelligence in World War II.*   New York: Macmillan, 1978.
Drawing on documentary sources, studies the intelligence efforts of Nazi Germany in World War II.   Describes the internal rivalries, the inefficiency and administrative confusion typical of the Third Reich.   Gives attention to four different military groups sharing military intelligence – the *Wehrmacht*, the Nazi Party, several ministerial bureaucracies and the private sector.

In general, shows the German intelligence effort to fall qualitatively short in comparison to that of the Allies.

802. KATZ, Robert. *Death in Rome*. New York: Macmillan, 1966. Details, for the first time in English, the World War II massacre of the Ardeatine caves, in which 335 Italians were shot in reprisal for the killing of thirty-three German soldiers by Partisans. The writer, who had lived in Rome, reconstructs the events of forty-eight hours, including the testimony of witnesses who had appeared before the Ardeatine Caves Commission of the U.S. Fifth Army.

803. *KELLEY, Douglas McGlashan. *22 Cells in Nuremberg: A Psychiatrist Examines the Nazi Criminals*. New York: Greenberg, 1947.
The psychiatrist charged with obtaining the case histories of the Nazis accused at Nuremberg presents the report of his interviews. Devotes one chapter to each defendant. Believes that there was nothing really unusual about these men and that their counterparts could be found in any society. A concluding chapter offers a composite portrait of Hitler as described by his associates.

804. KILLEN, John. *A History of the Luftwaffe*. Garden City, NY: Doubleday, 1968.
Relates the history of the *Luftwaffe* from 1915 to 1945. Offers capsule biographies of famous German airmen of both World Wars, the outstanding aircraft and Hermann Goering's record as *Luftwaffe* chief. Emphasizes developments in World War II.

805. KOEHL, Robert Lewis. *RKFDV: German Resettlement and Population Policy, 1939-1945: A History of the Reich Commission for the Strengthening of Germandom*. Cambridge, MA: Harvard University Press, 1957.
A study of the important aspects of the work of the Reich Commission for the Strengthening of Germandom and its attempts at resettlement, especially in Polish areas under Nazi control during World War II. Uses the extensive records of the Nuremberg Trial to discuss the operations of the Nazi élite, including the complex personal feuds of Hitler's underlings.

806. *LIDDELL HART, B. H. *The German Generals Talk*. London: Cassell, 1948, under title *The Other Side of the Hill*; New York: Morrow, 1948.

British military historian B. H. Liddell Hart discusses the top
secret history of the German High Command. Presents dictator
Hitler as his military commanders knew him, and explains why
German commanders acted as they did – and why they failed.
Uses many interviews with German officers in English prison
camps, and writes about the disastrous schisms in the German
High Command, differences which weakened the German war
effort. Gives special attention to the Battle of Britain.

807. MACKSEY, Kenneth. *Afrika Korps*. London: Ballantine,
1968.
An illustrated popular treatment of the *Afrika Korps* by a
British officer serving in the Royal Tank Regiment, who fought
with the Royal Armoured Corps in North Africa. Pays tribute
to General Erwin Rommel and his "company of soldiers," honored by Winston Churchill: "We have a very daring and skillful
opponent against us, and, may I say across the havoc of war, a
great general." In February 1941 the situation looked black for
the Axis in North Africa following defeat after defeat of the
Italians by a small British task force. Two months later, the
situation had changed – the British were in confusion and
Rommel's troops were on the frontiers of Egypt.

808. MARTIENSSEN, Anthony K. *Hitler and His Admirals*. New
York: Dutton, 1948.
This study of Hitler's failure to understand and use naval power
does in the naval field what B. H. Liddell Hart did for the Army
in *The German Generals Talk* (1948). Depending mostly upon
German documents and the evidence given at Nuremberg, de-
scribes the intense belief Hitler had in his own ability as a war
strategist and how he overruled the advice of professionals.
Gives his attention to the personalities and careers of Karl
Doenitz and Erich Raeder, the two most important admirals,
and describes the war at sea as seen by the top command of the
German Navy.

809. MASER, Werner. *Nuremberg, A Nation on Trial*. Translated
from the German by Richard Barry. New York: Scribner,
1979.
Werner Maser's study, originally published as *Nürnberg:
Tribunal der Sieger* (1977), criticizes the Nuremberg Trial for its
legal shortcomings as well as its "historical inaccuracies." Presents the view, popular in Germany, that Nuremberg was not
an international court but "a victors' tribunal." Accuses the

triumphant Allies of creating new rules of law in their zealous attempt to punish the Nazis.   Emphasizes the well-known concept of *ex post facto* laws, and rejects the idea of a Nazi conspiracy.   Denies that his book is an apology for Nazism.

810.   MASON, David.   *U-Boat: The Secret Menace.*   New York: Ballantine, 1972.
An account of U-Boat warfare as an important aspect of combat in World War II.   Maintains that, although Allied propaganda portrayed its merchant seamen as gallant and the German U-boat crews as cold-hearted criminals, actually all seamen, "theirs and ours," were courageous men with high morale, whose technical skills compel admiration.

811.   McKEE, Alexander.   *Dresden, 1945: The Devil's Tinderbox.*   New York: Dutton, 1984.
During the night of 13 February 1945, the British Command of the Royal Air Force launched an all-out attack upon the city of Dresden.   The next day, American Flying Fortresses pressed home the attack.   The once beautiful city was turned into a blast furnace.   More than 35,000 people died.   Basing his text on interviews with eyewitnesses, offers an account of what it was like to be caught in the inferno.

812.   MEINCK, Gerhard.   *Hitler und die deutsche Aufrüstung* (Hitler and German Rearmament).   Wiesbaden: Steiner, 1959.
Examines Hitler's rearmament program from 1934 on.   It was obvious that as soon as he attained political power, Hitler would prepare Germany for what he conceived a coming showdown with the Allies.   He had already indicated that he would "right the wrongs of the Treaty of Versailles" and that he would demand "living space" for Germany.

813.   MENDELSSOHN, Peter.   *Design for Aggression: The Inside Story of Hitler's War Plans.*   New York: Harper, 1947.
The British title, *Nuremberg Documents,* more accurately describes the contents of this book.   The author, a German-born English journalist, examined all the documents presented by the prosecution at the International Military Tribunal at Nuremberg, and offers a logical series of selections with his own commentaries.   Explains Hitler's techniques in starting the war as well as the military planning which led to the conflict.

814. MERLE, Marcel. *Le procès de Nuremberg, et châtiment des criminels de guerre* (The Nuremberg Process, and the Punishment of the War Criminals). Paris: Pedone, 1949.
French publishers show intense interest in the Nuremberg Trial. This study concerns "chastisement," the punishment, of the accused.

815. MESSENGER, Charles. *The Blitzkrieg Story*. New York: Scribner, 1976.
Discusses the early development of "lightning war" as a reaction to the stalemated trench warfare of World War I, the controversial struggles to win adherents and the application of the new strategy in World War II. The author, a graduate of Sandhurst, the British military academy, and an officer in the British Royal Tank Regiment, analyzes *Blitzkrieg* as a technique of war, and shows how planes and tanks were used to win greater mobility and protection in a fast advance.

816. MESSERSCHMIDT, Manfred. *Die Wehrmacht im NS-Staat. Zeit der Indoktrination* (The *Wehrmacht* in the National Socialist State. Time of Indoctrination). Hamburg: Decker, 1969.
Analyzes indoctrination of the German army by the National Socialist German Workers' Party. Explains that the upper echelons, far from trying to preserve their ideological independence, actively cooperated with Hitler. By emphasizing military virtues, rearmament and the army's vital role in the Third Reich, Hitler was able to attract the support of many officers. His propaganda was enormously effective in winning the loyalty of the military.

817. MORRISON, Wilbur H. *Fortress Without a Roof: The Allied Bombing of the Third Reich*. New York: St. Martin's Press, 1982.
Studies Allied bombing of the Third Reich, the development of Allied strategy, and the controversies involved in carrying these out. Describes the working relationships among Allied military and political leaders, and offers the story of the Eighth Air Force in detail. Includes narratives of battle scenes, as well as interviews and memoirs of key participants.

818. MÜLLER, Klaus-Jürgen. *Das Heer und Hitler* (The Army and Hitler). Stuttgart: Deutsche Verlagsanstalt, 1969.

Discusses the relations between the German Army and the National Socialist regime from 1933 to 1940, including the rivalry for power in the Nazi state.

819. NEAVE, Airey. *Nuremberg: A Personal Record of the Trial of the Major Nazi War Criminals in 1945-6.* London: Hodder & Stoughton, 1979; also under the title *On Trial at Nuremberg.* Boston: Little, Brown, 1979.
Airey Neave, an attorney, was a major in the British army at the time of the Nuremberg Trial and served as a minor official on the Tribunal. His main task was to serve the defendants in their cells with copies of the indictment. Offers biographical portraits and capsule biographies of the prisoners based on Neave's reactions to their behavior as they were handed the indictments. Defends the Nuremberg concept against its detractors and praises the British representatives. There is a foreword by Rebecca West.

820. NOBÉCOURT, Jacques. *Hitler's Last Gamble: The Battle of the Bulge.* Translated from the French by R. H. Barry. New York: Schocken, 1967.
A correspondent for *Le Matin* describes the military and political aspects of the Battle of the Bulge. Emphasizes the psychological factors involved in this battle, which he calls Hitler's last gamble, the relations between Hitler and his generals, and the mistakes made by both. Describes the thinking of the high commands on both sides.

821. O'DONNELL, James P. *The Bunker: The History of the Reich Chancellery Group.* Boston: Houghton Mifflin, 1978.
A one-time *Newsweek* bureau chief in Berlin attempts to update and correct the classic account of H. R. Trevor-Roper's *The Last Days of Hitler* (1947). Interviewed witnesses, generals, staff officers, Hitler's personal pilot, telephone operators and secretaries, in all, about 150 survivors of the debacle. Uses these notes to present a day-by-day account of events in the underground shelter. Reveals many hitherto unpublished anecdotes.

822. PAULUS, Friedrich von. *Paulus and Stalingrad.* Translated from the German. London: Methuen, 1963.
Friedrich von Paulus (1890-1957), German Field Marshal, was the losing commander at the Battle of Stalingrad in the winter of 1942-43. Caught in a pocket with his Sixth Army under severe Russian pressure, he saw his supplies cut off and his

ammunition dwindling. Recommended a temporary retreat, but Hitler refused to allow him to move an inch backward: "I am not leaving the Volga." After the siege, Paulus and 12,000 ragged and hungry German troops emerged from the cellars and caves of Stalingrad. Paulus surrendered to the Russians and joined a Soviet puppet organization. Following his release from a Soviet prison in 1953, he settled in the German Democratic Republic. Justifies his actions in the Stalingrad disaster.

823. PHILLIPS, Cecil Ernest Lucas. *Alamein*. London: Heinemann, 1962.
A detailed account of the Battle of El Alamein in the North African desert between the British Eighth Army and Italo-German forces from 23 October to 4 November 1942, one of the important turning points of the war – the beginning of the collapse of Hitler's fortunes.

824. PIRIE, A. *Operation Bernhard*. London: Cassell, 1961.
Operation Bernhard was the code name for a Nazi plan to drop forged British banknotes on England by plane early in World War II, a scheme devised by Alfred Helmut Naujocks, assistant to Reinhard Heydrich, head of the Reich Security Service. Offers details of the unsuccessful operation.

825. PRICE, Alfred. *Luftwaffe: Birth, Life and Death of an Air Force*. London: Ballantine Books, 1970.
Explains that from its triumphant role in Hitler's opening *Blitzkrieg* campaigns in the war to its last futile efforts to stem the Allied and Russian advances, the *Luftwaffe* waged a savage war against the enemy only to be overcome by Allied power in the air. There is an introduction by General Adolf Galland, *Luftwaffe* organizer and German fighter ace.

826. RAUSCHENBACH, Hermann. *Der Nürnberger Prozess gegen die Organisationen* (The Nuremberg Trial against the Organizations). Bonn: Röhrscheid, 1954.
In addition to the 22 Nazi leaders placed on trial before the International Military Tribunal, several leading Nazi organizations were condemned as criminal: the Nazi *Führer-Korps*, the *Gestapo*, the SS (*Schutzstaffel*) and the SA (*Sturmabteilung*). Offers details of the court proceedings against these bulwarks of the Nazi regime.

827. *RICH, Norman. *Hitler's War Aims.* Volume 1. *Ideology, the Nazi State, and the Course of Expansion;* Volume 2. *The Establishment of the New Order.* New York: Norton, 1973, 1974.

These two volumes are designed to explain the interaction of Hitler's words and deeds and the record and development of German war aims on the basis of the policies of the *Führer* actually pursued in Germany and German-occupied countries. Discusses Hitler's ideology, instruments of power and conquest. The documentation is based largely on material from the Nuremberg Tribunal, other war crimes trials and published diplomatic papers. Concludes that Hitler, indeed, did have a definite program of expansion, a view denied by A. J. P. Taylor in his revisionist *The Origins of the Second World War* (1961).

828. RUGE, Friedrich. *Sea Warfare, 1939-1945: A German Viewpoint.* Translated from the German by M. G. Saunders. London: Cassell, 1957.

Describes Hitler's attempt to wrest control of the seas from Great Britain during World War II, as seen by a German admiral. Seeks to explain Hitler's lack of success in challenging Allied sea power.

829. RUMPF, Hans. *The Bombing of Germany.* Translated from the German by Edward Fitzgerald. London: White Lion, 1961.

Designed as an addendum to Great Britain's official report of the bombing of Germany, seeks to give as accurate as possible a picture of the bombing as it affected German territory – "neither in anger nor indignation." In addition, it aims to provide an introduction to the political and military discussions relating to the urgently topical question of strategic air warfare as it affected victors and vanquished. Reports vast areas devastated, 600,000 Germans killed and twice as many injured, thirteen million homeless, and priceless art treasures destroyed. The Allied Strategic Bomber Command insisted that the fierce air attacks were in response to Nazi bombings of Warsaw, Rotterdam and Coventry. Germans felt that the smashing of Hamburg and Dresden in fire-bomb attacks was "an atrocity greater than that of Hiroshima or Nagasaki." Maintains that the inevitable result of Allied strategic air warfare was "indiscriminate terrorism." Doubts that it shattered the morale of the German people.

830. SEATON, Albert. *The German Army, 1933-45.* New York: St. Martin's Press, 1982.
This study of the German Army during the years from Hitler's accession to political power in 1933 to the end of World War II traces how the German dictator increased his control of the armed forces by limiting the powers of the General Staff. Presents the history of units and describes the changes in weapons during that era. Writes about the incompetence of those Army leaders who allowed Hitler to dominate them. Gives attention to the personalities of important military figures.

831. SIMONOV, Konstantin. *Moscow.* Moscow: Foreign Languages Publishing House, 1943.
A Soviet reporter records the German defeat on Soviet soil in early January 1942. "Moscow was calm and stern in those days."

832. *SMITH, Bradley F. *Reaching Judgment at Nuremberg.* New York: Basic Books, 1977.
Using previously unavailable sources, seeks to move beyond the polemics of the past to show, in all its complications and complexities, how judgment was reached by the International Military Tribunal at Nuremberg. Demonstrates the substantial degree to which the judges were independent of the prosecution and their governments. The defendants faced a court surprisingly free of outside control. Concludes that "the judges attitude toward legal process and the situation's complexities were the decisive factors." Although the Nuremberg court did not produce perfect justice, the trial did prevent an anarchic bloodbath that might have occurred had the Nazi leaders been subjected to summary execution. In the debate over the legality of the Nuremberg Trial, this study demands a corrective for the charge that Nuremberg represented simply "victors' justice."

833. *SMITH, Bradley F. *The Road to Nuremberg.* New York: Basic Books, 1981.
Bradley Smith previously told the story of the Nuremberg Trial in *Reaching Judgment at Nuremberg* (1977). Analyzes the predominantly American planning of the trials, including the rejection of the Morgenthau Plan to make Germany an agricultural state and the acceptance of the idea of Secretary of War Henry Stimson to try the Nazi leaders before the International Military Tribunal at Nuremberg. The choice was for judicial prosecution and not summary execution. Believes that

American authorities wanted to atone for the folly of the Unites States' pre-1933 isolation.

834. SPEIDEL, Hans. *Invasion, 1944.* Tübingen: Wunderlich, 1949.
An account of the 1944 Normandy invasion by General Hans Speidel (b. 1897), *Wehrmacht* general, Rommel's Chief of Staff in France, and secret member of the Resistance movement. This is an inside account of German response to the gigantic enterprise. Provides a detailed description of the conspiracy against Hitler and condemns the *Führer's* moral principles. Asserts that the rank and file of the army as well as its leaders had full confidence in Rommel rather than Hitler, and supported the plot to terminate the Third Reich.

835. *STOWE, Leland. *Nazi Means War.* New York: McGraw-Hill, 1934.
Leland Stowe, Paris correspondent of *The New York Herald-Tribune*, following two months of observation in the new Third Reich, reports on the remilitarization of Germany under the Nazi regime and the means taken by Hitler's Propaganda Ministry to create a war psychology. Describes the militant tone in the new German official educational system, which prescribed military training even for small children. Concludes that the Nazi regime was heading directly for war.

836. TAYLOR, A. J. P. *The Origins of the Second World War.* London: Hamish Hamilton, 1961.
A revisionist study of war responsibility by an Oxford University historian and journalist. Believes that Hitler was not a maniac bent upon world conquest, but a traditional German statesman in the category of Frederick the Great, Bismarck and Stresemann. The *Führer* wanted merely a revision of the Treaty of Versailles, not a war with Great Britain or France in 1939 or at any other time. The Hitler who turned on the Soviet Union in 1941 was not the Hitler of the prewar era. The only conflict desired in 1939 was a war of nerves, in which he excelled. He had no way of knowing that Great Britain and France would go to war over Danzig. *Mein Kampf*, far from being a blueprint for war, was only a grandiose daydream. Criticizes the documents produced at Nuremberg as only "lawyers' briefs."

837. *TAYLOR, Telford. *Sword and Swastika: Generals and Nazis in the Third Reich.* New York: Simon & Schuster, 1952.

Taylor, military officer, lawyer and historian, a specialist on the German High Command, and chief of counsel for the prosecution of accused "war criminals" at Nuremberg contends that the alliance of German military leaders with Nazi officials led directly to war and turned the course of history. On the one side was the honored class of tight-lipped professional warriors; on the other an incredible aggregation of misfits, demagogues and thugs intoxicated by a revolutionary surge of lethal energy. Traces the changing relationships between these two forces, one archaic, the other atavistic. Hitler and his generals found in each other a necessary adjunct for attaining desired military goals.

838. *TAYLOR, Telford. *The Breaking Wave: The Second World War in the Summer of 1940.* New York: Simon & Schuster, 1967.

Already known for his *Sword and Swastika* (1952), Taylor discusses the events of World War II in the summer of 1940. Sees the Battle of Britain as one of the most decisive engagements in history. "Marked on a map, the conquests of the *Wehrmacht* were awesome, but the combination of decisions that led to them was military madness." Regards this situation as in no small measure due to Hitler's flawed strategy.

839. *TOLAND, John. *Battle: The Story of the Bulge.* New York: Random House, 1959.

A reconstruction of the Battle of the Bulge, Hitler's last offensive of the war, based on official documents and military records, interviews with hundreds of former GI's, SHAEF officials and Nazi officers. Renders an account of the strategic and tactical picture of the confrontation as well as the experiences of the fighting men and civilians caught in the maelstrom. Relates stories and anecdotes of panic, terror and courage. Praises the American fighting men and ridicules British General Bernard Law Montgomery as a pompous peacock.

840. TREVOR-ROPER, Hugh R. "A. J. P. Taylor, Hitler and the War." *Encounter*, XVII (1961), 88-96.

Hugh R. Trevor-Roper, Regius Professor of Modern History at Oxford University, presents a polemical review of his colleague A. J. P. Taylor's *The Origins of the Second World War* (1961). Denounces Taylor's revisionist views as a whitewashing of Hitler and an apology for appeasement. Accuses Taylor of wilfully misusing documents and unconsciously strengthening the forces of neo-fascism. Considers Taylor's thesis demonstrably false and erroneous. Hitler's "patience" was indecision that drove the *Führer's* followers wild. Gives the impression that Taylor's revisionism was too painful to be accepted by any scholar of academic standing.

841. TUSA, Ann and John TUSA. *The Nuremberg Trial.* New York: Atheneum, 1984.
This narrative survey of the Nuremberg Trial explains the reasons for the tribunal, the courtroom, behind-the-scenes actions, and the judgments, sentences and executions. The authors conclude that under the circumstances the Nuremberg court performed a necessary task in a generally efficient and just manner.

842. UEBERSCHÄR, Gerd R. and Wolfram WETTE, eds. *"Unternehmen Barbarossa"* (Operation Barbarossa). Paderborn: Schöningh, 1984.
Reports, analyses and documents on Operation Barbarossa, the invasion of the Soviet Union in 1941. Claims that the operation was not a desperate response to a Soviet threat but rather an ultimate gesture of ideologically and racially motivated aggression. Some authors argue that this attitude was held not only by Hitler but was also supported by the leaders of the *Wehrmacht* and the "civilized élites" of Nazi Germany.

843. VAN CREFELD, Martin L. *Hitler's Strategy, 1940-1941: The Balkan Clue.* Cambridge (Eng.): Cambridge University Press, 1973.
This account of Hitler's military strategy from the defeat of France in June 1940 to the outbreak of war against the Soviet Union a year later, concerns the Balkans, with stress on the "peripheral strategy" against Great Britain in the eastern Mediterranean. Surveys Hitler's role in the planning of war against the Soviet Union.

844. VOGEL, Rolf. *Ein Weg aus der Vergangenheit* (A Road from the Past). Frankfurt am Main: Verlag Ullstein, 1969.
This documentation about the prosecution of Nazi leaders accused of war crimes and the judgments reached at Nuremberg in 1946 extends the record from 1946 to 1968, with attention to the work of courts in the occupying powers – Great Britain, the United States, France and the Soviet Union. Also discusses

court judgments against Nazis in the East German Republic and the Federal Republic of Germany.

845. WAGNER, Alfred. "Die Rüstung im 'Dritten Reich' unter Albert Speer" (The Arming of the Third Reich under Albert Speer). *Technikgeschichte*, XXXIII (1966), 205-27. Studies the role Albert Speer played in the rearmament of the Third Reich. Speer was Hitler's personal architect and after 1942 Minister of Armaments and War Production. Stresses the technical aspects of Speer's work, and the change from master architect to complete technician. Speer's production miracles, achieved despite opposition from the other Nazi leaders and under heavy Allied bombings, undoubtedly prolonged the course of the war.

846. WARLIMONT, Walther. *Inside Hitler's Headquarters, 1939-1945.* Translated from the German by R. H. Barry. London: Weidenfeld & Nicolson, 1964; New York: Praeger, 1964. Nazi general Walther Warlimont (b. 1895) was General Alfred Jodl's deputy in the Armed Forces Operations Staff during World War II. Together with Jodl he drew up the preliminary plans for Operation Barbarossa, code name for the proposed attack on the Soviet Union. On 1 April 1944 he was made General of Artillery and was one of the officers present in the barracks hut at Rastenburg when the 20 July 1944 attempt on Hitler's life was made, but he was not injured. After the war he was arrested and condemned to life imprisonment; he served eighteen years. Presents an account of the milieu in Hitler's field headquarters. Gives special attention to his role in drawing up Directive 21, originally called "Fritz," but later "Barbarossa," a general plan for operations against Soviet Russia.

847. WHALEY, Barton. *Codeword Barbarossa.* Cambridge, MA: Massachusetts Institute of Technology Press, 1973. This account of how Hitler achieved strategic surprise in his attack on the Soviet Union examines the various Nazi intelligence services and the information they were able to obtain. The more important Soviet codes remained unbroken. Hitler succeeded in misleading Stalin about his intentions. Stalin apparently believed that Hitler had no ulterior motives in strengthening his border forces. Contends that Hitler expected Americans to

intervene in the war eventually and decided to conquer the
Soviet Union before this happened.

848. WHITING, Charles. *Gehlen: Germany's Master Spy.* New
      York: Ballantine, 1972.
      Relates the story of Reinhard Gehlen, who served twenty-six
      years as Germany's master spy, and as a long-term man of
      mystery who dominated European intelligence. This "first
      technocrat of espionage," although at great cost in human life
      and suffering, changed espionage from its old cloak-and-dagger
      form with false whiskers and thrilling chase to work of clean-
      cut, middle-class graduates from the great universities. After
      the war, from 1956 to 1968, Gehlen was the head of the West
      German Intelligence Service. A rival once called him "the
      product of a moment of mental lovemaking between Mata Hari
      and General Ludendorff."

849. WIGTON, Charles and Gunter PEIS. *Hitler's Spies and
      Saboteurs.* New York: Holt, Rinehart & Winston, 1958.
      The authors relate the story of Nazi spies and saboteurs in
      action, based on the secret war diary of General Erwin von
      Lahousen of the German Secret Service, who was a witness for
      the Allied prosecution at Nuremberg. Give attention to the four
      German espionage agents who were landed from a U-boat on
      the south shore of Long Island in June, 1942. They aim to re-
      veal the top-secret details of Germany's international spy ring
      during World War II.

850. WINTERBOTHAM, F. W. *The Ultra Secret.* New York:
      Harper & Row, 1974.
      This account of the extraordinary cryptanalysis coup of World
      War II reveals how the British broke the German code and read
      most of the signals between Hitler and his generals throughout
      the war. With the help of a Polish defector and the Polish Secret
      Service, the British obtained an exact copy of the highly secret
      and complex German coding machine known as Enigma. The
      supposedly unbreakable Enigma system was solved with the aid
      of another highly sophisticated machine, and as a result top-
      secret German signals became available to Allied commanders.

INDEX OF AUTHORS

N.B. The numbers following the names refer to individual book and article entries, not to pages.